Navigating the BIBLE

THE

5-MINUTE GUIDE

TO UNDERSTANDING **GOD'S WORD**

CHRISTOPHER D. HUDSON

BARBOUR BOOKS

An Imprint of Barbour Publishing, Inc.

PHOTO CREDITS:
Page 24 (map): Christopher D. Hudson. *Bible Atlas & Companion*. Ulrichsville, OH: Barbour, 2008.

Pages 57 and 78 (charts): *New International Version QuickView Bible: Visual Snapshots of God's Word*. Grand Rapids, MI: Zondervan, 2012.

Pages 1, 11, 16, 20, 26, 33, 45, 64, 65, 66, 72, 74, 80, 85, 89, 95, 98, 100, 101, 103, 105, 109, 114, 132, 133, 134, 135, 136, 137, 141, 142, 144, 146, 152, 155, 166, 200, 202, 204, 206, 208, 211, 213, 215, 219, 221, 223, 227, 229, 233, 235, 237, 238, 241, 243, and 245: SHUTTERSTOCK

Pages 15, 36, 61, 116, 181, 183, and 254: THINKSTOCK

Pages: 14, 17, 31, 32, 52, 58, 60, 62, 68, 87, 93, 113, 119, 121, 126, 131, 139, and 148: COMMONS WIKIMEDIA

Pages 160, 164, 168, 173, 185, 189, 231, 256, 258, 264, and 272: DOVER

All other paintings, image, charts, maps and timelines © TheBiblePeople.com. Used by permission.

Cover Design: Greg Jackson, Thinkpen Design

Published by Barbour Books, an imprint of Barbour Publishing, Inc., P.O. Box 719, Uhrichsville, Ohio 44683 www.barbourbooks.com

Our mission is to publish and distribute inspirational products offering exceptional value and biblical encouragement to the masses.

ecpa Member of the
Evangelical Christian
Publishers Association

CONTENTS

INTRODUCTION
Your Guide to Understanding the Bible, Five Minutes at a Time

The Bible can be a daunting book. Most editions are big and thick, and they simply feel imposing. Although most of us would say we want to read it more, we often don't know where to start. When we do sit down to read, we give up because we have trouble making sense of what's going on. The task of understanding God's Word feels so overwhelming that many of us close the Bible soon after we've opened it. That leads to another set of frustrations: If the Bible is God's Word, shouldn't we be able to get through it? Shouldn't we be able to understand it?

If you can relate to that experience, then this book is for you. Here's what you'll find inside.

Quick Five-Minute Overviews
At the conclusion of the introduction for each Bible book, you'll find a brief outline that lists all the five-minute overviews that you can find for that book.

Next to each overview (which begins with a big number 5) you'll find a short paragraph that describes a section of the Bible. Following that paragraph you'll find a handful of verses next to an hourglass. Most people will be able to read the paragraph and the short passages in about five minutes.

Read Each 5-Minute Overview in Romans		
○ 1:1–2:29	The Righteousness of God	Page 203
○ 3:1–4:25	Justification by Faith Alone, before the Law	Page 203
○ 5:1–6:23	The Effect of Salvation	Page 204
○ 7:1–8:39	Life in the Spirit	Page 204
○ 9:1–10:21	Israel's Rejection	Page 205
○ 11:1–12:21	Israel's Unchanging Role in God's Plan of Redemption	Page 205
○ 13:1–15:13	The Believer's Place	Page 206
○ 15:14–16:27	Paul's Fellow Ministers	Page 206

THE RIGHTEOUSNESS OF GOD (1:1–2:29)
Paul writes his letter to the Romans before ever visiting Rome, yet his heartfelt concern for the believers there is evident throughout this epistle. Paul writes about the absence of righteousness in humankind. He later contrasts this with God's righteousness. When humans reject God, their behavior is reflected in how they respond to sinful desires and natural lusts. No law-abiding person—Jew or Gentile—is righteous enough on his or her own merit to avoid God's wrath. ✤ *ROMANS 1:18–32; 2:1–29*

Putting History in Context
One understandable difficulty people have in reading the Bible is that the chapters and books are not always arranged chronologically. The running time line at the bottom of every page will help you put the characters and events in

10 AD	20 AD	30 AD	40 AD	50 AD	60 AD
◆ 8 Jesus visits temple		◆ 30 Jesus raised	◆ 45 James written		◆ 60 Eph–Col
◆ 5 Birth of Paul (?)		◆ 32 Stephen martyred		◆ 55 1 & 2 Corinthians	◆ 64 R
	◆ 14 Tiberius (Rome)	◆ 37 Paul converts		◆ 57 Romans	◆ 65

historical perspective. To help you connect the Bible's stories with world history, you'll also find some historical information. While the time line is helpful, it is not exhaustive. Sometimes dates are approximate, and even their placements on the time line may not be precise because of space. Regardless, the time line will provide a sense of when these stories take place.

Who's Who?
The Bible includes hundreds of characters. Keeping them all straight is a difficult challenge in itself. You will find short biographies (quick cheat sheets) of forty of the most significant Bible characters.

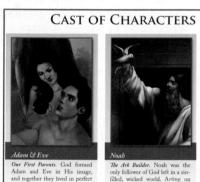

CAST OF CHARACTERS   IN GENESIS

Adam & Eve
Our First Parents. God formed Adam and Eve in His image, and together they lived in perfect harmony with Him in a beautiful garden. Adam and Eve chose

Noah
The Ark Builder. Noah was the only follower of God left in a sin-filled, wicked world. Acting on nothing but faith, Noah obeyed God and built an ark to prepare

Abraham
Patriarch of Israel. God promised land, many descendants, and blessing to the whole world through Abraham. Abraham believed God for everything even

Joseph
Jacob's Favorite Son. Joseph was Jacob's favorite son. His jealous brothers sold him into slavery. Wrongly thrown into prison in Egypt, Joseph interpreted a dream

Bottom-of-the-Page Boxes
At the bottom of many pages are boxes that answer questions readers often ask while working through the Bible. These answers usually provide historical background, interesting information, or tips on how to read the Bible.

Finally, Don't Give up!
I understand that reading the Bible can feel so overwhelming that it's tempting not to begin. Don't give in to that temptation. If the Bible is God's Word and contains the most important message humanity has ever received (and I believe both are true), then we should work hard at reading and understanding it. It's my hope that you'll commit to reading the Bible—five minutes at a time—and better understanding the message God has for you. As you work through God's Word, I would love to hear from you and find out how this book has helped you.

Christopher D. Hudson
Facebook.com/Christopher.D.Hudson.books
Twitter: @ReadEngageApply

ACKNOWLEDGMENTS
The people who helped make this book happen

This book exists because of the contributions of many people. First and foremost is Karen Engle, who framed the manuscript, edited the character profiles, and created the running time line throughout the book. I am so grateful for your contribution, your passion for God's Word, and your regular help.

Thank you also to Benjamin Irwin and Dr. Stephen Leston, who made a number of suggestions and contributions. As always, I'm grateful to Mary Larsen, who consistently offers me strong editorial support.

In creating this manuscript, I leaned heavily on the content and scholarship of Barbour's Layman's Bible Commentary Set. I am indebted to the contributors of that series: Tremper Longman, Mark Strauss, Carol Smith, Peter Barnes, Stan Campbell, Ralph Davis, Robert Deffinbaugh, Ian Fair, Rev. Joe Guglielmo, David Guzik, John Hanneman, W. Hall Harris III, David Hatcher, J. Hampton Keathley III, Stephen Magee, Doug McIntosh, Eugene H. Merrill, Jeffrey Miller, Richard D. Patterson, Robert Rayburn, and Derek W. H. Thomas.

I am invariably grateful to Paul Muckley and the amazing team at Barbour Publishing, Inc. Thank you for allowing me to create books that help people understand the Bible.

And most importantly, thank you to Amber, my beautiful wife, who has been my faithful coworker and trustworthy companion for twenty years. Thanks for walking this road with me.

THE 5-MINUTE GUIDES

The Creation of the World and the Fall of Humankind	Wickedness Increases, but God Is Faithful	God's Promise of Land, Descendants, and Blessing	God Tests Abraham's Heart
1:1–5:32	6:1–11:32	12:1–17:27	18:1–23:20

INTRODUCTION TO GENESIS

Author: Moses
Dates of Events: ?–1859 BC

Genesis, a book of beginnings, is a sketch of human history that sets the stage for the rest of the Bible. In it God's profound grace and plan of restoration for His creation are introduced. Genesis records the beginning not only of the heavens and the earth—and of plant, animal, and human life—but also of all human institutions and relationships.

This first book of the Bible paints a beautiful picture of God's created universe, good and free from sin, with humans living in intimate relationship with Him. However, human depravity and sin are introduced as well. Adam and Eve's disobedience ushers in spiritual death and evil, and from that point on, all humankind finds itself separate and far from God. Sin's destructive effects are seen in the wickedness of people, and the grave consequences of God's righteous judgment are seen in the curse, in the flood, in the confusion of languages at Babel, and in

GENESIS

1

????	????	????	????	????	????	3200 BC	3100 BC	3000 BC

✦ Creation of the world

✦ 3200 Sumerian alphabet

✦ The flood

✦ 3100 King Menes (Egypt)

✦ Tower of Babel

✦ 3000 Stonehenge erected

The Creation of the World and the Fall of Humankind	Wickedness Increases, but God Is Faithful	God's Promise of Land, Descendants, and Blessing	God Tests Abraham's Heart
1:1–5:32	6:1–11:32	12:1–17:27	18:1–23:20

the obliteration of Sodom and Gomorrah. But piercing this darkness is the light of God's grace, seen in His provision for humankind's salvation. God provides a promise of redemption in Genesis 3:15, and His grace is further evidenced in the ark and His covenant with Noah, in the rescue of Lot and his family, and in the covenant with Abraham. From Abraham, an entire nation is built; it is here

Creation of Adam *by Michelangelo (1475–1564) (Sistine Chapel)*

in Genesis that God is seen preserving a remnant of people so that His promise of redemption and restoration will come to pass—with the birth of Christ, our promised Redeemer.

The whole of the Bible looks toward the reversal of this curse upon humankind and on the earth, and toward the restoration of all things. It is here in Genesis that the story begins.

????	????	????	????	????	????	3200 BC	3100 BC	3000 BC

◆ Creation of the world

◆ The flood

◆ Tower of Babel

◆ 3200 Sumerian alphabet

◆ 3100 King Menes (Egypt)

◆ 3000 Stonehenge erected

Jacob Deceives Esau and Isaac	Sold into Slavery	God Preserves a Remnant	Jacob's Family Arrives in Egypt
24:1–33:20	34:1–39:23	40:1–45:28	46:1–50:26

THE CREATION OF THE WORLD AND THE FALL OF HUMANKIND (1:1–5:32)

God, who existed before the beginning (Psalms 90:1–2; 93:2), creates the heavens, the earth, and everything in it. He then fashions His masterpiece, Adam and Eve, in His own image. God gives Adam and Eve charge over the entire earth. However, tempted by Satan, Adam and Eve choose to disobey God, be their own authority, and eat from a forbidden tree. God covers their shame and nakedness with animal skins—the first sacrifice. He removes Adam and Eve from His presence in the garden. However, God promises to redeem humankind from

2900 BC	2800 BC	2700 BC	2600 BC	2500 BC	2400 BC	2300 BC	2200 BC	2100 BC	2090 BC

• 2700 Construction of ancient pyramids begins in Egypt   • 2166 Birth of Abraham

• 2500 Iron manufactured

• 2500 Egyptians use papyrus

The Creation of the World and the Fall of Humankind	Wickedness Increases, but God Is Faithful	God's Promise of Land, Descendants, and Blessing	God Tests Abraham's Heart
1:1–5:32	6:1–11:32	12:1–17:27	18:1–23:20

this spiritual death through a human offspring who will crush Satan. The story of atonement and redemption begins. ⏳ *GENESIS 1:1–5, 26–31; 3:9–15, 23–24*

WICKEDNESS INCREASES, BUT GOD IS FAITHFUL (6:1–11:32)

The depravity in the world escalates, and every human thought is evil continually; there is not one aspect of human nature that is not corrupted by sin. God will not allow humankind to stay in this rebellious state forever. Noah, a blameless man, finds favor in the eyes of the Lord. God tells Noah to build an ark and gives him detailed instructions. Noah obeys, and when the rains pour down, flooding the earth and destroying all life, Noah's family and two of every creature on earth find salvation, safety, and hope in that ark. After 150 days, the flood-waters recede; God promises He will never again destroy the earth with a flood, and He places a rainbow in the sky to remind all subsequent generations of this promise. People become prideful yet again; God confuses their speech and scatters them throughout the earth. ⏳ *GENESIS 6:1–22; 9:8–17*

GOD'S PROMISE OF LAND, DESCENDANTS, AND BLESSING (12:1–17:27)

God calls Abram to leave his home country and sojourn to a different land. God promises Abram that he will have many descendants, that he will become a great nation, and that all families on earth will be blessed through him. Abram believes God and moves his family to Canaan. God promises Abram a

---

How does the story of the fall (Genesis 3) impact the Bible?

Genesis 3:15 is one of the foundational verses of the Bible. Many see this verse as the first glimpse of the Gospel of Jesus. The hostility described here certainly exists between snakes and people, but God's intention in this verse seems to include the person behind the snake (Satan) even more than the snake itself. The snake's offspring would remain in opposition to the woman's offspring. In this case, Eve's offspring points to one individual—the Messiah, Jesus, who would come forth from the Jewish people.

????	????	????	????	????	????	3200 BC	3100 BC	3000 BC

◆ Creation of the world

◆ 3200 Sumerian alphabet

◆ The flood

◆ 3100 King Menes (Egypt)

◆ Tower of Babel

◆ 3000 Stonehenge erected

Jacob Deceives Esau and Isaac	Sold into Slavery	God Preserves a Remnant	Jacob's Family Arrives in Egypt
24:1–33:20	34:1–39:23	40:1–45:28	46:1–50:26

son and reaffirms Abram will possess the land. Abram's wife, Sarah, is barren and doubts God's plan; she sends Abram to her maidservant, Hagar, to ensure a male child will be born. The child born to Hagar, Ishmael, is not the child of the promise. God changes Abram's name to Abraham, which means "father of

GENESIS

5

Tower of Babel *by Pieter Bruegel (1525–1569)*

2900 BC	2800 BC	2700 BC	2600 BC	2500 BC	2400 BC	2300 BC	2200 BC	2100 BC	2090 BC

◆ 2700 Construction of ancient pyramids begins in Egypt ◆ 2166 Birth of Abraham

◆ 2500 Iron manufactured

◆ 2500 Egyptians use papyrus

The Creation of the World and the Fall of Humankind	Wickedness Increases, but God Is Faithful	God's Promise of Land, Descendants, and Blessing	God Tests Abraham's Heart
1:1–5:32	6:1–11:32	12:1–17:27	18:1–23:20

many nations." God commands Abraham and the male members of his household to undergo circumcision, a sign showing they received the promise by faith. ☒ *GENESIS 12:1–9; 15:1–7; 17:1–10*

GOD TESTS ABRAHAM'S HEART (18:1–23:20)

The Lord confirms His promise to Abraham of a son. Sarah reacts by laughing; she is well past childbearing age. Then God reveals to Abraham the fate of Sodom and Gomorrah, two wicked and depraved cities. True to His word, God rains burning sulfur on Sodom and Gomorrah; Abraham's nephew Lot and his family escape. God fulfills His promise to Abraham and Sarah, and Isaac is born. Jealous of Ishmael, Sarah orders Hagar and Ishmael to be sent away. To test Abraham's faith, God asks him to sacrifice Isaac; believing God can raise Isaac from the dead, Abraham obeys. Just before slaying his son, God tells Abraham to stop—Abraham's obedience had revealed his true heart of faith. Sarah dies, and Abraham buys a field and buries his wife. ☒ *GENESIS 21:1–20; 22:1–18*

JACOB DECEIVES ESAU AND ISAAC (24:1–33:20)

Isaac marries Rebekah. Abraham dies, leaving his inheritance to Isaac. Isaac and Rebekah have twin boys, Esau and Jacob. Esau swears his birthright over to Jacob for a bowl of stew. Rebekah convinces her son Jacob to trick his aging father into giving him the blessing that is intended for Esau, the firstborn. Jacob agrees. Isaac and Esau realize what Jacob did, and Esau threatens to kill his brother. Later Jacob agrees to work for seven years for his uncle Laban, in exchange for his daughter Rachel's hand in marriage. Laban tricks Jacob into

---

What is the birthright, and why does Jacob want it so badly (25:32–33)?
First Chronicles 5:1–2 tells us the birthright involves both a material and a spiritual blessing. The son of the birthright receives a double portion of the inheritance, and he also becomes head of the family and the spiritual leader upon the passing of the father. And, in the case of this family, the birthright determines who will inherit the covenant God made with Abraham—the covenant of a land, a nation, and the Messiah.

2080 BC	2070 BC	2060 BC	2050 BC	2040 BC	2030 BC	2020 BC	2010 BC	2000 BC

◆ ???? Life of Job   ◆ 2050 Abraham offers Isaac as a sacrifice   ◆ 2005 Birth of Jacob

◆ 2100–2000? Ziggurats built in Mesopotamia   ◆ 2010? Silk use in China

Jacob Deceives Esau and Isaac	Sold into Slavery	God Preserves a Remnant	Jacob's Family Arrives in Egypt
24:1–33:20	34:1–39:23	40:1–45:28	46:1–50:26

marrying Rachel's less-than-attractive older sister, Leah. After confronting his uncle on his deception, Jacob agrees to work seven more years to marry Rachel. ⌛ *GENESIS 27:1–40*

SOLD INTO SLAVERY (34:1–39:23)

In one of the most shameful incidents in Israel's history, a local prince of Shechem violates Dinah, Leah's daughter, and then wants to marry her. After cleverly immobilizing the men of Shechem, Simeon and Levi destroy and plunder the city and rescue Dinah. Rachel and Isaac die. Joseph, Jacob's favored son, is sold into slavery by his own brothers, who lie to their father and tell him

The Sacrifice of Isaac *by Caravaggio (1571–1610)*

1990 BC	1980 BC	1970 BC	1960 BC	1950 BC	1940 BC	1930 BC	1920 BC	1910 BC

◆ 1950 Amorites conquer Mesopotamia   ◆ 1914 Birth of Joseph

◆ 1940 City of Ur falls

◆ 1991 Death of Abraham

The Creation of the World and the Fall of Humankind	Wickedness Increases, but God Is Faithful	God's Promise of Land, Descendants, and Blessing	God Tests Abraham's Heart
1:1–5:32	6:1–11:32	12:1–17:27	18:1–23:20

CAST OF CHARACTERS

Adam & Eve

Our First Parents. God formed Adam and Eve in His image, and together they lived in perfect harmony with Him in a beautiful garden. Adam and Eve chose to disobey God, by eating from a forbidden tree. Their actions severed their communion with God and ushered sin into a perfect world.

Noah

The Ark Builder. Noah was the only follower of God left in a sin-filled, wicked world. Acting on nothing but faith, Noah obeyed God and built an ark in preparation for a worldwide flood. After the flood, Noah planted a vineyard and became drunk; his embarrassed sons covered his nakedness.

1900 BC	1890 BC	1880 BC	1870 BC	1860 BC	1850 BC	1840 BC	1830 BC	1820 BC	1810 BC

• 1898 Sodom and Gomorrah destroyed • 1859 Death of Jacob

• 1876–1446 Sojourn in Egypt

• 1900 Wheel spokes invented in ancient Near East • 1856 First immigration into Greece

Jacob Deceives Esau and Isaac	Sold into Slavery	God Preserves a Remnant	Jacob's Family Arrives in Egypt
24:1–33:20	34:1–39:23	40:1–45:28	46:1–50:26

IN GENESIS

GENESIS

9

Abraham

Patriarch of Israel. God promised land, many descendants, and blessing to the whole world through Abraham. Abraham believed God for everything, even when he was asked to sacrifice his son Isaac. God spared Isaac; through him and his son Jacob, the great nation of Israel came into being.

Joseph

Jacob's Favorite Son. Joseph was Jacob's favorite son. His jealous brothers sold him into slavery. Wrongly thrown into prison in Egypt, Joseph interpreted a dream for Pharaoh about a coming famine, earning him favor. The famine drove Joseph's brothers to Egypt for food. Joseph revealed himself and forgave his brothers.

1800 BC	1790 BC	1780 BC	1770 BC	1760 BC	1750 BC	1740 BC	1730 BC	1720 BC	1710 BC

◆ 1800 Code of Hammurabi created   ◆ 1766 Shang Dynasty (China)

(Sojourn in Egypt continues. Begins in 1876. Ends in 1446.)

◆ 1800 Old Babylonian Period begins

Jacob Deceives Esau and Isaac	Sold into Slavery	God Preserves a Remnant	Jacob's Family Arrives in Egypt
24:1–33:20	34:1–39:23	40:1–45:28	46:1–50:26

Joseph has been killed; Jacob is devastated. God blesses Joseph in Egypt, even while in prison. ⌛ *GENESIS 37:12–36; 39:20B–23*

GOD PRESERVES A REMNANT (40:1–45:28)

Joseph interprets the dreams of two men while in prison; the dreams come true. Word gets out of Joseph's abilities, and two years later, Joseph is called in to interpret Pharaoh's dream, which reveals that a terrible famine is ahead. Joseph is promoted to a position of authority under Pharaoh, and he stores up food in anticipation of the coming famine. Back in Israel, the famine hits; Jacob sends his sons to Egypt to find food. After testing his brothers, who do not recognize him, and seeing his brother Judah stand up for his younger brother Benjamin, Joseph reveals himself to his brothers. He tells them to return home and bring their father back to Egypt to find protection from the famine. Thus, a remnant of Hebrews is preserved. ⌛ *GENESIS 41:14–57; 45:1–7*

JACOB'S FAMILY ARRIVES IN EGYPT (46:1–50:26)

Jacob and his family head for Egypt, and God encourages Jacob not to fear. Joseph and his father have an emotional reunion, and Pharaoh gives Joseph's father and brothers the best part of the land of Egypt. The Israelites grow in number and prosper. Jacob dies after passing on some cryptic blessings to his sons. His body is brought back to Canaan, and Joseph comforts his worried brothers that he is not out for revenge for selling him into slavery. Joseph dies, and his body is placed in a coffin in Egypt. ⌛ *GENESIS 47:1–12; 50:15–26*

> **Why did Joseph encourage his family to settle in Goshen?**
> Joseph encouraged his family to be completely honest with Pharaoh when asked about their occupation so that he would send them to live in Goshen (46:34). Goshen had some of the best pastureland in Egypt. It would be a place to keep the Hebrews isolated and insulated from the culture and religion of Egypt, since the Egyptians considered sheep unclean and Hebrews detestable (43:32). One of the greatest dangers to the covenant promises of God was intermarriage between the Hebrews and the Egyptians, because intermarriage would inevitably lead to spiritual compromise and the worship of the false gods of the Egyptians.

1900 BC	1890 BC	1880 BC	1870 BC	1860 BC	1850 BC	1840 BC	1830 BC	1820 BC	1810 BC

♦ 1898 Sodom and Gomorrah destroyed   ♦ 1859 Death of Jacob

♦ 1876–1446 Sojourn in Egypt

♦ 1900 Wheel spokes invented in ancient Near East   ♦ 1856 First immigration into Greece

Moses: Israel's Deliverer	The Reality of Bondage	Plagues, Passover, and Deliverance	Learning to Obey	The Tyranny of the Urgent	The Ten Command- ments and Beyond	God's Loving Insruction for His People	The Presence of God among His People
1:1 4:31	5.1–7:13	7:14–14·31	15:1–16:36	17:1–18:27	19:1–23:33	24:1–33:11	34:10–40:38

INTRODUCTION TO EXODUS–DEUTERONOMY

Author: Moses
Dates of Events: 1526–1410 BC

G od expands on His plan to redeem humankind and reveals more of His divine purpose, plan, and instruction in the books of Exodus, Leviticus, Numbers, and Deuteronomy. Exodus describes how God faithfully rescues His enslaved people and makes them into a great nation, in spite of the Israelites' continued stubborn rebellion against Him. Exodus also provides detailed instructions for how the people of Israel are to build God's holy dwelling place, the tabernacle. God establishes His holy priesthood in the book of Leviticus and gives practical regulations and guidelines to the priesthood for leading the people in how to worship God and live out holiness in everyday life. Leviticus also introduces the sacrificial system, which reveals human sinfulness and the need of a substitutionary blood sacrifice.

The instructions included in the book of Numbers are intended to prepare God's people for their entrance into the promised land. Numbers follows the

1800 BC	1790 BC	1780 BC	1770 BC	1760 BC	1750 BC	1740 BC	1730 BC	1720 BC	1710 BC

• 1800 Code of Hammurabi created   • 1766 Shang Dynasty (China)

(Sojourn in Egypt continues. Begins in 1876. Ends in 1446.)

• 1800 Old Babylonian Period begins

Moses: Israel's Deliverer	The Reality of Bondage	Plagues, Passover, and Deliverance	Learning to Obey
1:1–4:31	5:1–7:13	7:14–14:31	15:1–16:36

rebellious nation as the people wander for thirty-nine years from Mount Sinai to the plains of Moab.

The book of Deuteronomy is a reiteration and expansion of the Law given in Exodus, and it calls the people of Israel to renew their covenant with God by pledging their obedience.

Moses with the Commandments *by Rembrandt (1606–1669)*

1710 BC	1700 BC	1690 BC	1680 BC	1670 BC	1660 BC	1650 BC	1640 BC	1630 BC	1620 BC

◆ 1700 Egyptian papyrus document describes medical and surgical procedures

(Sojourn in Egypt continues. Begins in 1876. Ends in 1446.)

◆ 1700 Assyrian monarchy founded by Bel-kap-kapu

The Tyranny of the Urgent	The Ten Commandments and Beyond	God's Loving Instruction for His People	The Presence of God among His People
17:1–18:27	19:1–23:33	24:1–33:11	34:10–40:38

Read Each 5-Minute Overview in Exodus

EXODUS

13

MOSES: ISRAEL'S DELIVERER (1:1–4:31)

It seems like God is not speaking to His people at the beginning of Exodus. Although He appears to be keeping silent, God continues to orchestrate His plan of redemption behind the scenes. He never leaves His children, continues to work in their lives, and keeps a watchful eye on the tiny nation. God continues to watch over Israel, His treasured possession, by allowing Pharaoh's daughter to rescue Moses out of the waters of the Nile, thus preserving Israel's future deliverer. God then shifts His work with the nation of Israel and begins to work directly through Moses. God breaks His silence and instructs Moses from a burning bush to command Pharaoh to release God's people from captivity, but Moses is far from excited. He tells God to find someone else for the job because the task is too big for him. ☒ *EXODUS 1:1–22; 3:1–22*

1610 BC	1600 BC	1590 BC	1580 BC	1570 BC	1560 BC	1550 BC	1540 BC	1530 BC	1520 BC

◆ 1570 New kingdom of Egypt begins (extends through 1130)

(Sojourn in Egypt continues. Begins in 1876. Ends in 1446.)

◆ 1600 Hittites defeat Babylon; rise of the Hittites   ◆ 1556 Athens founded   ◆ 1526 Moses' birth

Moses: Israel's Deliverer	The Reality of Bondage	Plagues, Passover, and Deliverance	Learning to Obey
1:1–4:31	5:1–7:13	7:14–14:31	15:1–16:36

THE REALITY OF BONDAGE (5:1–7:13)

After Moses meets with God, he returns to Egypt. As expected, Pharaoh resists God's demands to let the Israelites go. The genealogy in Exodus 6 testifies to God's faithfulness and work across generations in space and time.
EXODUS 5:1–6:1; 6:28–7:13

PLAGUES, PASSOVER, AND DELIVERANCE (7:14–14:31)

God deploys ten plagues to bring judgment on Pharaoh and his people for oppressing the Israelites. God uses the tenth plague, the slaughter of the Egyptians' firstborn sons, to release His people from slavery. Simultaneously, God introduces the idea of a substitutionary sacrifice for Israel—the Passover lamb. Even though God's judgment is evident, so is His salvation effort. Sadly,

The Death of the Firstborn *by Lawrence Alma-Tadema (1836–1912)*

1610 BC	1600 BC	1590 BC	1580 BC	1570 BC	1560 BC	1550 BC	1540 BC	1530 BC	1520 BC

• 1570 New kingdom of Egypt begins (extends through 1130)

(Sojourn in Egypt continues. Begins in 1876. Ends in 1446.)

• 1600 Hittites defeat Babylon; rise of the Hittites   • 1556 Athens founded   • 1526 Moses' birth

The Tyranny of the Urgent	The Ten Commandments and Beyond	God's Loving Instruction for His People	The Presence of God among His People
17:1–18:27	19:1–23:33	24:1–33:11	34:10–40:38

the Egyptians continue in their refusal to acknowledge God, which ultimately leads to the nation's destruction. Incredibly, the sea that destroys the Egyptians is the same instrument God uses to deliver the Israelites. ⏳ *EXODUS 11:1–12:40*

top: African bullfrog
bottom: hail

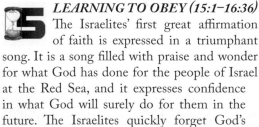 **LEARNING TO OBEY (15:1–16:36)**
The Israelites' first great affirmation of faith is expressed in a triumphant song. It is a song filled with praise and wonder for what God has done for the people of Israel at the Red Sea, and it expresses confidence in what God will surely do for them in the future. The Israelites quickly forget God's faithfulness, however, and slip into sinful behaviors of greed and grumbling. In spite of their lack of trust, God continues to care for His people and meet their basic needs by providing manna. However, He regulates the gathering and use of the manna to test His people's faith and obedience. ⏳ *EXODUS 15:19–16:35*

 THE TYRANNY OF THE URGENT (17:1–18:27)
Leaving the Desert of Sin, where the provision of manna had commenced, the Israelites wander from place to place as the Lord directs their steps. Moses grows weary with the many responsibilities of leading the nation. He receives a visit from his father-in-law, Jethro, who has heard how God protected and delivered Israel. Jethro reunites Moses with his wife and children and also offers advice to help Moses lead his people with balance. ⏳ *EXODUS 17:1–18:27*

THE TEN COMMANDMENTS AND BEYOND (19:1–23:33)
God introduces His commandments, or instruction, for how to live as a set-apart nation. The Ten Commandments are one of the keys to

EXODUS

15

1510 BC	1500 BC	1490 BC	1480 BC	1470 BC	1460 BC	1450 BC	1440 BC	1430 BC	1420 BC

◆ 1510 Thutmose II (Egypt); sundials used in Egypt   ◆ 1446 The Exodus (assumes the "high date")

(Sojourn in Egypt continues. Begins in 1876. Ends in 1446.)   ◆ 1445 The Ten Commandments (Mt. Sinai)

◆ 1500 The creation of Nuzi Tablets; Aryans invade India   ◆ 1446–1406 The Hebrews wander 40 years

Moses: Israel's Deliverer	The Reality of Bondage	Plagues, Passover, and Deliverance	Learning to Obey
1:1–4:31	5:1–7:13	7:14–14:31	15:1–16:36

NAVIGATING THE BIBLE

understanding the Old Testament; they offer a broad view of God's Law for His people and outline how to relate to God and honor His image in others. After proclaiming the Ten Commandments, God follows by giving the lengthier and more specific Mosaic Law. In the Mosaic Law, God reveals His design for protecting servants, persons, and property. He also delivers His expectations for His people to act with mercy and justice toward others. ⌛ *EXODUS 19:1–20:21*

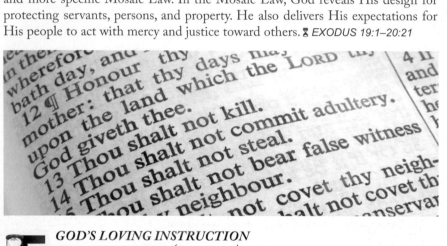

16

GOD'S LOVING INSTRUCTION FOR HIS PEOPLE (24:1–33:11)

God formally imposes the Mosaic Covenant on Israel. After giving Moses the Law, God follows by giving the Israelites instructions to construct a place where His presence can dwell among them—the tabernacle. The people need a place where they can worship God. Before Moses can even communicate God's holy instruction to the people, they impatiently construct and worship a

---

The Ten Commandments: Do they still apply today?
Jesus said He came to the world not to abolish God's law but to fulfill it (Matthew 5:17). Specifically, He fulfilled the Law by making it possible for us to follow its original intent. So what was the Law's original intent? To teach people how to love God with their whole heart and to love their neighbor as themselves. Love is the key to obeying God's commandments.

1610 BC	1600 BC	1590 BC	1580 BC	1570 BC	1560 BC	1550 BC	1540 BC	1530 BC	1520 BC

◆ 1570 New kingdom of Egypt begins (extends through 1130)

(Sojourn in Egypt continues. Begins in 1876. Ends in 1446.)

◆ 1600 Hittites defeat Babylon; rise of the Hittites   ◆ 1556 Athens founded   ◆ 1526 Moses' birth

The Tyranny of the Urgent	The Ten Commandments and Beyond	God's Loving Instruction for His People	The Presence of God among His People
17:1–18:27	19:1–23:33	24:1–33:11	34:10–40:38

golden calf. Even though God is angry at Israel's sin, He continues leading His people from a distance as they travel through the wilderness. ⌛ *EXODUS 32:1–33:23*

THE PRESENCE OF GOD AMONG HIS PEOPLE (34:10–40:38)

Moses returns from the mountain a second time, his face glowing—a reflection of the glory of God. Every time he speaks to the Israelites with his beaming face, the people know that God is speaking to them through Moses, giving him credentials that they dare not ignore. Soon the tabernacle is completed, and the glory of God's presence descends into the middle of the camp. ⌛ *EXODUS 40:1–38*

EXODUS

17

Timna tabernacle altar of burnt offerings

1510 BC	1500 BC	1490 BC	1480 BC	1470 BC	1460 BC	1450 BC	1440 BC	1430 BC	1420 BC

• 1510 Thutmose II (Egypt); sundials used in Egypt

♦ 1446 The Exodus (assumes the "high date")

(Sojourn in Egypt continues. Begins in 1876. Ends in 1446.)

♦ 1445 The Ten Commandments (Mt. Sinai)

• 1500 The creation of Nuzi Tablets; Aryans invade India

♦ 1446–1406 The Hebrews wander 40 years

Rules for Approaching God	Principles of Priesthood	Clean and Unclean
1:1–7:38	8:1–10:20	11:1–15:33

Read Each 5-Minute Overview in Leviticus

RULES FOR APPROACHING GOD (1:1–7:38)

God gives Moses instruction for five different tabernacle offerings, establishing how His people are to appropriately draw near to Him. (1) The burnt offering, which illustrates God's principle of atonement, appeases God's wrath as an acceptable ransom price and makes fellowship possible through the sacrificial shedding of blood. The burnt offering becomes a "pleasing aroma" to God and points to Christ, who "gave himself up for us as a fragrant offering and sacrifice to God" (Ephesians 5:2). (2) The grain offering is a gift that reveals the Israelites' faith that God will continue to provide for them in the desert where grain is scarce. It looks forward to Jesus as our true bread of life (John 6:35). (3) The only optional offering is the fellowship offering, which focuses on Israel's dependence on God and ends with a sacrificial meal. An animal without defect or blemish is presented, and the worshipper identifies with the animal while it is being sacrificed by placing a hand on the animal's head. This offering foreshadows Christ as our peace (Ephesians 2:14, 17; Colossians 1:20) and reminds us of the communion meal as a means of fellowship. (4) The sin offering cleanses the worshipper from the defilement of sin and deals with sin's consequences. The sin offering is for specific, unintentional sins. It typifies Christ, who cleanses believers from sin (Hebrews 9:12–14; 1 John 1:7). (5) Finally, the guilt offering serves the

1610 BC	1600 BC	1590 BC	1580 BC	1570 BC	1560 BC	1550 BC	1540 BC	1530 BC	1520 BC

♦ 1570 New kingdom of Egypt begins (extends through 1130)

(Sojourn in Egypt continues. Begins in 1876. Ends in 1446.)

♦ 1600 Hittites defeat Babylon; rise of the Hittites   ♦ 1556 Athens founded   ♦ 1526 Moses' birth

The Day of Atonement	Rules for Holy Living	The Value of a Vow
16:1–34	17:1–26:46	27:1–34

same purpose as the sin offering, but it is offered in cases where restitution is possible (such as with sins involving stolen property). ⁑ *LEVITICUS 5:1–13*

PRINCIPLES OF PRIESTHOOD (8:1–10:20)

The Aaronic priesthood's ordination is described in detail. Aaron and his sons are commanded to offer sacrifices, first for their own sins and then for the sins of the nation. Two of Aaron's sons, Nadab and Abihu, die because they exercise their priestly duties in a way that dishonors God. God's presence is seen as a consuming fire, and the priesthood is seen as an exceedingly dangerous job. ⁑ *LEVITICUS 10:1–20*

CLEAN AND UNCLEAN (11:1–15:33)

God now defines what is considered clean and unclean, holy and profane, and these terms become prominent themes in Leviticus. Because the people of Israel are in a covenant relationship with God, they are to be holy as He is holy. Serious skin diseases and abnormal discharges make an individual unacceptable before a holy God and unacceptable within the Israelite community. God then gives people direction for how to purify themselves and the tabernacle. ⁑ *LEVITICUS 11:1–28*

Unusual laws: Why don't Christians follow all the Levitical laws today?

The Levitical laws were designed to help the Israelites worship God and maintain their distinct identity as God's people. The Old Testament legal code provided boundaries that protected the Israelites and nurtured their relationships with God and with one another. When Jesus came, He offered to transform people's hearts by showing them how to follow the original intent of God's law—that is, to love Him and to love others with their entire beings. To obey the intent of the Law means you no longer need specific rules to govern your actions. Your instincts are being transformed as you seek to bring glory to God. In Romans 13:9–10, Paul wrote, "The commandments, 'You shall not commit adultery,' 'You shall not murder,' 'You shall not steal,' 'You shall not covet,' and whatever other command there may be, are summed up in this one command: 'Love your neighbor as yourself.' Love does no harm to a neighbor. Therefore love is the fulfillment of the law." When we read Leviticus today, we do not need to approach it as a set of rules to be followed. Instead, we should ask how we might fulfill the "heart behind the commands"—that is, how we might love God and others.

1510 BC	1500 BC	1490 BC	1480 BC	1470 BC	1460 BC	1450 BC	1440 BC	1430 BC	1420 BC

◆ 1510 Thutmose II (Egypt); sundials used in Egypt

◆ 1446 The Exodus (assumes the "high date")

(Sojourn in Egypt continues. Begins in 1876. Ends in 1446.)

◆ 1445 The Ten Commandments (Mt. Sinai)

◆ 1500 The creation of Nuzi Tablets; Aryans invade India

◆ 1446–1406 The Hebrews wander 40 years

| GEN | EXOD | LEV | NUM | DEUT | JOSH | JUDG | RUTH | 1 SAM | 2 SAM | 1 KGS | 2 KGS | 1 CHR | 2 CHR | EZRA | NEH | ESTH | JOB | PSALMS | PROV | ECCL | SONG |

Rules for Approaching God	Principles of Priesthood	Clean and Unclean	The Day of Atonement	Rules for Holy Living	The Value of a Vow
1:1–7:38	8:1–10:20	11:1–15:33	16:1–34	17:1–26:46	27:1–34

NAVIGATING THE BIBLE

20

THE DAY OF ATONEMENT (16:1–34)

God addresses the expectations of the Aaronic priesthood. God gives instruction to Moses for cleansing the nation of Israel—the people and the tabernacle—and commands the high priest to make atonement through a blood sacrifice; this provides an acceptable "ransom price" for the sins of the nation of Israel once a year to cleanse sins. The Day of Atonement looks forward to Christ's once-for-all sacrifice (Hebrews 9:12). *LEVITICUS 16:1–34*

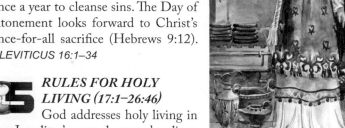

RULES FOR HOLY LIVING (17:1–26:46)

God addresses holy living in the Israelites' normal, everyday lives. Freed from slavery in Egypt, God's people are under a new order with a high standard. God establishes the Mosaic Covenant so Israel might be a holy, set-apart nation. The people of Israel need instruction for special ceremonies, holy days, and how to approach and care for the tabernacle. The people are instructed to love their neighbors, but they are also given details for dealing with serious sin through capital punishment. *LEVITICUS 18:1–37*

THE VALUE OF A VOW (27:1–34)

God lays out various things that His people may promise to dedicate to Him, along with appropriate regulations for each and provisions for vows made irresponsibly. *LEVITICUS 27:1–34*

1610 BC	1600 BC	1590 BC	1580 BC	1570 BC	1560 BC	1550 BC	1540 BC	1530 BC	1520 BC

◆ 1570 New kingdom of Egypt begins (extends through 1130)

(Sojourn in Egypt continues. Begins in 1876. Ends in 1446.)

◆ 1600 Hittites defeat Babylon; rise of the Hittites   ◆ 1556 Athens founded   ◆ 1526 Moses' birth

Israel at Sinai	From Sinai to Kadesh Barnea	Israel's Rebellion at Kadesh Barnea	Near, Yet So Far: Lessons along the Way	In Anticipation of Taking the Promised Land	Looking Back at God's Faithfulness
1:1–10:10	10:11–12:16	13:1–20:13	20:14–22:1	22:2–32:42	33:1–36:13

Read Each 5-Minute Overview in Numbers

ISRAEL AT SINAI: PREPARING TO DEPART FOR THE PROMISED LAND (1:1–10:10)

The book of Numbers opens with a counting of the people one year after leaving Egypt to identify those fit for battle once the people enter the land. The Levites are given care of the tabernacle and will live off a portion of the offerings brought by the people. God instructs the Israelites to rid their camp of spiritual impurities and make restitution for personal sin. The tabernacle is dedicated,

Modern-day unleavened bread

1510 BC	1500 BC	1490 BC	1480 BC	1470 BC	1460 BC	1450 BC	1440 BC	1430 BC	1420 BC

♦ 1510 Thutmose II (Egypt); sundials used in Egypt

♦ 1446 The Exodus (assumes the "high date")

(Sojourn in Egypt continues. Begins in 1876. Ends in 1446.)

♦ 1445 The Ten Commandments (Mt. Sinai)

♦ 1500 The creation of Nuzi Tablets; Aryans invade India

♦ 1446–1406 The Hebrews wander 40 years

Israel at Sinai	From Sinai to Kadesh Barnea	Israel's Rebellion at Kadesh Barnea
1:1–10:10	10:11–12:16	13:1–20:13

followed by a twelve-day festival. Three very important aspects to the nation of Israel are established—Passover, the presence of God in the cloud covering the tabernacle, and the use of the silver trumpets. ⏳ *NUMBERS 9:1–23*

FROM SINAI TO KADESH BARNEA (10:11–12:16)

God's presence leads the Israelites out of Sinai toward the land God said He would give His people. The ark of the covenant goes before them. But the people are frustrated with their circumstances and begin to complain. They have lost sight of God's promises and are focused on their immediate suffering. God provides manna and quail for them, but He strikes the people with a plague because His anger is so great against them. The people set up camp in the Desert of Paran. ⏳ *NUMBERS 11:1–35*

ISRAEL'S REBELLION AT KADESH BARNEA (13:1–20:13)

The Israelites arrive at Canaan, and twelve spies enter the land. Ten see only obstacles and report that the people in the land are too powerful to overtake. Two others, Joshua and Caleb, see opportunities and confidently rest in God's power to complete the task. Unfortunately, the people focus on the fear

Moses Striking the Rock *by Bartolomé Esteban Murillo (1617–1682)*

1610 BC	1600 BC	1590 BC	1580 BC	1570 BC	1560 BC	1550 BC	1540 BC	1530 BC	1520 BC

• 1570 New kingdom of Egypt begins (extends through 1130)

(Sojourn in Egypt continues. Begins in 1876. Ends in 1446.)

• 1600 Hittites defeat Babylon; rise of the Hittites   • 1556 Athens founded   • 1526 Moses' birth

Near, Yet So Far: Lessons along the Way	In Anticipation of Taking the Promised Land	Looking Back at God's Faithfulness
20:14–22:1	22:2–32:42	33:1–36:13

and danger of what's ahead, and because of their unbelief, God detains them in the wilderness for almost forty more years. God gives instructions for the people who now know they will wander in this wilderness until their deaths. He also reestablishes correct worship. The people continue to complain and rise up against Aaron's authority and his priestly line. God affirms the position of the Levites as guardians of the tabernacle, and He spells out their roles, responsibilities, regulations, and rewards. He establishes the ceremonial cleansing process for anyone who has been in contact with a dead body. A series of sad events, beginning with Miriam's death, highlights the seriousness with which God's instructions must be treated, and God's continued faithfulness to Israel allows the next generation to emerge and carry on God's plan. ☥ *NUMBERS 14:1–40*

NEAR, YET SO FAR: LESSONS ALONG THE WAY (20:14–22:1)

After Aaron's death, Moses alone leads the Israelites closer to Canaan. The people, as usual, grumble along the way. Israel defeats the Amorites, but moving northward, the king of Arad attacks them and takes captives. This first battle establishes a pattern: God will do the winning. The Israelites acknowledge that unless God gives their foes into their hands, they will not have any success. ☥ *NUMBERS 21:1–9*

IN ANTICIPATION OF TAKING THE PROMISED LAND (22:2–32:42)

The Israelites, poised on the border of the promised land, encamp at the base of the mountains of Moab. A sorcerer, Balaam, repeats God's covenant of blessing on the Hebrew people, foretells the deaths of pagan kings, and prophesies of a "star" that would come out of Jacob—pointing to Christ. The king of Moab, Balak, is angered that Balaam blesses, rather than curses, the Hebrews. A more subtle assault on Israel also spreads through the nation, through Moabite women sent to seduce the men of Israel and lead the whole nation to ruin through idolatry. A census is taken to count the people before entering the land, once again revealing God's faithfulness: Even though the people continually rebelled

1510 BC	1500 BC	1490 BC	1480 BC	1470 BC	1460 BC	1450 BC	1440 BC	1430 BC	1420 BC

◆ 1510 Thutmose II (Egypt); sundials used in Egypt   ◆ 1446 The Exodus (assumes the "high date")

(Sojourn in Egypt continues. Begins in 1876. Ends in 1446.)   ◆ 1445 The Ten Commandments (Mt. Sinai)

◆ 1500 The creation of Nuzi Tablets; Aryans invade India   ◆ 1446–1406 The Hebrews wander 40 years

Israel at Sinai	From Sinai to Kadesh Barnea	Israel's Rebellion at Kadesh Barnea	Near, Yet So Far: Lessons along the Way	In Anticipation of Taking the Promised Land	Looking Back at God's Faithfulness
1:1–10:10	10:11–12:16	13:1–20:13	20:14–22:1	22:2–32:42	33:1–36:13

against God, He did not wipe out every tribe. The Lord prescribes specific daily and yearly observances for the people of Israel to keep when they enter into the land; the nation is to be governed by worship. The Israelites make a commitment over and above what is required by the Law, and Moses reminds the leaders of Israel of the seriousness of following through with those vows. Israel is called to war with the Midianites, and the Lord tells Moses that he is to treat them as enemies and destroy them. Two tribes, Reuben and Gad, request to be allowed to settle in the Transjordan region rather than going across the Jordan into Canaan.
⏳ *NUMBERS 32:1–27*

 LOOKING BACK AT GOD'S FAITHFULNESS (33:1–36:13)

Before taking the promised land, Moses reviews God's faithfulness in leading the Israelites out of Egypt to the land promised to them through Abraham. Many were children when the Lord delivered them from their bondage and might not remember. Moses reminds them that God is the One who delivers. Portions of the land are assigned to each tribe, and the Levites are given a portion of each tribe's inheritance. ⏳ *NUMBERS 33:50–56*

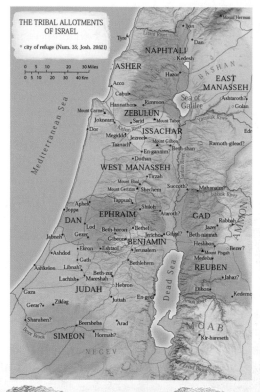

24

1610 BC	1600 BC	1590 BC	1580 BC	1570 BC	1560 BC	1550 BC	1540 BC	1530 BC	1520 BC

◆ 1570 New kingdom of Egypt begins (extends through 1130)

(Sojourn in Egypt continues. Begins in 1876. Ends in 1446.)

◆ 1600 Hittites defeat Babylon; rise of the Hittites   ◆ 1556 Athens founded   ◆ 1526 Moses' birth

Ready to Enter the Land	Restating the Covenant	Details of Worship	Under God's Authority	Further Stipulations	God Is Holy and He Is Everywhere	Transitions
1:1–4:43	4:44–11:32	12:1–16:17	16:18–20:20	21:1–24:22	25:1–30:20	31:1–34:12

Read Each 5-Minute Overview in Deuteronomy

READY TO ENTER THE LAND (1:1–4:43)

The nation of Israel is poised on the eastern bank of the Jordan River opposite Jericho. Two months later, the people will cross the river, on dry land, into the promised land for the first time. It is at this juncture in Israel's history that God initiates a renewal of the covenant. Moses reminds the Israelites of everything God has done but also reminds them of their rebellion—the reason they spent so many years wandering. Moses retells the story of Israel's forty-year sojourn in the wilderness, which is now coming to an end. Israel is ready to conquer and claim the land. At this point, Moses begins to lay out the commandments the nation must obey in response to God's faithfulness. ⏳ *DEUTERONOMY 1:26–46*

RESTATING THE COVENANT TO A NEW GENERATION (4:44–11:32)

The stipulations of the covenant are also restated, this time to the current generation of Israelites. God exhorts parents to nurture their children in the faith, to ensure the covenant is passed down to generations to come. God's people are

1510 BC	1500 BC	1490 BC	1480 BC	1470 BC	1460 BC	1450 BC	1440 BC	1430 BC	1420 BC

♦ 1510 Thutmose II (Egypt); sundials used in Egypt   ♦ 1446 The Exodus (assumes the "high date")

(Sojourn in Egypt continues. Begins in 1876. Ends in 1446.)   ♦ 1445 The Ten Commandments (Mt. Sinai)

♦ 1500 The creation of Nuzi Tablets; Aryans invade India   ♦ 1446–1406 The Hebrews wander 40 years

| GEN | EXOD | LEV | NUM | DEUT | JOSH | JUDG | RUTH | 1 SAM | 2 SAM | 1 KGS | 2 KGS | 1 CHR | 2 CHR | EZRA | NEH | ESTH | JOB | PSALMS | PROV | ECCL SONG |

Ready to Enter the Land	Restating the Covenant	Details of Worship	Under God's Authority
1:1–4:43	4:44–11:32	12:1–16:17	16:18–20:20

reminded that they are holy to the Lord, and if they follow God's instruction, their nation will be blessed more than any other nation. Moses knows what the human heart is capable of. He knows when the Israelites enter the lush and fruitful land God is giving them, they might forget about the time of wandering and all that God had done for them and take credit for the Lord's achievement. Moses calls them to give their whole hearts to God and understand the key to staying in the land is obedience that stems from love. ⏳ *DEUTERONOMY 5:1–22*

DETAILS OF WORSHIP (12:1–16:17)

Moses gives stipulations, or legislation, for matters such as worship and management of criminal cases in court. Israel is warned about worshipping other gods, given a brief account of the laws of cleanliness, and made aware of God's concern for the poor and disadvantaged—in this case, those in debt and those who have to sell themselves as servants. God also summarizes the three yearly pilgrimage festivals the Israelites are to keep. ⏳ *DEUTERONOMY 12:1–32*

UNDER GOD'S AUTHORITY (16:18–20:20)

Israel is to live under God's authority. Judges, trials, and punishment all demonstrate God's requirement that His will be done in the community of His people. God communicates His presence directly to His people's hearts through the Holy Spirit and uses people as instruments of His presence. He speaks to Israel through prophets, maintains fellowship with them through priests, and will continue to rule over them through kings. God's underlying rules about murder and punishment point to a bigger requirement: Innocent blood should not be shed on the land. ⏳ *DEUTERONOMY 17:1–20*

1610 BC	1600 BC	1590 BC	1580 BC	1570 BC	1560 BC	1550 BC	1540 BC	1530 BC	1520 BC

♦ 1570 New kingdom of Egypt begins (extends through 1130)

(Sojourn in Egypt continues. Begins in 1876. Ends in 1446.)

♦ 1600 Hittites defeat Babylon; rise of the Hittites   ♦ 1556 Athens founded   ♦ 1526 Moses' birth

Further Stipulations	God Is Holy and He Is Everywhere	Transitions
21:1–24:22	25:1–30:20	31:1–34:12

FURTHER STIPULATIONS (21:1–24:22)

A variety of laws for difficult situations are given, including laws related to the themes of the sanctity of life and marriage. ⌛ *DEUTERONOMY 24:1–22*

GOD IS HOLY AND HE IS EVERYWHERE (25:1–30:20)

The people of Israel are to recognize God's presence every day. Some of the rituals they must follow when they enter the land are listed. Blessings and curses will result from keeping or breaking the covenant they are renewing. The importance of obedience cannot be overstated. Even though God knows His people will fall into exile because of their tendency toward idolatry, they will eventually be brought out of exile: God will never abandon them. ⌛ *DEUTERONOMY 28:1–14*

TRANSITIONS (31:1–34:12)

At the end of their journey through the wilderness and at the doorstep of the conquest, Moses prepares to step out of the way and transfer leadership from himself to Joshua. Moses' priority is ensuring that the next generation prioritizes their relationship with God. Moses' song reminds the people of Israel of their sin and rebellion and that the people's hearts are far from God. Before his death, Moses blesses Israel, and although he does not lead the people into the land, God allows him to see it from afar. ⌛ *DEUTERONOMY 34:1–12*

Legal interpretation: What is the best way to read the Law?

No one can be made right with God by keeping the Law through the power of their own flesh (Romans 3:20–22). So how should we read the law of God if it is has no power to save? Here are three things to remember:

1. The Law was not written to save people but to show people their sin (1 Timothy 1:9).
2. Through Jesus the Law has been fulfilled on our behalf (Matthew 5:17).
3. The Law should cause us to treasure Jesus as our source of life (Romans 5:20–21).

Reading the Law can help us realize the depth of our sin and the righteous requirements of God. But we shouldn't stop there. The Law is a reminder that the only way to fulfill its requirements is through faith in Jesus. Therefore, as we read the Law, we should find that our love and appreciation of Jesus is ever growing.

1510 BC	1500 BC	1490 BC	1480 BC	1470 BC	1460 BC	1450 BC	1440 BC	1430 BC	1420 BC

• 1510 Thutmose II (Egypt); sundials used in Egypt

(Sojourn in Egypt continues. Begins in 1876. Ends in 1446.)

• 1500 The creation of Nuzi Tablets; Aryans invade India

• 1446 The Exodus (assumes the "high date")

• 1445 The Ten Commandments (Mt. Sinai)

• 1446–1406 The Hebrews wander 40 years

Ready to Enter the Land	Restating the Covenant	Details of Worship	Under God's Authority
1:1–4:43	4:44–11:32	12:1–16:17	16:18–20:20

CAST OF CHARACTERS

Moses

Great Hebrew Prophet. As Israel's anointed leader, Moses led the nation from slavery in Egypt, through the desert, and eventually to the promised land. Moses built the tabernacle and delivered God's law to the people. Because of disobedience, Moses didn't cross into the land but only saw it from afar.

Aaron

Moses' Influential Brother. Aaron stood alongside Moses as he confronted Pharaoh. Aaron often compensated for Moses' weakness by serving as Moses' spokesperson. Though he made mistakes, Aaron held an important position of influence over Israel. Aaron and his sons became the first Hebrew priests appointed by God.

1610 BC	1600 BC	1590 BC	1580 BC	1570 BC	1560 BC	1550 BC	1540 BC	1530 BC	1520 BC

♦ 1570 New kingdom of Egypt begins (extends through 1130)

(Sojourn in Egypt continues. Begins in 1876. Ends in 1446.)

♦ 1600 Hittites defeat Babylon; rise of the Hittites   ♦ 1556 Athens founded   ♦ 1526 Moses' birth

Further Stipulations	God Is Holy and He Is Everywhere	Transitions
21:1–24:22	25:1–30:20	31:1–34:12

IN EXODUS–DEUTERONOMY

Miriam

Worship Leader. Miriam, an Israelite slave girl, watched over her baby brother Moses when Pharaoh commanded all baby boys be killed. She arranged for Moses' nursemaid when he was discovered floating in a basket in the Nile by Pharaoh's daughter. Miriam led the Israelites in song after crossing the Red Sea.

Caleb

A Different Spirit. Caleb was one of twelve spies sent to explore Canaan. Alongside Joshua, Caleb tried to convince Israel to obey God and take the land. The people did not listen. God rewarded Caleb for his devotion and tenacity by assuring him a place in the promised land.

1510 BC	1500 BC	1490 BC	1480 BC	1470 BC	1460 BC	1450 BC	1440 BC	1430 BC	1420 BC

- ✦ 1510 Thutmose II (Egypt); sundials used in Egypt
- ✦ 1446 The Exodus (assumes the "high date")
- (Sojourn in Egypt continues. Begins in 1876. Ends in 1446.)
- ✦ 1445 The Ten Commandments (Mt. Sinai)
- ✦ 1500 The creation of Nuzi Tablets; Aryans invade India
- ✦ 1446–1406 The Hebrews wander 40 years

NAVIGATING THE BIBLE

INTRODUCTION TO JOSHUA, JUDGES, AND RUTH

Authors: Unknown
Dates of Events: 1300–1000 BC

God had promised Abraham many descendants, land, and blessing in Genesis, and His faithfulness in orchestrating the fulfillment of this promise continues to be seen in the books of Joshua, Judges, and Ruth. He has done for Israel exactly what He has said. The fulfillment of God's promise begins with Isaac's birth to Abraham and Sarah, followed by generations of descendants. Now Joshua provides an overview of the military campaigns to conquer the land that God had promised. Following the Exodus from Egypt and the subsequent forty years of wilderness wanderings, the newly formed nation is ready to enter and occupy Canaan. God intervenes on behalf of His people against all kinds of tremendous odds, and Israel conquers and possesses the land with its fortified cities—but only with God's blessing and power. Joshua teaches that victory is accomplished through faith and that only God can provide deliverance.

From the time of Joshua's death until the rise of Samuel, the Israelites fight many wars of deliverance to defeat the Canaanites and the Philistines. The book of Judges is a tragic account of how, during this time period, God was taken for granted by His disobedient and idolatrous children over and over again. Yet Judges reveals God's consistent and merciful response to Israel's repetitive cycle of sin. He never fails to open His loving arms to His people whenever they turn to Him and call on His name. Fifteen different colorful and imperfect judges lead Israel in righteous living, and through them God graciously honors His promise to Abraham to protect and bless his offspring. Through these types of saviors, God

1410 BC	1400 BC	1390 BC	1380 BC	1370 BC	1360 BC	1350 BC	1340 BC	1330 BC	1320 BC

◆ 1400 Chopstick use begins in China   ◆ 1372 Amenhotep (Egypt)   ◆ 1340 First use of iron tools

◆ 1406 Moses dies; Joshua appointed leader   ◆ 1373–1334 Othniel (judge)

◆ 1400 Creation of cuneiform tablets in Ugarit   ◆ 1360 King Tut (Egypt)

Israel's Promised Inheritance Realized	Allotment for the Rest of the Land	The Covenant Renewed
11:1–14:15	15:1–19:51	20:1–24:33

draws His children back to Himself. The Israelites' poor decisions during these centuries directly correlate, however, to their eventual downfall.

Ruth, a small book of four chapters, was written to the Israelites and teaches that although genuine love may require uncompromising sacrifice at times, it will be rewarded. Ruth reveals God's work of providence in the details of people's lives. Specifically the book shows how God provides for a non-Israelite to become a faithful follower of Israel's God—fulfilling God's promise to Abraham of blessing to all peoples. God guides Ruth, a Moabite, in her every step to become His child and fulfill His plan for her to become an ancestor of Jesus Christ. Ruth reminds readers that God's plan will continue in spite of sin, obstacles, and mistakes. His plan of redemption will be accomplished.

Ruth and Boaz *by Barent Fabritius (1624–1673)*

1310 BC	1300 BC	1290 BC	1280 BC	1270 BC	1260 BC	1250 BC	1240 BC	1230 BC	1220 BC

◆ 1304–1238 Ramses II (Egypt)

◆ 1316–1237 Ehud (judge)   ◆ 1237 Deborah (judge) & Barak

◆ 1300 Shalmaneser (Assyria)

The Battle Is the Lord's	Learning to Trust God for Victory	Walking by Faith, Not by Sight
1:1–5:15	6:1–8:35	9:1–10:43

Read Each 5-Minute Overview in Joshua

THE BATTLE IS THE LORD'S (1:1–5:15)

God commissions Joshua as Israel's new leader after Moses and charges Israel to take control of the promised land. God's people listen and obey. Joshua and the people are called to accomplish tasks far beyond their abilities, but Joshua trusts in God's promises and courageously prepares the Israelites for what's ahead. The priests carry the ark of the covenant ahead of the people and step into the Jordan River; the waters miraculously stop flowing, and the people of Israel cross on dry ground. Wisely concerned that His people will forget what He has done for them, God instructs the Israelites to build a monument as a memorial for crossing the Jordan. Before the Israelites begin taking the land, Joshua

The Harlot of Jericho and the Two Spies by James Tissot (1836–1902)

1410 BC	1400 BC	1390 BC	1380 BC	1370 BC	1360 BC	1350 BC	1340 BC	1330 BC	1320 BC

◆ 1400 Chopstick use begins in China   ◆ 1372 Amenhotep (Egypt)   ◆ 1340 First use of iron tools

◆ 1406 Moses dies; Joshua appointed leader   ◆ 1373–1334 Othniel (judge)

◆ 1400 Creation of cuneiform tablets in Ugarit   ◆ 1360 King Tut (Egypt)

Israel's Promised Inheritance Realized	Allotment for the Rest of the Land	The Covenant Renewed
11:1–14:15	15:1–19:51	20:1–24:33

prepares their hearts by dedicating them to God's divine purpose, and the people humbly submit to God's instruction. ⏳ *JOSHUA 3:1–17*

LEARNING TO TRUST GOD FOR VICTORY (6:1–8:35)

God directs the Israelites to a miraculous victory at Jericho with an unlikely strategy. According to God's instruction, the Israelites march around Jericho for seven days; on the seventh day the priests sound a long trumpet blast. The whole army shouts, the city wall collapses, and Israel takes Jericho. This first great victory precedes an initial terrible defeat at Ai as a result of the Israelites' slip back into unfaithfulness. However, God's grace and restoration overpower the people's failure, and Israel victoriously defeats Ai. ⏳ *JOSHUA 6:1–27*

WALKING BY FAITH, NOT BY SIGHT (9:1–10:43)

Next, the Israelites learn the importance of trusting God and His plans rather than walking by sight. There are enemy nations that still need to be taken, one in particular that had deceived Israel into committing  to a treaty of peace. The five kings of the Amorites then join forces against Israel. Joshua trusts God for a victory over the Amorites and prays for extended daylight, and miraculously the sun does not set for a full day. This allows for a quick victory over a number of enemies at once. Israel wipes out the southern part of Canaan and once again testifies to God's faithfulness. ⏳ *JOSHUA 10:1–15*

Holy war: Why is God so violent?

God is not a violent God as much as He is a holy God. In other words, God hates sin. As the Judge of the world, God has the right and the responsibility to bring justice to our world. God intervenes in this world and demonstrates not only grace and mercy but also judgment and justice. Because God is the final Judge of the world, there are times when He must bring judgment upon individuals as well as upon nations—especially those that have tried to thwart His purposes in the world. Such intervention is not gratuitous violence but righteous and perfect judgment. In response, we should pray as the prophet Habakkuk did: "In wrath remember mercy" (Habakkuk 3:2).

1310 BC	1300 BC	1290 BC	1280 BC	1270 BC	1260 BC	1250 BC	1240 BC	1230 BC	1220 BC

◆ 1304–1238 Ramses II (Egypt)

◆ 1316–1237 Ehud (judge)   ◆ 1237 Deborah (judge) & Barak

◆ 1300 Shalmaneser (Assyria)

The Battle Is the Lord's	Learning to Trust God for Victory	Walking by Faith, Not by Sight	Israel's Promised Inheritance Realized	Allotment for the Rest of the Land	The Covenant Renewed
1:1–5:15	6:1–8:35	9:1–10:43	11:1–14:15	15:1–19:51	20:1–24:33

ISRAEL'S PROMISED INHERITANCE REALIZED (11:1–14:15)

Joshua finally takes the entire remaining land of the north; this realizes the victory promised to Israel back in Genesis. The land enjoys rest from war. A list of all the kings conquered testifies to the power and faithfulness of God to accomplish His purposes. Caleb receives the first portion of land, as he and Joshua were the only two men who believed God would be faithful to do what He said He would do. ⧗ *JOSHUA 11:1–23*

ALLOTMENT FOR THE REST OF THE LAND (15:1–19:51)

The largest portion of land is then given to the largest tribe—the tribe of Judah. In years past, Jacob had included Joseph's two children, Ephraim and Manasseh, in his inheritance; thus, Joshua gives their tribes land as well. Seven more tribes finally receive their allotment. The Israelites move the tent of meeting, the place where the presence of God resides, to Shiloh—the center of the entire nation. ⧗ *JOSHUA 18:1–10*

THE COVENANT RENEWED (20:1–24:33)

God next gives further instruction to the Israelites for how they are to live in the land He has given them. He commands them to set up cities of refuge for anyone who accidentally kills another person. He also gives cities and pasturelands to the Levites so they may raise families and care for cattle; however, they must remain set apart primarily for service to God. The eastern tribes return home but sadly act inappropriately, and civil war almost destroys the newly formed nation. God faithfully continues to protect the Israelites but teaches them some serious lessons about true worship. Joshua, nearing the end of his life, gives a farewell address expressing his deep concern for Israel's growing complacency toward the Canaanite remnants. He warns the people they will only experience God's blessing if they obey God. Finally, Joshua meets with the people of Israel for the last time at Shechem, and the Israelites renew their covenant with God. ⧗ *JOSHUA 23:1–16*

34

1410 BC	1400 BC	1390 BC	1380 BC	1370 BC	1360 BC	1350 BC	1340 BC	1330 BC	1320 BC

◆ 1400 Chopstick use begins in China ◆ 1372 Amenhotep (Egypt) ◆ 1340 First use of iron tools

◆ 1406 Moses dies; Joshua appointed leader ◆ 1373–1334 Othniel (judge)

◆ 1400 Creation of cuneiform tablets in Ugarit ◆ 1360 King Tut (Egypt)

The Vicious Cycle after Joshua	Othniel, Ehud, Deborah, and Jael	The Call to Gideon	Set Apart for God	Dan's Deceit	Idolatry Leads to Immorality
1:1–3:16	3:7–5:31	12:1–16:17	16:18–20:20	17:1–18:31	19:1–21:25

Read Each 5-Minute Overview in Judges

○ 1:1–3:6	The Vicious Cycle after Joshua	Page 35
○ 3:7–5:31	Othniel, Ehud, Deborah, and Jael	Page 35
○ 6:1–12:15	The Call to Gideon	Page 36
○ 13:1–16:31	Set Apart for God	Page 36
○ 17:1–18:31	Dan's Deceit	Page 37
○ 19:1–21:25	Idolatry Leads to Immorality	Page 37

THE VICIOUS CYCLE AFTER JOSHUA (1:1–3:6)

After Joshua leads the Israelites in conquering Canaan and assigns portions of the land to each of the twelve tribes that make up the nation of Israel, the people compromise and fail to obey God's next commands completely. Consequences dramatically affect their occupation of the land. God had instructed them to drive out any people who refused to follow Yahweh, but the Israelites are convinced their half attempts to claim their territories are justified and still represent victories. They begin to serve other gods and suffer consequences for this sin. They too easily forget the great works the Lord had done in bringing them out of Egypt. ⚱ *JUDGES 2:6–23*

OTHNIEL, EHUD, DEBORAH, AND JAEL (3:7–5:31)

Suffering from the consequences of disobedience, God's people cry out again for help. Hearing their cries, God sends judges to instruct them in righteous living. Through two exemplary judges, Othniel and Ehud, God's sovereign goodness and grace are evident in both His chastisements and His deliverance. God then raises two female leaders: Deborah, a judge, and Jael.

1310 BC	1300 BC	1290 BC	1280 BC	1270 BC	1260 BC	1250 BC	1240 BC	1230 BC	1220 BC

◆ 1304–1238 Ramses II (Egypt)

◆ 1316–1237 Ehud (judge)　　　　　　　　　　　　　　　　　　　◆ 1237 Deborah (judge) & Barak

◆ 1300 Shalmaneser (Assyria)

The Vicious Cycle after Joshua	Othniel, Ehud, Deborah, and Jael	The Call to Gideon
1:1–3:6	3:7–5:31	6:1–12:15

NAVIGATING THE BIBLE

Deborah prevails on Barak, the head captain of Israel's army, to fight against King Jabin. Jael completes the victory by killing Sisera, the captain of Jabin's army. ☷ *JUDGES 4:1–24*

THE CALL TO GIDEON (6:1–12:15)

The cycle of falling away from faith, becoming oppressed, and praying for deliverance begins again. Gideon's battle with the Midianites illustrates the people's weakness versus God's strength. Gideon exemplifies what a faithful follower of God looks like but also reminds readers that faithfulness doesn't exempt one from future temptation. After Gideon, Israel experiences forty years of peace, followed once again by sin and compromise. Great judgment comes on Israel, serving as a warning for future generations. Next, Jephthah—a mighty warrior, judge, and brilliant military strategist—leads the Gileadites to defeat the Ammonites, in spite of a terrible vow he makes (and apparently fulfills) to God. ☷ *JUDGES 7:1–25*

SET APART FOR GOD (13:1–16:31)

Once again, the Israelites rebel against God, and He delivers them into the hands of the Philistines for forty years. An angel of the Lord comes

The death of Samson

1210 BC	1200 BC	1190 BC	1180 BC	1170 BC	1160 BC	1150 BC	1140 BC	1130 BC	1120 BC

◆ 1190–1180 Trojan War

◆ 1151 Abimelek (judge)   ◆ 1126 Jair (judge)

◆ 1191–1151 Gideon (judge)

◆ 1149 Tola (judge)

◆ 1200 Beginning of the Iron Age; fall of the Hittite Empire

◆ 1150 Chou Dynasty (China)

Set Apart for God	Dan's Deceit	Idolatry Leads to Immorality
13:1–16:31	17:1–18:31	19:1–21:25

to Manoah's barren wife and announces she will miraculously conceive a son, who will be set apart for the Lord from birth. The Spirit of the Lord moves on this son, Samson, who begins to deliver a "sleeping" Israel. His actions are surprising and instill fear of a mighty and holy God in the people. Samson's love for Delilah, however, marks the beginning of his downfall and eventual demise. Samson becomes bound, blinded, and imprisoned. Then in one sacrificial act that leads to his death, he slaughters more enemies than he had killed in all the battles of his life. ⧗ *JUDGES 16:1–31*

DAN'S DECEIT (17:1–18:31)

The Israelites continue in their corrupt practices of idolatry. An Ephraimite named Micah sets up an idol of silver in a shrine in his home. A Levite from Bethlehem comes to Micah and becomes his priest. This Levite later steals Micah's idol and joins a group of Danites to become their priest instead. The Danites, who were seeking a place to conquer and settle, defeat Laish and rename the city Dan. They settle in Dan, where they set up and worship Micah's idol. While Moses had delivered the people of Israel and established a house of worship, a priesthood, and promise of conquest of land, we see in Judges 17–18 how the Israelites pervert this history of an established worship and priesthood, as well as the land conquest. ⧗ *JUDGES 18:1–31*

IDOLATRY LEADS TO IMMORALITY (19:1–21:25)

A Levite comes to the city of Gibeah in Benjamin, and the men of the city rape and murder his concubine. The Levite reacts by cutting her corpse into twelve pieces and sending a piece to each of the twelve tribes in Israel. The tribes respond by attacking Gibeah on behalf of the crime committed against the Levite and his concubine. The men of Benjamin defend their city but are defeated, and only six hundred Benjamites survive. God uses this awful event to show that idolatry leads to immorality. The Levites have been unable to protect the people from idolatry and immorality, and thus judgment falls hard on the house of the Lord. ⧗ *JUDGES 19:1–30*

The Journey	God's Provision
1:1–22	2:1–23

Read Each 5-Minute Overview in Ruth

THE JOURNEY (1:1–22)

God's providence is certain, and He makes no mistakes. God unfolds the intricacies of His divine purpose: to redeem humankind. Naomi and Ruth's tender relationship is introduced in Ruth 1. Naomi, an Ephrathite, lives in Moab. Her husband and two sons die, so she prepares to return to Bethlehem. Ruth insists on staying with Naomi and adopts Naomi's God as her own. They both return to Bethlehem, Naomi's hometown, at the beginning of the barley harvest. ⏳ *RUTH 1:1–22*

GOD'S PROVISION (2:1–23)

The Old Testament laws of gleaning provided for the poor and for the widows. Naomi has a relative on her late husband's side named Boaz, and Naomi instructs Ruth to glean in Boaz's barley fields. Boaz, out of compassion and obedience to the laws, allows Ruth, a stranger, to glean. He also purposefully leaves leftover grain for her. Ruth tells Naomi about her day, and Naomi realizes Boaz could serve to provide an heir for Ruth's late husband and also provide security for Ruth. Because Boaz is Naomi's wealthy close relative, he has the option of redeeming—or buying back—the land Naomi's late husband had lost. ⏳ *RUTH 2:1–23*

THE AGREEMENT (3:1–18)

Naomi has an idea. She encourages Ruth to seek marriage with Boaz, a guardian-redeemer. Ruth obeys Naomi, who instructs her to uncover and

1210 BC	1200 BC	1190 BC	1180 BC	1170 BC	1160 BC	1150 BC	1140 BC	1130 BC	1120 BC

◆ 1190–1180 Trojan War

◆ 1151 Abimelek (judge) ◆ 1126 Jair (judge)

◆ 1191–1151 Gideon (judge)

◆ 1149 Tola (judge)

◆ 1200 Beginning of the Iron Age; fall of the Hittite Empire

◆ 1150 Chou Dynasty (China)

The Agreement	The Legacy
3:1–18	4:1–22

lay at Boaz's feet, a normal custom of the time. When Boaz wakes up and realizes there is a woman lying at his feet, he is surprised and asks her to reveal her identity. Ruth responds by asking Boaz to spread his covering over her, or to protect her, as her legal guardian-redeemer. Boaz agrees to the marriage request, but he mentions he must first offer the proposal to another man. Naomi actually has a relative closer than Boaz who is legally first in line to redeem her land and marry Ruth.
⌛ *RUTH 3:1–18*

THE LEGACY (4:1–22)

Boaz heads to the city gate, where the men execute business transactions, to find the man able to redeem Ruth and Naomi's land. At first the man agrees to buy back the land; however, he is not interested in marrying Ruth. Quite possibly this would have affected his inheritance for his own children. Boaz marries Ruth, and she gives birth to a son named Obed, who becomes the grandfather of King David. God's provision of Boaz as the guardian-redeemer fulfills His plan not only for Naomi and Ruth but also for the lineage of Christ the Messiah. ⌛ *RUTH 4:1–22*

Ruth's Descendants

One of the surprising details in the story of Ruth is that she became an ancestor of King David (and ultimately Jesus Christ). Below is her abbreviated family tree.

Ruth — Boaz
Obed
Jesse
David
Jesus

1110 BC	1100 BC	1090 BC	1080 BC	1070 BC	1060 BC	1050 BC	1040 BC	1030 BC	1020 BC

♦ 1100 Life of Ruth?   ♦ 1075 Elon (judge)   ♦ 1060–1020 Samuel (judge/prophet)

♦ 1100 Eli (judge)   ♦ 1087 Jephthah (judge)   ♦ 1065 Abdon (judge)   ♦ 1051–1011 Saul (united kingdom)

♦ 1100 Greece enters Dark Ages   ♦ 1069 Samson (judge)?   ♦ 1050 Zhou Dynasty (China)

The Journey	God's Provision
1:1–22	2:1–23

CAST OF CHARACTERS

Joshua

Faithful Leader. Born a slave in Egypt, Joshua became Moses' primary aide after Israel was freed. Joshua explored the promised land as a spy, led Israel's successful military battles, joined Moses on the mountain of God, and eventually ushered the Israelites into the promised land after Moses' death.

Deborah

Prophetess and Judge. Deborah, a prophetess, led the Israelites and settled disputes among them. The Lord told Deborah a man named Barak was to lead Israel in the fight against the Canaanites. Barak trusted Deborah and requested Deborah lead alongside him. The two celebrated a great victory over the Canaanites.

1210 BC	1200 BC	1190 BC	1180 BC	1170 BC	1160 BC	1150 BC	1140 BC	1130 BC	1120 BC

• 1190–1180 Trojan War

• 1151 Abimelek (judge) • 1126 Jair (judge)

• 1191–1151 Gideon (judge)

• 1149 Tola (judge)

• 1200 Beginning of the Iron Age; fall of the Hittite Empire

• 1150 Chou Dynasty (China)

IN JOSHUA, JUDGES, AND RUTH

Samson

Israel's Strongman. Called from birth to judge and deliver Israel from enemy oppression, Samson was gifted with supernatural strength. However, he lost sight of his calling and gave up his strength trying to please a woman. Finally, at the end of his life, Samson realized his utter dependence on God.

Ruth

Naomi's Daughter-in-Law. Ruth, a Moabite widow, stayed with her Jewish mother-in-law after both of their husbands died in Moab. Back in Israel, Ruth helped provide food by gleaning in nearby fields. There she met Boaz, who subsequently married her. They had a son, Obed, King David's grandfather.

1110 BC	1100 BC	1090 BC	1080 BC	1070 BC	1060 BC	1050 BC	1040 BC	1030 BC	1020 BC

- 1100 Life of Ruth? ◆ 1075 Elon (judge) ◆ 1060–1020 Samuel (judge/prophet)
- 1100 Eli (judge) ◆ 1087 Jephthah (judge) ◆ 1065 Abdon (judge) ◆ 1051–1011 Saul (united kingdom)
- 1100 Greece enters Dark Ages ◆ 1069 Samson (judge)? ◆ 1050 Zhou Dynasty (China)

NAVIGATING THE BIBLE

INTRODUCTION TO 1 & 2 SAMUEL

Author: Unknown. Perhaps Samuel contributed.
Dates of Events: 1100–971 BC

O riginally one book, 1 and 2 Samuel pick up after a very dark period in Israel's history. They tell the story of the transition of leadership in Israel from judges to kings. Because the Israelites did not trust and obey God under Moses' leadership, that generation of God's people did not enter Canaan. The next generation of Israelites, led by Joshua, did cross into the promised land, but the nation quickly fell apart and cycled repeatedly from blessing to discipline—the result of disobedience and rebellion.

The Israelites' enemies dominate them until the people repent. When God's people cry out to God for help, He sends judges to intervene and temporarily free them. Born to a prayerful and faithful woman, Samuel, Israel's last judge, becomes a prophet, a priest, and an adviser of kings. Samuel faithfully mediates between the people and the Lord, though the people eventually reject his advice. God answers Israel's petition to be ruled by kings like the nations around them, and Saul is anointed as the first king of Israel. However, Saul falls short of being a good king. David's journey from shepherd boy to second heir to the throne follows. David—from young musician to valiant warrior to creative leader—follows after God's own heart. Throughout 1 Samuel, the blessing of obedience versus the consequence of disobedience is illustrated, as well as the importance of seeking God's guidance and direction. First Samuel ends with King Saul turning against David, his loyal servant and friend. Saul fails to obey God, bringing about his own downfall and demise.

1110 BC	1100 BC	1090 BC	1080 BC	1070 BC	1060 BC	1050 BC	1040 BC	1030 BC	1020 BC

◆ 1100 Life of Ruth?   ◆ 1075 Elon (judge)   ◆ 1060–1020 Samuel (judge/prophet)

◆ 1100 Eli (judge)   ◆ 1087 Jephthah (judge)   ◆ 1065 Abdon (judge)   ◆ 1051–1011 Saul (united kingdom)

◆ 1100 Greece enters Dark Ages   ◆ 1069 Samson (judge)?   ◆ 1050 Zhou Dynasty (China)

God Rejects Saul	David's Defeat of Goliath	A Fugitive Models Mercy	The Kingdom Is Given to Another
15:1–16:23	17:1–23:14	23:15–25:44	26:1–31:13

King Saul's death marks the beginning of David's journey toward establishing his throne. In the book of 2 Samuel, Israel is divided when David first comes to power, foreshadowing the nation's future. David is not without shortcomings. His sin with Bathsheba brings a long list of tragic consequences along with it, but his repentance is what characterizes him as a man after God's own heart. God's great promise to David to establish his throne forever is a concept that runs throughout the book. Every book of Hebrew prophecy that follows reflects or interprets this Davidic promise, or covenant. Second Samuel's many contrasts—the blessing and curse of power, the sinfulness present even in God's greatest servants, and the power of temptation, lust, and covetousness—serve as a reminder and warning that even great world leaders can fail. The true kingdom, glory, and power belong to the Lord alone.

David with Goliath before Saul *by Rembrandt (1606–1669)*

1010 BC	1000 BC	990 BC	980 BC	970 BC	960 BC	950 BC	940 BC	930 BC	920 BC

♦ 1011–971 David (united kingdom)   ♦ 971–931 Solomon (united kingdom)   ♦ 930 Kingdom divides

♦ 1000 Glazing bricks begins in Near East   ♦ 959 Temple in Jerusalem completed

♦ 1000 Mayan Empire founded (Central America)   ♦ 950 Gold vessels and jewelry popular in Europe

The Son and the Song of Hannah	Israel Insists on a King	Saul Is Anointed as King	King Saul's Fatal Mistake
1:1–4:22	5:1–8:22	9:1–11:13	11:14–14:52

Read Each 5-Minute Overview in 1 Samuel

THE SON AND THE SONG OF HANNAH (1:1–4:22)

The book of 1 Samuel begins with the story of a humble but barren young woman, Hannah, who longs for and begs God for a baby. God answers her prayers with the birth of Samuel. Hannah gives Samuel to Eli the priest to live in the temple and serve God all the days of his life. Samuel is a special person, clearly called by God, who matures and moves into the office of the priesthood. He also takes the role of a prophet. God appears to Samuel and tells of the coming fall of Eli's house. Samuel apprehensively relates the bad news to Eli, who accepts the prophecy as the will of God. The Philistines defeat the Israelites, who suffer thirty thousand casualties. Priests are among the dead, including Eli's two sons. Eli, after hearing the ark of God is captured by the Philistines, falls backward off his chair and dies as well. ⏳ *1 SAMUEL 1:1–11, 20–28; 3:11–21; 4:10–18*

1110 BC	1100 BC	1090 BC	1080 BC	1070 BC	1060 BC	1050 BC	1040 BC	1030 BC	1020 BC
	◆ 1100 Life of Ruth?		◆ 1075 Elon (judge)		◆ 1060–1020 Samuel (judge/prophet)				
	◆ 1100 Eli (judge)	◆ 1087 Jephthah (judge)		◆ 1065 Abdon (judge)		◆ 1051–1011 Saul (united kingdom)			
	◆ 1100 Greece enters Dark Ages			◆ 1069 Samson (judge)?		◆ 1050 Zhou Dynasty (China)			

God Rejects Saul	David's Defeat of Goliath	A Fugitive Models Mercy	The Kingdom Is Given to Another
15:1–16:23	17:1–23:14	23:15–25:44	26:1–31:13

ISRAEL INSISTS ON A KING (5:1–8:22)

After defeating the Israelites and capturing the ark of the covenant, the Philistines put the ark in their temple, but God comes down hard on their city. Their false god falls on its face before the ark. Eventually they return the ark to Israel out of fear. Samuel warns the Israelites that if they are serious about returning to God, they need to cleanse their lives of foreign gods and worship Yahweh alone. Despite the judges God faithfully provided and

Model of the ark of the covenant

Samuel's strong leadership, the Israelites want to be like other nations, and they beg God for a king; Samuel warns sternly against it. ⌛ *1 SAMUEL 5:1–12; 6:1–6, 13–16, 21; 7:3–5, 15–17; 8:1–9, 19–20*

SAUL IS ANOINTED AS KING (9:1–11:13)

The Lord tells Samuel that Saul will be Israel's first king. Saul is searching for his father's lost donkeys when he intercepts the prophet Samuel, who invites Saul to dinner. The following day, Samuel tells Saul details about things that are about to happen—things Saul would not know about unless they were revealed to him supernaturally. The Spirit of the Lord comes on Saul, who prophesies. ⌛ *1 SAMUEL 9:1–6, 14–27; 10:1–7, 17–24; 11:12–13*

KING SAUL'S FATAL MISTAKE (11:14–14:52)

Asking for a king in spite of Samuel's clear warning against it was Israel's rejection of both Samuel's and God's leadership. God anoints Saul as Israel's first king, and at first King Saul has the people's full support. However, Saul begins to disobey God in numerous situations. The Israelites face the Philistines, and out of desperation and self-interest, Saul makes an offering to God that Samuel rebukes him for, and Samuel tells him he is doomed to lose the monarchy. Saul later issues a foolish oath that almost leads to his son Jonathan's death! ⌛ *1 SAMUEL 11:14–15; 12:1–18; 13:1–14; 14:24–45*

1 SAMUEL

45

1010 BC	1000 BC	990 BC	980 BC	970 BC	960 BC	950 BC	940 BC	930 BC	920 BC
◆ 1011–971 David (united kingdom)				◆ 971–931 Solomon (united kingdom)				◆ 930 Kingdom divides	

- ◆ 1000 Glazing bricks begins in Near East
- ◆ 959 Temple in Jerusalem completed
- ◆ 1000 Mayan Empire founded (Central America)
- ◆ 950 Gold vessels and jewelry popular in Europe

The Son and the Song of Hannah	Israel Insists on a King	Saul Is Anointed as King	King Saul's Fatal Mistake
1:1–4:22	5:1–8:22	9:1–11:13	11:14–14:52

46

GOD REJECTS SAUL (15:1–16:23)

Saul is off to a pretty good start as Israel's first king, but as time passes, he begins to make poor decisions. Saul is given specific instructions to follow, but he doesn't quite obey them fully. The results will be worse than he ever anticipated. Samuel ends up walking away from Saul forever, but God puts Samuel on another assignment: to anoint Saul's replacement as king of Israel. Samuel obeys but does not know ahead of time who the new king will be. ⌛ *1 SAMUEL 15:7–19; 16:1–7, 13–14*

DAVID'S DEFEAT OF GOLIATH BREWS JEALOUSY IN SAUL (17:1–23:14)

David and Jonathan, Saul's son, become fast friends, and David quickly becomes like a member of Saul's family. David's courageous defeat of Goliath gives him instant fame in Israel. Initially, Saul gives David a high rank in the army.

David and Goliath *by Michelangelo (1475–1564) (Sistine Chapel)*

1110 BC	1100 BC	1090 BC	1080 BC	1070 BC	1060 BC	1050 BC	1040 BC	1030 BC	1020 BC
	◆ 1100 Life of Ruth?		◆ 1075 Elon (judge)		◆ 1060–1020 Samuel (judge/prophet)				
	◆ 1100 Eli (judge)	◆ 1087 Jephthah (judge)		◆ 1065 Abdon (judge)		◆ 1051–1011 Saul (united kingdom)			
	◆ 1100 Greece enters Dark Ages			◆ 1069 Samson (judge)?		◆ 1050 Zhou Dynasty (China)			

God Rejects Saul	David's Defeat of Goliath	A Fugitive Models Mercy	The Kingdom Is Given to Another
15:1–16:23	17:1–23:14	23:15–25:44	26:1–31:13

However, loyalties change and rivalries intensify, and the closeness between Saul and David soon ends. Saul becomes jealous of David; Saul's envy soon turns to hostility, and he attempts to kill David a few times. David, now a fugitive, flees for his life. ⌛ *1 SAMUEL 17:26–50; 18:1–9; 19:1–18; 20:1–4, 12–17, 30–32; 23:9–14*

A FUGITIVE MODELS MERCY, PATIENCE, AND FORGIVENESS (23:15–25:44)

David continues to hide from Saul, moving from place to place to avoid being killed. David and Jonathan make a covenant with each other. In spite of his situation, David displays his dependence on God in a number of difficult situations. After the death of Samuel, David moves to the Desert of Paran, where he asks a wealthy man named Nabal for provisions. Nabal refuses the request and is almost killed by David. Nabal's wife, Abigail, secretly gives food and drink to David and his men. Nabal dies, and David takes Abigail as his wife. ⌛ *1 SAMUEL 23:15–18; 24:1–13; 25:1–19, 36–41*

THE KINGDOM IS GIVEN TO ANOTHER (26:1–31:13)

Saul continues to chase David, who sneaks into Saul's camp and steals his personal items while he is sleeping. David flees to Philistia, plunders the neighboring cities, and tricks the Philistines into thinking he has raided Judah. Saul realizes God is removing the kingdom from him and giving it to David, who has already been anointed to take his place. After many months of conflict, Saul, who is further away from God than ever, commits suicide by falling on his own sword and is buried. ⌛ *1 SAMUEL 26:1–9; 27:1–12; 31:1–13*

> **Command or description: How do you tell the difference?**
> The books of the Bible addressed specific audiences and situations. As you study, it's good to ask the following questions: *Is the text describing events, or is it giving some kind of instruction? Who were the intended recipients?* Some of the laws in Leviticus, for example, applied to a certain group of people at a certain time. Other texts, like the Ten Commandments, reveal timeless principles about the character of God and what He values. Still others, like the story of Jephthah's rash vow in Judges 11:30–39, simply describe events. Yet even these stories may contain indirect lessons from which we can benefit.

1010 BC	1000 BC	990 BC	980 BC	970 BC	960 BC	950 BC	940 BC	930 BC	920 BC

◆ 1011–971 David (united kingdom)   ◆ 971–931 Solomon (united kingdom)   ◆ 930 Kingdom divides

◆ 1000 Glazing bricks begins in Near East   ◆ 959 Temple in Jerusalem completed

◆ 1000 Mayan Empire founded (Central America)   ◆ 950 Gold vessels and jewelry popular in Europe

Still Grieving, David Becomes King	King David's House	David's Desire to Build God's House	David's Dark Sin
1:1–2:32	3:1–5:25	6:1–10:19	11:1–12:31

Read Each 5-Minute Overview in 2 Samuel

STILL GRIEVING, DAVID BECOMES KING (1:1–2:32)

David and his men are grateful for the defeat of the Amalekites and the recovery of their families and possessions. But this victory is overshadowed by David's concern for the massive force attacking Israel. On his third day back in Ziklag, a young man approaches David with news of Israel's defeat and the deaths of Saul and Jonathan. David composes a lament for them. After grieving, David takes his rightful place as the second king over the united kingdom of Israel, but he faces some big obstacles. ⏳ 2 SAMUEL 1:17–27; 2:1–32

KING DAVD'S HOUSE (3:1–5:25)

David moves to Hebron and is anointed king of Israel. The conflict continues to work itself out, and David is forced to wait patiently on the Lord to reunite the nation. Another of Saul's sons, Ish-bosheth, is murdered. This event concludes a difficult, bloody phase of David's entrance to the monarchy.

1110 BC	1100 BC	1090 BC	1080 BC	1070 BC	1060 BC	1050 BC	1040 BC	1030 BC	1020 BC
	◆ 1100 Life of Ruth?		◆ 1075 Elon (judge)		◆ 1060–1020 Samuel (judge/prophet)				
	◆ 1100 Eli (judge)	◆ 1087 Jephthah (judge)		◆ 1065 Abdon (judge)		◆ 1051–1011 Saul (united kingdom)			
	◆ 1100 Greece enters Dark Ages		◆ 1069 Samson (judge)?		◆ 1050 Zhou Dynasty (China)				

Tragedy and Tears in the Royal Family	David's Darkest Days	David Returns to Jerusalem
13:1–17:20	17:21–19:8	19:9–24:25

There are new lessons for David to learn as he takes Jerusalem from the Jebusites and makes it his stronghold. David is forced to deal with the Philistines yet again.
⧗ *2 SAMUEL 3:1, 6–11; 4:1–12; 5:4–25*

DAVID'S DESIRE TO BUILD GOD'S HOUSE (6:1–10:19)

David gathers his people to transfer the ark, which he brings to Jerusalem. He begins to formulate a plan to build a house for God. However, Nathan reveals that God has rejected that request; David's son will be the one to build God's house. God does promise, however, that He will perpetuate David's dynasty forever. David uses his newfound power in the war with Israel's enemies. David wishes to honor one of Jonathan's descendants. He finds Jonathan's son Mephibosheth and grants him land and servants. Assembling his army, David routs the Ammonite and Aramean armies. ⧗ *2 SAMUEL 6:1–2, 17–22; 7:1–15; 8:1–2; 9:1–13; 10:17–19*

DAVID'S DARK SIN (11:1–12:31)

From the pinnacle of success, David makes a choice that takes him to the depths of failure. David succumbs to temptation: He commits adultery and then kills the woman's husband. (His actions are proof that spiritual highs don't necessarily guard against future sin.) The prophet Nathan confronts David about his sin, and David humbly admits he has sinned against God. Nathan comforts David by telling him God will forgive his sin; however, there will be a terrible consequence: David' son born to Bathsheba will die. ⧗ *2 SAMUEL 11:1–27; 12:7–19*

TRAGEDY AND TEARS IN THE ROYAL FAMILY (13:1–17:20)

God, in His grace, allows for David to become powerful, rich, and prosperous, but not because David deserves it. Because of his sin, David's

49

Foreshadowing: Why do I feel a sense of déjà vu when reading about Jesus?
Jesus' family fled to Egypt, just like Jacob's family. Jesus spent forty days in the desert, echoing Israel's forty-year wilderness sojourn. Jesus was betrayed on the Mount of Olives, the spot where David fled when he was betrayed by Absalom. The Bible uses these echoes of past events to connect Jesus to Israel's story.

1010 BC	1000 BC	990 BC	980 BC	970 BC	960 BC	950 BC	940 BC	930 BC	920 BC
◆ 1011–971 David (united kingdom)				◆ 971–931 Solomon (united kingdom)				◆ 930 Kingdom divides	
	◆ 1000 Glazing bricks begins in Near East				◆ 959 Temple in Jerusalem completed				
	◆ 1000 Mayan Empire founded (Central America)				◆ 950 Gold vessels and jewelry popular in Europe				

Still Grieving, David Becomes King	King David's House	David's Desire to Build God's House	David's Dark Sin
1:1–2:32	3:1–5:25	6:1–10:19	11:1–12:31

CAST OF CHARACTERS

Saul

The First King. As far as disasters go, Saul's time on the throne was an unmitigated one. Although he began his reign with great promise, he proved erratic and unstable. More than once he failed to listen to the prophet Samuel; as a result, Samuel announced that the throne would be taken from Saul. Saul's life ended in humiliating defeat to the Philistines.

David

King of Israel. Young David killed Goliath, a Philistine giant. As king of Israel, David fought many battles and established Israel as a dominant power. He committed adultery, but he repented. Because of his faith, God called him "a man after [my] own heart." David made preparations to build the temple and composed many psalms.

1110 BC	1100 BC	1090 BC	1080 BC	1070 BC	1060 BC	1050 BC	1040 BC	1030 BC	1020 BC

◆ 1100 Life of Ruth?   ◆ 1075 Elon (judge)   ◆ 1060–1020 Samuel (judge/prophet)

◆ 1100 Eli (judge)   ◆ 1087 Jephthah (judge)   ◆ 1065 Abdon (judge)   ◆ 1051–1011 Saul (united kingdom)

◆ 1100 Greece enters Dark Ages   ◆ 1069 Samson (judge)?   ◆ 1050 Zhou Dynasty (China)

Tragedy and Tears in the Royal Family	David's Darkest Days	David Returns to Jerusalem
13:1–17:20	17:21–19:8	19:9–24:25

IN 1 & 2 SAMUEL

Solomon

King of Israel. Solomon succeeded David as king and devoted himself to cultivating wisdom, forging diplomatic alliances with regional powers, and building the temple in Jerusalem. His wisdom did not prevent him from plunging into the dangerous pursuit of wealth and women. Over time, the once wise king descended into folly.

Jezebel

Evil Queen of Israel. A pagan princess, Jezebel married Israel's King Ahab and brought hundreds of cult priests with her. Overpowering her husband, she ordered the extermination of God's prophets, erected altars to Baal, and proved herself wicked. Eventually Jezebel was thrown out a window to her death and trampled by horses.

1010 BC	1000 BC	990 BC	980 BC	970 BC	960 BC	950 BC	940 BC	930 BC	920 BC

❖ 1011–971 David (united kingdom)

❖ 971–931 Solomon (united kingdom)

❖ 930 Kingdom divides

❖ 1000 Glazing bricks begins in Near East

❖ 959 Temple in Jerusalem completed

❖ 1000 Mayan Empire founded (Central America)

❖ 950 Gold vessels and jewelry popular in Europe

Tragedy and Tears in the Royal Family	David's Darkest Days	David Returns to Jerusalem
13:1–17:20	17:21–19:8	19:9–24:25

family and the nation of Israel experience serious tragedies and trials, including the nation's eventual division into two kingdoms. The people's alliance shifts to Absalom, and David learns a full-scale rebellion is brewing. David flees from Jerusalem, followed only by his true friends. ⌛ *2 SAMUEL 13:1–4, 8–14; 15:1–15; 16:5–23; 17:1–20*

While fleeing from his son, David wept at the Mount of Olives

52

DAVID'S DARKEST DAYS (17:21–19:8)

Still fleeing for his life, David and his army cross the Jordan River. David organizes his forces and then stands by the city gate as his whole army marches out to fight against Absalom. Israel's army is badly defeated, and Absalom dies. David is brokenhearted over his son's death. He will return to Jerusalem to resume his reign over the nation of Israel. ⌛ *2 SAMUEL 17:21–29; 18:1–17, 33; 19:1–8*

DAVID RETURNS TO JERUSALEM (19:9–24:25)

Before resuming his reign over the nation of Israel, David removes Joab as commander of his armed forces and replaces him with Amasa. For three years, the Israelites experience a famine—a consequence for the actions of King Saul years earlier when he violated a four-century-old covenant with the Gibeonites. David must now rectify and reconcile Saul's sin. David reflects on his reign as king and expresses thanks to God in song for His many acts of deliverance. He is confident God will remain faithful to the everlasting covenant He made with the house of David. David slips into distrust once again but quickly begs God for forgiveness and prays for Jerusalem to be spared from disaster. God listens. ⌛ *2 SAMUEL 20:21:1–14; 22:1–7, 47–51; 24:1–14*

1110 BC	1100 BC	1090 BC	1080 BC	1070 BC	1060 BC	1050 BC	1040 BC	1030 BC	1020 BC

• 1100 Life of Ruth? • 1075 Elon (judge) • 1060–1020 Samuel (judge/prophet)

• 1100 Eli (judge) • 1087 Jephthah (judge) • 1065 Abdon (judge) • 1051–1011 Saul (united kingdom)

• 1100 Greece enters Dark Ages • 1069 Samson (judge)? • 1050 Zhou Dynasty (China)

Solomon Becomes King	Solomon Builds the Temple	The Dedication of the Temple	Solomon's Decline and a Divided Kingdom	A Long List of Evil Kings	Elijah's Victory at Carmel	The Beginning of Jehoshaphat's Reign
1:1–4:34	5:1–7:51	8:1–10:29	11:1–14:31	15:1–17:24	18:1–20:43	21:1–22:53

INTRODUCTION TO 1 & 2 KINGS AND 1 & 2 CHRONICLES

Authors: Unknown. Some suggest Ezra and Jeremiah.
Dates of Events: 1000–576 BC

The narrative of 1 and 2 Kings is actually two parts of the same book and covers almost five hundred years of the history of Israel and Judah. Likely written between 560 and 540 BC, it describes the last days of the monarchy under David to the capture of both kingdoms by enemy nations. Together the books warn of the consequences of falling away from faith versus consistent obedience. First Kings explains God's judgment of the northern kingdom's idolatry and calls the southern kingdom to repentance for following Israel's example. The unknown author reminds the people of Judah of the hope promised through the royal—and ultimately messianic—line of David. First Kings provides a historical framework for each of the kingships by including the dates, length, and place of reign, and whether each king did right in the Lord's eyes. Second Kings underscores God's patience as prophets continually call His people to repentance and repeatedly warn them of the consequences of disobedience.

Written for a Hebrew audience and originally penned as one book, 1 and 2 Chronicles tell of a time of uncertainty, if not despair, for the people of the southern kingdom. Likely written between 450 and 425 BC, 1 and 2 Chronicles cover mostly the same information as 1 and 2 Samuel and 1 and 2 Kings. However, 1 and 2 Chronicles focus more on the priestly aspect of the time period and serve as an evaluation of the nation's religious history.

1010 BC	1000 BC	990 BC	980 BC	970 BC	960 BC	950 BC	940 BC	930 BC	920 BC

◆ 1011–971 David (united kingdom)   ◆ 971–931 Solomon (united kingdom)   ◆ 930 Kingdom divides

◆ 1000 Glazing bricks begins in Near East   ◆ 959 Temple in Jerusalem completed

◆ 1000 Mayan Empire founded (Central America)   ◆ 950 Gold vessels and jewelry popular in Europe

Solomon Becomes King	Solomon Builds the Temple	The Dedication of the Temple
1:1–4:34	5:1–7:51	8:1–10:29

The book of 1 Chronicles was written to help those returning to Judah from Babylon know how to worship God and understand their history in order to live well in the present. As the people return home and look toward rebuilding their ruined temple, the Chronicler assures them God is present. He also reminds the people how God has provided for and delivered them in the past. The book of 2 Chronicles is more of a commentary and guide for the remnant of God's people returning to Jerusalem. The writer helps connect the exiles with their national history, instructs how to live well in light of that history, and warns of the dangers of religious compromise and vanity in seeking or serving anything besides God.

Kings of the Northern and Southern Kingdoms

UNITED KINGDOM
Saul
David
Solomon

KINGS OF THE NORTHERN KINGDOM	KINGS OF THE SOUTHERN KINGDOM
Jeroboam	Rehoboam
Nadab	Abijah
Baasha	Asa
Elah	Jehoshaphat
Zimri	Joram
Omri	Queen Athaliah
Ahab	Joash
Ahaziah	Amaziah
Joram	Uzziah
Ahaziah	Jotham
Jehu	Ahaz
Jehoahaz	Hezekiah
Jehoash	Manasseh
Jeroboam II	Amon
Zechariah	Josiah
Shallum	Jehoahaz
Menahem	Jehoiakim
Pekahiah	Jehoiachin
Pekah	Zedekiah
Hoshea	

1010 BC	1000 BC	990 BC	980 BC	970 BC	960 BC	950 BC	940 BC	930 BC	920 BC

◆ 1011–971 David (united kingdom)　　　◆ 971–931 Solomon (united kingdom)　　　◆ 930 Kingdom divides

◆ 1000 Glazing bricks begins in Near East　　　◆ 959 Temple in Jerusalem completed

◆ 1000 Mayan Empire founded (Central America)　　　◆ 950 Gold vessels and jewelry popular in Europe

Solomon's Decline and a Divided Kingdom	A Long List of Evil Kings	Elijah's Victory at Carmel	The Beginning of Jehoshaphat's Reign
11:1–14:31	15:1–17:24	18:1–20:43	21:1–22:53

SOLOMON BECOMES KING (1:1–4:34)

King David's oldest living son, Adonijah, would like to take over the throne, but God has a different plan. David gives final instructions to his son Solomon, God's choice for the next king. David passes away and is buried in the City of David. God offers Solomon the opportunity to ask for anything; Solomon requests wisdom, which God generously grants. Solomon leads well with organization and creativity, and he enjoys prosperity. ⌛ *1 KINGS 1:15–21, 28–37; 2:1–12; 3:4–14*

SOLOMON BUILDS THE TEMPLE (5:1–7:51)

Solomon nurtures his father's friendship with the king of neighboring Tyre, who supplies Solomon with needed materials and manpower to build the temple. Solomon begins building the temple—using only the very best skills, workers, and materials of the day—but God reminds him that what is most important is not a fancy building but obedience. The temple is completed in seven

910 BC	900 BC	890 BC	880 BC	870 BC	860 BC	850 BC	840 BC	830 BC	820 BC
✦ 909 Baasha (Israel)			✦ 886 Elah (Israel)	✦ 870 Elijah (prophet)		✦ 845 Elisha (prophet)			
✦ 913 Abijah (Judah)			✦ 885 Zimri & Omri (Israel)		✦ 853 Joram (Israel)		✦ 835 Joash (Judah)		
✦ 911 Asa (Judah)				✦ 874 Ahab (Israel)		✦ 841 Athaliah (Judah)			

Solomon Becomes King	Solomon Builds the Temple	The Dedication of the Temple
1:1–4:34	5:1–7:51	8:1–10:29

NAVIGATING THE BIBLE

years, but Solomon takes almost twice that long to build his own palace. With the temple finished, Solomon now hires skilled workers to craft its bronze and gold furnishings. ⏳ *1 KINGS 5:1–12; 6:1–13; 7:1–5, 9–12, 45–51*

THE DEDICATION OF THE TEMPLE AND A VISIT FROM A QUEEN (8:1–10:29)

Solomon assembles the elders of Israel and the heads of the tribes to dedicate God's new dwelling place. The glory of God fills the temple. Solomon blesses the people, and he boldly and passionately praises God for His faithfulness. God then gives Solomon a promise and a warning. The queen of Sheba travels thousands of miles to see Solomon's riches and wisdom for herself; his wisdom, vast wealth, and possessions take her breath away. ⏳ *1 KINGS 8:1–21; 9:1–9; 10:6–13*

SOLOMON'S DECLINE AND A DIVIDED KINGDOM (11:1–14:31)

Solomon lusts after many foreign women, who turn his heart away from God to idols. This leads to his downfall. Despite Solomon's sin, God delays judgment and extends mercy. He does announce, however, that the kingdom will be divided. Adversaries begin to rise as Solomon approaches death. Solomon's son Rehoboam becomes king, but he opens the door for the kingdom's split when he is rejected as king of the northern ten tribes and rules instead over the southern kingdom of Judah. His opponent, Jeroboam, takes the throne and rules over the

The Judgment of Solomon *by Rubens (1577–1640)*

56

1010 BC	1000 BC	990 BC	980 BC	970 BC	960 BC	950 BC	940 BC	930 BC	920 BC

• 1011–971 David (united kingdom)   • 971–931 Solomon (united kingdom)   • 930 Kingdom divides

• 1000 Glazing bricks begins in Near East   • 959 Temple in Jerusalem completed

• 1000 Mayan Empire founded (Central America)   • 950 Gold vessels and jewelry popular in Europe

Solomon's Decline and a Divided Kingdom	A Long List of Evil Kings	Elijah's Victory at Carmel	The Beginning of Jehoshaphat's Reign
11:1–14:31	15:1–17:24	18:1–20:43	21:1–22:53

northern kingdom, but he sadly brings practices of pagan worship along with him. A prophet comes from the south testifying against evil Jeroboam, and the reigns of both Jeroboam and Rehoboam end terribly. ⧗ *1 KINGS 11:1–13; 12:15–33; 13:1–5, 33–34; 14:25–31*

A LONG LIST OF EVIL KINGS (15:1–17:24)

Four more kings rule Judah and Israel, but only one, Asa, does right before the Lord; God grants Asa a long reign. Five successive kings of Israel after Asa come to power, culminating in Ahab and his wicked wife, Jezebel. Jezebel, like Solomon's foreign wives, leads Ahab and the nation into deep idolatry. Ahab did more to anger the Lord than all the kings of Israel before him. Next, the prophet Elijah comes on the scene and will soon challenge Ahab. Elijah performs two miracles for a widow: he provides an unlimited supply of food for her and heals her son. ⧗ *1 KINGS 15:8–24; 16:29–33; 17:10–24*

ELIJAH'S VICTORY AT CARMEL (18:1–20:43)

Elijah returns to Israel and meets faithful Obadiah in Ahab's court. Elijah duels with the prophets of Baal on Mount Carmel, and Baal is shown to be an inefficacious deity. The one true God shows His power and miraculously consumes Elijah's sacrifice. The prophets of Baal are killed,

The Kingdom Divides
1 Kings 11–15

Solomon forsakes the covenant by worshiping other gods
11:1–13

A prophet tells Jeroboam of God's plan to give him rule over ten tribes of Israel 11:29–39

Solomon attempts to kill Jeroboam, who flees to Egypt until Solomon dies 11:40

Rehoboam succeeds Solomon as king 11:41–43

Rehoboam refuses to show kindness to the Israelites, who rebel against him 12:1–19

Jeroboam becomes king over Israel; the tribe of Judah remains loyal to Rehoboam 12:20

Jeroboam sets up golden calves for the people to worship, provoking God's wrath 12:25–33; 14:7–16

The people of Judah, under Rehoboam's rule, turn away from worshiping God and provoke his wrath 14:21–28

Continual warfare takes place between Israel and Judah 14:30; 15:6,16

Source: The QuickView Bible

910 BC	900 BC	890 BC	880 BC	870 BC	860 BC	850 BC	840 BC	830 BC	820 BC

◆ 909 Baasha (Israel)   ◆ 886 Elah (Israel)   ◆ 870 Elijah (prophet)   ◆ 845 Elisha (prophet)

◆ 913 Abijah (Judah)   ◆ 885 Zimri & Omri (Israel)   ◆ 853 Joram (Israel)   ◆ 835 Joash (Judah)

◆ 911 Asa (Judah)   ◆ 874 Ahab (Israel)   ◆ 841 Athaliah (Judah)

| GEN | EXOD | LEV | NUM | DEUT | JOSH | JUDG | RUTH | 1 SAM | 2 SAM | 1 KGS | 2 KGS | 1 CHR | 2 CHR | EZRA | NEH | ESTH | JOB | PSALMS | PROV | ECCL | SONG |

Solomon Becomes King	Solomon Builds the Temple	The Dedication of the Temple	Solomon's Decline and a Divided Kingdom	A Long List of Evil Kings	Elijah's Victory at Carmel	The Beginning of Jehoshaphat's Reign
1:1–4:34	5:1–7:51	8:1–10:29	11:1–14:31	15:1–17:24	18:1–20:43	21:1–22:53

Ahab flees, and Elijah prays for much-needed rain. Elijah sinks into depression, and God ministers to him and sends him to anoint his successor, Elisha. After laying siege to Samaria, Ben-Hadad, king of Aram, is defeated by Ahab's small army. A second battle ensues, and Ahab is once again victorious; however, an unnamed prophet rebukes Ahab for releasing Ben-Hadad. ⏳ *1 KINGS 18:1–46; 19:3–9, 15–18; 20:28–43*

THE BEGINNING OF JEHOSHAPHAT'S REIGN (21:1–22:53)

Evil Ahab and Jezebel deceitfully arrange Naboth's death, all because Ahab desires Naboth's vineyard. Elijah strongly condemns Naboth's murder and predicts Ahab's death because of it. God promises to annihilate Ahab's family but delays the punishment because Ahab fearfully repents. Ahab is eventually killed in an unsuccessful battle with the Arameans, in the very spot God had said he would die. The reigns of Jehoshaphat, king of Judah, and Ahaziah, king of Israel, are described next. Jehoshaphat, like his father, did what was right in the eyes of the Lord, but he did not do everything he should have done as king. Ahaziah, on the other hand, did evil in the sight of the Lord. ⏳ *1 KINGS 21:1–29; 22:41–53*

The cliffs of Mount Carmel may have made escape difficult for the prophets of Baal.

890 BC	880 BC	870 BC	860 BC	850 BC	840 BC	830 BC	820 BC	810 BC	800 BC

♦ 886 Elah (Israel)   ♦ 870 Elijah (prophet)   ♦ 845 Elisha (prophet)   ♦ 814 Jehoahaz (Israel)

♦ 885 Zimri & Omri (Israel)   ♦ 853 Joram (Israel)   ♦ 835 Joash (Judah)

♦ 874 Ahab (Israel)   ♦ 841 Athaliah (Judah)

Ahaziah, Elijah, and Elisha	Elisha Is Established as a True Prophet	Jehu Takes the Throne of Israel	Jehu's Reforms
1:1–2:25	3;1–6:33	7:1–9:37	10:1–12:21

Read Each 5-Minute Overview in 2 Kings

AHAZIAH, ELIJAH, AND ELISHA (1:1–2:25)

After King Ahab's death, his son Ahaziah ascends the throne. Moab takes the opportunity to move out from under Israel's domination. Ahaziah consults the idol Baal-Zebub, and Elijah prophesies Ahaziah will now die. Ahaziah sends men to kill Elijah, but they are consumed by fire. Elijah confronts Ahaziah, and Ahaziah dies. A chariot of fire appears in a whirlwind and takes Elijah to heaven. Elisha takes Elijah's cloak, divides the water of the Jordan River, and succeeds Elijah as prophet. 🕭 *2 KINGS 1:1–18; 2:1–25*

ELISHA IS ESTABLISHED AS A TRUE PROPHET (3:1–6:33)

An army of Israelites, Judahites, and Edomites lays waste to the land of Moab. Unlike Israel's kings, many of the people live with profound

790 BC	780 BC	770 BC	760 BC	750 BC	740 BC	730 BC	720 BC	710 BC

✦ 792 Uzziah (Judah)   ✦ 760 Isaiah (prophet)   ✦ 722 Israel falls

✦ 798 Jehoash (Israel)   ✦ 770 Jonah (prophet)   ✦ 753 Zechariah (Israel)   ✦ 732 Ahaz (Judah)

✦ 796 Amaziah (Judah)   ✦ 755 Amos/Hosea (prophets)   ✦ 732 Hoshea (Israel)

Ahaziah, Elijah, and Elisha	Elisha Is Established as a True Prophet	Jehu Takes the Throne of Israel	Jehu's Reforms	Jehoahaz and Jehoash, Elisha's Death
1:1–2:25	3:1–6:33	7:1–9:37	10:1–12:21	13:1–14:29

faith. The prophet Elisha, Elijah's successor, tells a Shunammite woman that she will have a son. That son dies, but Elisha revives him. Elisha cleanses the food at Gilgal, heals the commander of the Aramean army of leprosy, and miraculously recovers an iron axhead from the Jordan River. These miracles establish Elijah's credibility as a prophet of God. The king of Aram sends an army to capture Elisha, but the Lord blinds the army. ⧗ *2 KINGS 3:14–27; 4:8–20, 31–35; 5:9–15; 6:1–7, 18–20*

Elisha Refusing Gifts from Naaman
by Pieter Fransz de Grebber (ca. 1600–1653)

NAVIGATING THE BIBLE

60

JEHU TAKES THE THRONE OF ISRAEL (7:1–9:37)

God frightens the Arameans, they abandon their camp, and the Israelites enjoy the booty. An Israelite is killed for questioning Elisha's prophecy of wealth, which comes true. Elisha also predicts seven years of famine. Ben-Hadad, the king of Aram, is assassinated by Hazael, who assumes the throne. The reigns of kings Jehoram and Ahaziah of Judah are described, and the story shifts back to the northern kingdom of Israel. Jehu is anointed king of Israel and murders King Joram, son of Ahab. Jehu also brutally murders Ahaziah and Jezebel, the queen mother. ⧗ *2 KINGS 7:1–7, 16–20; 8:7–29; 9:21–37*

JEHU'S REFORMS (10:1–12:21)

Jehu, anointed king of Israel, wipes out Ahab's house. He orders the deaths of King Ahab's seventy sons and grandsons. Ahaziah's mother,

---

Foreshadowing: Elijah and John the Baptist
Identifying Elijah by his clothes also connects him to the ministry of John the Baptist, who dressed in hairy skins from animals (Matthew 3:4). When the priests and Levites saw him, they asked, "Are you Elijah?" (John 1:19–21).

---

890 BC	880 BC	870 BC	860 BC	850 BC	840 BC	830 BC	820 BC	810 BC	800 BC

◆ 886 Elah (Israel)　　◆ 870 Elijah (prophet)　　◆ 845 Elisha (prophet)　　◆ 814 Jehoahaz (Israel)

◆ 885 Zimri & Omri (Israel)　　◆ 853 Joram (Israel)　　◆ 835 Joash (Judah)

◆ 874 Ahab (Israel)　　◆ 841 Athaliah (Judah)

The Fall of the Northern Kingdom of Israel	Hezekiah's Reign and Assyria's Threat	The Decline of Judah	The Fall of Jerusalem and Judah's Exile
15:1–17:41	18:1–20:21	21:1–23:37	24:1–25:30

Athaliah, has plans for Judah's throne. She kills Ahaziah's descendants and becomes queen. Ahaziah's sister hides Ahaziah's son Joash for six years. The people soon declare Joash king of Judah and kill Athaliah. Joash collects money to repair the temple and appeases Hazael, king of Aram, with the temple's vessels, but he is assassinated by his own officials. ⌛ *2 KINGS 10:1–10; 11:1–16; 12:4–22*

⌛ ## JEHOAHAZ AND JEHOASH, ELISHA'S DEATH, AND THE REIGNS OF AMAZIAH AND JEROBOAM II (13:1–14:29)

Jehoahaz's reign begins the fulfillment of the promise that Jehu's descendants would rule Israel to the fourth generation. Jehoash replaces Jehoahaz as king and defeats the Arameans in battle. The prophet Elisha dies and is buried. Amaziah becomes king of Judah and defeats the Edomites. Jehoash, king of Israel, decimates the Judahites. Jerusalem is plundered, Amaziah is murdered, and Azariah becomes king in Judah. Jeroboam becomes king of Israel and conquers much land. ⌛ *2 KINGS 13:1–20; 14:1–4, 8–25*

⌛ ## THE FALL OF THE NORTHERN KINGDOM OF ISRAEL (15:1–17:41)

Six more kings of Israel take the throne before Israel is exiled: Zechariah, Shallum, Menahem, Pekahiah, Pekah, and Hoshea. Each king passes the thread of evil to the next. State-sponsored idolatry in Israel is the norm. Shalmaneser, king of Assyria, exiles the Israelites when he learns of Hoshea's deceitful dealings. Because the people of Israel continued to forsake God and ignore His guidance and correction, God allows the northern kingdom of Israel to fall. Foreigners resettle the land and worship pagan deities. ⌛ *2 KINGS 15:8–31; 17:1–41*

Relief of Assyrian weapons. Israel falls in 722 BC.

790 BC	780 BC	770 BC	760 BC	750 BC	740 BC	730 BC	720 BC	710 BC

◆ 792 Uzziah (Judah)   ◆ 760 Isaiah (prophet)   ◆ 722 Israel falls

◆ 798 Jehoash (Israel)   ◆ 770 Jonah (prophet)   ◆ 753 Zechariah (Israel)   ◆ 732 Ahaz (Judah)

◆ 796 Amaziah (Judah)   ◆ 755 Amos/Hosea (prophets)   ◆ 732 Hoshea (Israel)

The Fall of the Northern Kingdom of Israel	Hezekiah's Reign and Assyria's Threat	The Decline of Judah	The Fall of Jerusalem and Judah's Exile
15:1–17:41	18:1–20:21	21:1–23:37	24:1–25:30

NAVIGATING THE BIBLE

62

HEZEKIAH'S REIGN AND ASSYRIA'S THREAT (18:1–20:21)

While Israel is being exiled, Hezekiah rises to Judah's throne. Hezekiah learns a valuable lesson from Israel's destruction: Rejecting God and His Word and worshipping other gods leads to destruction. Hezekiah responds to his nation's crisis wisely by seeking God's guidance. He rebels against Assyria and defeats the Philistines. God promises Hezekiah protection, and an angel kills 185,000 Assyrians in one night. Sennacherib, king of Assyria, flees for his life but is killed by his own sons in Nineveh. Hezekiah recovers from an illness, and Isaiah warns him that the Babylonians will raid Jerusalem and plunder its wealth. ⌛ *2 KINGS 18:1–8; 19:14–37; 20:1–7, 14–18*

Angel destroying the Assyrian camp

THE DECLINE OF JUDAH (21:1–23:37)

After Hezekiah's death, Manasseh takes Judah's throne. Manasseh's evil heart leads Judah to unfaithfulness similar to Israel's. Amnon succeeds Manasseh as king of Judah, but he is quickly killed in a coup. His son Josiah becomes Judah's next king. Josiah is obedient to the Lord throughout his reign. A priest named Hilkiah finds the Book of the Law. Josiah hears the words of the book and laments how the people have abandoned God. A prophetess predicts the fall of Jerusalem. Pharaoh Necho kills Josiah and imprisons Josiah's son Jehoahaz. Jehoiakim becomes the next king and pays a hefty tribute to Necho. ⌛ *2 KINGS 21:1–25; 22:1–20; 23:31–35*

THE FALL OF JERUSALEM AND JUDAH'S EXILE (24:1–25:30)

Jehoiakim reigns in Judah during a tumultuous time. Jehoiachin succeeds him and surrenders Jerusalem to Nebuchadnezzar. Jerusalem is besieged, the temple is raided and destroyed, and most of the people of Judah are exiled. God's judgment has fallen on His disobedient people. ⌛ *2 KINGS 24:1–17; 25:1–21*

700 BC	690 BC	680 BC	670 BC	660 BC	650 BC	640 BC	630 BC	620 BC	610 BC

◆ 716 Hezekiah (Judah)

◆ 658 Nahum (prophet)

◆ 640 Zephaniah (prophet)   ◆ 620 Daniel born

◆ 697 Manasseh (Judah)

◆ 640 Josiah (Judah)   ◆ 620 Ezekiel (prophet)

◆ 701 Sennacherib invades

◆ 650 Jeremiah (prophet)

IMPORTANT FAMILY HISTORIES (1:1–6:81)

First Chronicles opens with lists of genealogies beginning with Adam. The genealogies include the descendants of Noah and Abraham. The descendants of Israel (Jacob) are listed next: Judah (including David and Solomon), Simeon, Reuben, Gad, the half-tribe of Manasseh, and Levi. The list of the descendants of Levi includes the names of the temple musicians and the locations of where the Levites were assigned to live. ⌛ *1 CHRONICLES 1:1–4, 28; 2:3–4; 3:1–16; 4:24; 5:1–3, 11, 23; 6:1–81*

600 BC	590 BC	580 BC	570 BC	560 BC	550 BC	540 BC	530 BC	520 BC	510 BC
	◆ 597 Zedekiah (Judah)		◆ 570 Confucius teaches in China					◆ 522 Zechariah/Haggai (prophets)	
◆ 600 Habakkuk (prophet)				◆ 559 Cyrus the Great (Persia)				◆ 521 Darius (Persia)	
	◆ 586 Fall of Jerusalem			◆ 560 Aesop's fables		◆ 539 Darius the Mede (Babylon)			

Important Family Histories	Tribal Genealogies, Levites, and Postexilic Jerusalem	David Anointed King	Ark Brought to Jerusalem
1:1–6:81	7:1–10:14	11:1–12:40	13:1–16:43

NAVIGATING THE BIBLE

TRIBAL GENEALOGIES, LEVITES, AND POSTEXILIC JERUSALEM (7:1–10:14)

The genealogies of Issachar, Benjamin, Naphtali, Manasseh, Ephraim, and Asher are set forth. Particular attention is paid to the militias in Jerusalem and Gibeon. The Israelites who resettled Jerusalem, the Levites who guarded and served in the temple, and King Saul's lineage are highlighted. The Philistines' defeat of King Saul in battle and how he chose to end his life by falling on a sword is retold. Although the Philistines desecrate Saul's body, the people of Jabesh Gilead give him and his sons a proper burial. ⧗ *1 CHRONICLES 7:1–40; 8:33; 9:2–16; 10:1–14*

DAVID ANOINTED KING (11:1–12:40)

King David

After lengthy genealogies and a brief account of King Saul's reign, the story of King David begins. The people acknowledge God's choice of David as shepherd and ruler of His people. David makes a covenant with Israel in God's presence and is anointed king, just as God had commanded through Samuel. David immediately conquers Jerusalem and captures it from the Jebusites. David's mighty men are listed, and soldiers who joined David's forces at the fortress in Ziklag are mentioned as well. Another list enumerates the soldiers who anointed David in Hebron. ⧗ *1 CHRONICLES 11:1–19; 12:1–22*

ARK BROUGHT TO JERUSALEM (13:1–16:43)

After Saul dies on the battlefield, David begins his reign over Israel. He has waited a decade to reign as king. He chooses to bring the ark to Jerusalem. A man named Uzza touches the ark when the oxen stumble, and God strikes him dead. David decides to house the ark of the covenant temporar-

64

1010 BC	1000 BC	990 BC	980 BC	970 BC	960 BC	950 BC	940 BC	930 BC	920 BC
◆ 1011–971 David (united kingdom)				◆ 971–931 Solomon (united kingdom)				◆ 930 Kingdom divides	
	◆ 1000 Glazing bricks begins in Near East				◆ 959 Temple in Jerusalem completed				
	◆ 1000 Mayan Empire founded (Central America)					◆ 950 Gold vessels and jewelry popular in Europe			

A Fair and Righteous Military Leader	Preparing to Build the Temple	David Organizes People	David's Final Days and Solomon's Debut
17:1–19:19	20:1–22:19	23:1–27:34	28:1–29:30

ily in Obed-Edom's house. David then enjoys a period of peace and prosperity in Jerusalem, and with God's approval, he defeats the Philistines twice in battle. The nations begin to fear him. David assembles the people in Jerusalem to celebrate the ark's return, but his wife Michal does not approve of David's enthusiasm. The Levites lead the congregation in praise,

David directs them to their posts, and the people return home. ⏳ *1 CHRONICLES 13:1–14; 14:8–17; 15:11–16; 16:1–6, 37–42*

5 A FAIR AND RIGHTEOUS MILITARY LEADER (17:1–19:19)

David is now king and has united the nation and built his palace. He is becoming a popular leader who is respected by the people. David desires to build a more permanent dwelling place for the ark, but God has a different idea. God rejects David's proposal but lets him know his son will be the one to build the temple. David attacks and defeats the neighboring Philistines, Moabites, Arameans, and Edomites; the victories bring him and his kingdom great wealth. He consecrates precious metals to God. His government rules the people with fairness and righteousness. The new Ammonite king ignores David's benevolent gestures and hires the Arameans to strengthen the Ammonite forces. David soundly defeats the Ammonites and Arameans, and Aram becomes David's vassal state. ⏳ *1 CHRONICLES 17:1–15; 18:1–6, 14; 19:1–19*

After God's own heart: How can flawed people be heroes of faith?
King David was not a perfect man. Yet he always returned to God when he sinned. Even at his darkest moments, he confessed his sin to God to be restored. The flawed heroes of the Bible remind us that being a man or woman "after God's own heart" doesn't mean you're perfect; it means that you give God the good, the bad, and the ugly of your life.

---

910 BC	900 BC	890 BC	880 BC	870 BC	860 BC	850 BC	840 BC	830 BC	820 BC

◆ 909 Baasha (Israel)   ◆ 886 Elah (Israel)   ◆ 870 Elijah (prophet)   ◆ 845 Elisha (prophet)

◆ 913 Abijah (Judah)   ◆ 885 Zimri & Omri (Israel)   ◆ 853 Joram (Israel)   ◆ 835 Joash (Judah)

◆ 911 Asa (Judah)   ◆ 874 Ahab (Israel)   ◆ 841 Athaliah (Judah)

Important Family Histories	Tribal Genealogies, Levites, and Postexilic Jerusalem	David Anointed King	Ark Brought to Jerusalem	A Fair and Righteous Military Leader	Preparing to Build the Temple	David Organizes People	David's Final Days and Solomon's Debut
1:1–6:81	7:1–10:14	11:1–12:40	13:1–16:43	17:1–19:19	20:1–22:19	23:1–27:34	28:1–29:30

PREPARING TO BUILD THE TEMPLE (20:1–22:19)

David's forces continue their winning streak, ransacking the cities of Ammon and crushing a Philistine revolt. Satan persuades David to count the people of Israel, which angers God and results in a plague that kills seventy thousand men. David buys a threshing floor, sets up an altar, and offers sacrifices that appease God and end the plague. David secures more than enough materials to build the temple and exhorts his son Solomon and the nation's leaders to follow Moses' law and get busy building God's permanent dwelling place with confidence. ⌛ *1 CHRONICLES 20:1–8; 21:1–24; 22:1–6, 17–19*

DAVID ORGANIZES PEOPLE TO SERVE (23:1–27:34)

David is growing old and appoints Solomon as the next king. Plans for the temple's construction are wrapping up, and David turns his attention to organizing the building staff. He divides the Aaronite priests and Levites into twenty-four divisions and assigns each a specific time of service. Musicians are also divided into twenty-four divisions and given specific times to serve. Finally, twelve groups of troops at David's disposal are listed, as well as tribal leaders, stewards of David's property, and the king's court servants. ⌛ *1 CHRONICLES 23:1, 6, 24–32; 24:1–6; 25:1–6; 26:20–32*

DAVID'S FINAL DAYS AND SOLOMON'S DEBUT (28:1–29:30)

David assembles Israel's leaders and directs Solomon to build the temple. David hands Solomon the building plans and encourages his son to proceed with perseverance. King David calls together all the leaders he has appointed and charges them to support Solomon as king. David describes his concern for the temple, and the people offer sacrifices and give donations to the treasury. David prays and hands the kingship over to his son Solomon. After ruling Israel forty years and enjoying long life, wealth, and honor, David dies. ⌛ *1 CHRONICLES 28:1–21; 29:1–9, 20–30*

1010 BC	1000 BC	990 BC	980 BC	970 BC	960 BC	950 BC	940 BC	930 BC	920 BC

◆ 1011–971 David (united kingdom)
◆ 971–931 Solomon (united kingdom)
◆ 930 Kingdom divides

◆ 1000 Glazing bricks begins in Near East
◆ 959 Temple in Jerusalem completed

◆ 1000 Mayan Empire founded (Central America)
◆ 950 Gold vessels and jewelry popular in Europe

TEMPLE COMPLETED, ARK ARRIVES (1:1–5:14)

Solomon begins his reign seeking and receiving God's blessing with boldness. God grants Solomon wisdom and success. Solomon almost immediately begins an elaborate and extensive building project, constructing the temple of the Lord as well as his own palace. He requests workers and materials from Hiram, king of Tyre, who agrees and sends Solomon all he asks for. With the help of a foreign king and a massive conscripted labor force, Solomon completes the construction of the temple. The building is decorated with gold and jewels, and two giant pillars are erected. The bronze altar, the Sea, the basins, the lampstands, the tables, and the sprinkling bowls are finished as well. Each item Hiram and

910 BC	900 BC	890 BC	880 BC	870 BC	860 BC	850 BC	840 BC	830 BC	820 BC

◆ 909 Baasha (Israel)   ◆ 886 Elah (Israel)   ◆ 870 Elijah (prophet)   ◆ 845 Elisha (prophet)

◆ 913 Abijah (Judah)   ◆ 885 Zimri & Omri (Israel)   ◆ 853 Joram (Israel)   ◆ 835 Joash (Judah)

◆ 911 Asa (Judah)   ◆ 874 Ahab (Israel)   ◆ 841 Athaliah (Judah)

Temple Completed, Ark Arrives	The Temple Dedication Continues	A Shift in Power and Division of the Kingdom	Further Trouble and Changing Times
1:1–5:14	6:1–7:22	8:1–11:23	12:1–14:15

NAVIGATING THE BIBLE

Solomon made is inventoried. Next, the ark of the covenant is brought into the new temple of the Lord with great joy, and God's presence in the form of a cloud envelops the temple. ⏳ *2 CHRONICLES 1:1–12; 2:1–18; 4:1–11; 5:1–14*

THE TEMPLE DEDICATION CONTINUES (6:1–7:22)

Solomon asks God to dwell in the temple and be responsive to the people's prayers. He praises God for keeping His promise given to David and asks Him to keep the promise that David would always have a descendant sitting on his throne. The people celebrate with sacrifice and song when God's glory fills the temple. They celebrate the Festival of Tabernacles, and God warns Solomon to be careful to follow His ways. ⏳ *2 CHRONICLES 6:1–21; 7:1–22*

A SHIFT IN POWER AND DIVISION OF THE KINGDOM (8:1–11:23)

Solomon continues to build Israel's infrastructure. He is known for his wisdom and his wealth, but the people stand ready to challenge their new leader. After Solomon dies, his son Rehoboam reigns in his place. When Jeroboam and the people ask King Rehoboam for reduced labor, he disregards their request. The people rebel and kill one of his emissaries. These events propel Israel to division. Rehoboam fortifies Judah's cities and appoints family members to powerful positions. ⏳ *2 CHRONICLES 8:1–11; 9:22–31; 10:12–19; 11:5–12, 18–23*

68

Rehoboam's Insolence *by Hans Holbein the Younger (1498–1543)*

1010 BC	1000 BC	990 BC	980 BC	970 BC	960 BC	950 BC	940 BC	930 BC	920 BC

◆ 1011–971 David (united kingdom)

◆ 971–931 Solomon (united kingdom)

◆ 930 Kingdom divides

◆ 1000 Glazing bricks begins in Near East

◆ 959 Temple in Jerusalem completed

◆ 1000 Mayan Empire founded (Central America)

◆ 950 Gold vessels and jewelry popular in Europe

Consequences of Not Trusting God	The Battle Is the Lord's	Turning from God	Judah Rapidly Declines and Is Taken Captive
15:1–19:11	20:1–22:9	22:10–28:27	29:1–36:23

FURTHER TROUBLE AND CHANGING TIMES (12:1–14:15)

At first, Rehoboam walks in the ways of David and Solomon, and the southern kingdom is strengthened. When the people of Judah disobey God, however, the Egyptian king is sent to plunder Judah. Rehoboam repents, and Jerusalem is spared. After Rehoboam dies, Abijah becomes king of Judah and destroys Jeroboam's army. Abijah dies and Asa, his son, is appointed as king. King Asa banishes idolatry from the land, fortifies Judah's cities, and defeats the Cushites. ⚱ *2 CHRONICLES 12:1–8; 13:1–20; 14:1–15*

CONSEQUENCES OF NOT TRUSTING GOD (15:1–19:11)

Azariah the prophet stirs the people to repent. But King Asa becomes prideful, and idolatry is still prevalent. When the Israelite king advances against Judah, Asa hires Aramean warriors to attack. Asa is rebuked for trusting Aram instead of God, and he dies. Jehoshaphat becomes king and uproots idolatry from the land. He forms an alliance with King Ahab, but Micaiah the prophet discourages the alliance. Ahab is killed in battle. ⚱ *2 CHRONICLES 15:1–8; 16:1–9; 17:1–9; 18:1–8, 18–22*

THE BATTLE IS THE LORD'S (20:1–22:9)

Judah begins to turn from God. God allows Judah's enemies to attack themselves, and Jehoshaphat's army enjoys the spoils of war. Jehoshaphat dies, and Jehoram replaces him. Elijah scolds the new king for killing his own siblings and worshipping idols. Jehoram's enemies conquer Jerusalem, and God punishes Jehoram with a fatal disease. Ahaziah, Jehoram's son, becomes king and does evil in the eyes of the Lord. Ahaziah also dies, and his mother, Athaliah, proceeds to destroy the whole royal family of the house of Judah. ⚱ *2 CHRONICLES 20:1–13, 22–30; 21:4–19, 22:7–12*

TURNING FROM GOD (22:10–28:27)

Joash is protected from being slaughtered by Athaliah, and he takes the throne at the age of seven. After Jehoiada the priest dies, the people

910 BC	900 BC	890 BC	880 BC	870 BC	860 BC	850 BC	840 BC	830 BC	820 BC

◆ 909 Baasha (Israel)　　◆ 886 Elah (Israel)　◆ 870 Elijah (prophet)　　◆ 845 Elisha (prophet)

◆ 913 Abijah (Judah)　　◆ 885 Zimri & Omri (Israel)　　◆ 853 Joram (Israel)　　◆ 835 Joash (Judah)

◆ 911 Asa (Judah)　　◆ 874 Ahab (Israel)　　◆ 841 Athaliah (Judah)

Temple Completed, Ark Arrives	The Temple Dedication Continues	A Shift in Power and Division of the Kingdom	Further Trouble and Changing Times	Consequences of Not Trusting God	The Battle Is the Lord's	Turning from God	Judah Rapidly Declines and Is Taken Captive
1:1–5:14	6:1–7:22	8:1–11:23	12:1–14:15	15:1–19:11	20:1–22:9	22:10–28:27	29:1–36:23

worship idols. Amaziah, Joash's son, is the next king, but he too is killed. The people make Uzziah king, and he does right in the eyes of the Lord and becomes powerful. However, he burns incense on the altar while in a fit of anger and is struck with leprosy. Jotham becomes king next and does right in the sight of the Lord. He builds fortresses in the hills and conquers the Ammonites. Ahaz follows as king, but he makes and worships idols. The Lord gives him over to Aram and Israel.

⏳ 2 CHRONICLES 22:10–12; 23:1–15; 24:17–19; 25:25–28; 26:1–15, 19–21; 27:1–9; 28:16–27

The Leper King Uzziah
by Rembrandt (1606–1669)

JUDAH RAPIDLY DECLINES AND IS TAKEN CAPTIVE (29:1–36:23)

Hezekiah becomes king of Judah and rules with righteousness, and the people return to the Lord. Many gather in Jerusalem to celebrate the Passover. After Sennacherib, king of Assyria, besieges Judah, Hezekiah and Isaiah cry out to the Lord, and the Assyrians are struck dead. Josiah, who loves the Lord, becomes Judah's next king. He repairs the temple and has the Book of the Law read out loud. Josiah celebrates the Passover, appoints priests to their duties, and provides offerings. Josiah dies, four evil kings rule consecutively after him, and judgment finally falls on Judah. Nebuchadnezzar takes the nation captive for seventy years.

⏳ 2 CHRONICLES 29:1–11, 31–35; 30:1–9; 32:1–5, 20–23; 34:1–8, 14–21; 36:1–21

The fall of Judah: How did it fit into God's plan?
When the kingdom of Judah fell to the Babylonian Empire in 586 BC, God used this tragedy to make His name known. The people of Judah were scattered across the empire. God commanded them to seek the welfare of their new hometowns so the inhabitants in those towns would know that He is holy.

700 BC	690 BC	680 BC	670 BC	660 BC	650 BC	640 BC	630 BC	620 BC	610 BC
◆ 716 Hezekiah (Judah)				◆ 658 Nahum (prophet)		◆ 640 Zephaniah (prophet)		◆ 620 Daniel born	
	◆ 697 Manasseh (Judah)					◆ 640 Josiah (Judah)		◆ 620 Ezekiel (prophet)	
	◆ 701 Sennacherib invades				◆ 650 Jeremiah (prophet)				

Introduction to Ezra and Nehemiah

Author: Potentially Ezra. Unknown.
Dates of Events: 540–440 BC

The books of Ezra and Nehemiah, originally one book and traditionally authored by Ezra, were likely written between 460 and 440 BC. Together they record about one hundred years of Israel's history. This "second exodus" from Babylon is less impressive than the escape from Egypt; only a remnant of Jews chooses to leave Babylon. The dramatic narrative actually begins in 538 BC and revolves around three epic tales: the struggle to rebuild the temple in Jerusalem under Zerubbabel, the reestablishment of the Law of Moses, and the rebuilding of Jerusalem. Through the eyes of Ezra and Nehemiah, God's faithfulness to His promises to His chosen people is seen as He restores them back to their land after seventy years of captivity.

Even though Ezra emphasizes the rebuilding of the temple, the book also beautifully reveals God's continued fulfillment of His promise to keep David's descendants alive. Written somewhere between 457 and 444 BC, this book relates two of three returns from Babylonia; the first led by Zerubbabel to rebuild the temple and the second under Ezra's leadership to restore the spiritual condition of the people. Through recounting historical events, the author of Ezra communicates God's love, power, and forgiveness; His activity and sovereignty in the world; His covenant with His people; and His unchanging grace. The book clearly emphasizes the power of the Word of God and the critical need to obey it in every area of life.

Nehemiah, one of the Old Testament's historical books, picks up naturally where Ezra leaves off. A contemporary of Ezra and cupbearer to the king of Persia,

600 BC	590 BC	580 BC	570 BC	560 BC	550 BC	540 BC	530 BC	520 BC	510 BC

◆ 597 Zedekiah (Judah)   ◆ 570 Confucius teaches in China   ◆ 522 Zechariah/Haggai (prophets)

◆ 600 Habakkuk (prophet)   ◆ 559 Cyrus the Great (Persia)   ◆ 521 Darius (Persia)

            ◆ 586 Fall of Jerusalem   ◆ 560 Aesop's fables   ◆ 539 Darius the Mede (Babylon)

GEN EXOD LEV NUM DEUT JOSH JUDG RUTH 1 SAM 2 SAM 1 KGS 2 KGS 1 CHR 2 CHR EZRA NEH ESTH JOB PSALMS PROV ECCL SONG

God Moves History	The Troubles Begin
1:1–3:13	4:1–5:17

Nehemiah leads the return of the third and final group of exiles from Babylon in 445 BC. Although the book of Nehemiah provides historical accounts of the rebuilding of Jerusalem's wall, it also documents the harder task of reviving and reforming the people of God within those rebuilt walls. After the walls are built, Ezra the priest consecrates the people and proclaims the law of the Lord to the nation. The people repent and weep, the covenant is renewed, and the people commit to obey God's commandments. Unfortunately, this revival is short-lived; Nehemiah, who had returned to Persia in 432 BC, returns to Jerusalem to reform the people yet again in 425 BC.

Nehemiah rebuilt the broken walls of Jerusalem.

Ezra and Nehemiah: How do they fit into the Bible's story line?

Ezra and Nehemiah are some of the last historical books of the Old Testament. They describe events in Jerusalem after the exiles were allowed to return. In other words, they reveal that exile was not the end of the story for God's people. God still had a plan for His people, no matter what happened.

600 BC	590 BC	580 BC	570 BC	560 BC	550 BC	540 BC	530 BC	520 BC	510 BC

- 597 Zedekiah (Judah)
- 570 Confucius teaches in China
- 522 Zechariah/Haggai (prophets)
- 600 Habakkuk (prophet)
- 559 Cyrus the Great (Persia)
- 521 Darius (Persia)
- 586 Fall of Jerusalem
- 560 Aesop's fables
- 539 Darius the Mede (Babylon)

The Strong Hand of God	Trouble in Covenant City
6:1–8:36	9:1–10:44

Read Each 5-Minute Overview in Ezra

GOD MOVES HISTORY (1:1–3:13)

Other major powers in the ancient Near East barely know Israel exists, yet God still cares about Israel. God had made promises to Israel, and He continues to work out the fulfillment of those promises through Cyrus, a Gentile king. Cyrus grants the Israelites the right to rebuild their temple in Jerusalem and returns the temple vessels that Nebuchadnezzar had stolen. The Jewish community makes preparations to leave Babylon, and many embark on the journey to Jerusalem. The first group is led by Zerubbabel—years before Ezra comes on the scene—and consists of Israelite priests, Levites, and singers, along with people of questionable descent. Upon arriving home, the returnees offer sacrifices, donate money to the temple treasury, and begin settling in cities. Even though life is hard, Israel celebrates the Festival of Tabernacles. ⏳ *EZRA 1:1–11; 2:62–70; 3:1–13*

THE TROUBLES BEGIN (4:1–5:17)

The rebuilding of the temple continues, but not everyone is excited about it. An unidentified group of locals offer their help in building the temple, but the Israelites reject their offer. They are insulted and convince King Artaxerxes to suspend the construction. The prophets Haggai and Zechariah speak to the exiles who have returned home, and the temple's construction resumes. When the governor questions the people about the operation's legality, they tell him to speak to King Darius. ⏳ *EZRA 4:1–24; 5:1–17*

500 BC	490 BC	480 BC	470 BC	460 BC	450 BC	440 BC	430 BC	420 BC	410 BC

♦ 509 Roman Republic begins ♦ 478 Esther ♦ 440 Malachi (prophet)

♦ 492–479 Greco-Persian Wars ♦ 460–445 Peloponnesian War

♦ 516 Jewish temple completed ♦ 469 Birth of Socrates ♦ 444 Nehemiah sent to Judah

NAVIGATING THE BIBLE

THE STRONG HAND OF GOD (6:1–8:36)

King Darius enthusiastically supports the temple's construction, which is soon completed, and the Jews celebrate with joy by observing the Festival of Passover. Ezra the scribe now steps into the story, decades after the first group of exiles returned with Zerubbabel from Babylonian captivity. King Artaxerxes authorizes Ezra to govern Judah and orders him to collect taxes, offer sacrifices, institute God's law, and appoint judges over the people. Ezra and the families that are listed travel to Jerusalem; they arrive safely to deliver the king's orders. They gratefully offer sacrifices at the temple. God's hand of protection on His people is evident. ⧗ *EZRA 6:13–22; 7:1–26; 8:31–36*

TROUBLE IN COVENANT CITY (9:1–10:44)

Ezra and his group of exiles have been in Jerusalem about four and a half months. Ezra is informed of the prevalence of intermarriage between the Jews and the people around them. This is an outright rejection of God's law and His demand for spiritual purity. Ezra laments the current state of affairs, confesses the people's sins to God, and begs for mercy. Ezra gathers the people in Jerusalem and criticizes the men severely for taking foreign wives; they repent of their sin and agree to change their ways. ⧗ *EZRA 9:1–15; 10:1–17*

74

600 BC	590 BC	580 BC	570 BC	560 BC	550 BC	540 BC	530 BC	520 BC	510 BC

◆ 597 Zedekiah (Judah) ◆ 570 Confucius teaches in China ◆ 522 Zechariah/Haggai (prophets)

◆ 600 Habakkuk (prophet) ◆ 559 Cyrus the Great (Persia) ◆ 521 Darius (Persia)

◆ 586 Fall of Jerusalem ◆ 560 Aesop's fables ◆ 539 Darius the Mede (Babylon)

Nehemiah Arrives	Rebuilding Efforts	The Foundation of Spiritual Reformation	The Israelites Repent
1:1–3:32	4:1–6:19	7:1–8:18	9:1–13:31

Read Each 5-Minute Overview in Nehemiah

NEHEMIAH ARRIVES (1:1–3:32)

Back in Susa, Nehemiah is informed of Jerusalem's desperate condition. He weeps, confesses the people's sins, and begs for mercy. Nehemiah then waits four months before approaching King Artaxerxes with his request to leave. King Artaxerxes grants Nehemiah permission to travel to Jerusalem and rebuild its wall. Soon after arriving in Jerusalem, Nehemiah inspects the wall and announces his plan to rebuild it. Men from surrounding nations discredit what Israel is doing, but Nehemiah trusts in God's faithfulness in allowing the Jews to complete the construction of the wall. Nehemiah gives a detailed account of the task, starting with the Sheep Gate. People who repaired specific sections of the wall are listed. ⧖ *NEHEMIAH 1:1–11; 2:1–20; 3:1–12*

REBUILDING EFFORTS (4:1–6:19)

Enemies plan to attack Jerusalem, so Nehemiah orders each worker to prepare for an ambush. He commands them to listen for a trumpet blast and trust God to fight for them. Nehemiah is certain God will grant success to those in the rebuilding effort. However, internal dissention is growing, and the people complain about their difficult economic situation. Nehemiah responds by charging the nobles and officials to forgive all outstanding loans. Jerusalem's wall is completed. Foreign enemies conspire to eliminate, or at least discredit, Nehemiah's exemplary leadership, but he avoids their traps. ⧖ *NEHEMIAH 4:1–20; 5:1–13; 6:12–19*

500 BC	490 BC	480 BC	470 BC	460 BC	450 BC	440 BC	430 BC	420 BC	410 BC

◆ **509 Roman Republic begins**   ◆ **478 Esther**   ◆ **440 Malachi (prophet)**

◆ **492–479 Greco-Persian Wars**   ◆ **460–445 Peloponnesian War**

◆ **516 Jewish temple completed**   ◆ **469 Birth of Socrates**   ◆ **444 Nehemiah sent to Judah**

Nehemiah Arrives	Rebuilding Efforts
1:1–3:32	4:1–6:19

CAST OF CHARACTERS

Ezra

Priest and Scribe. Ezra diligently studied and taught God's law. He led thousands of Jewish exiles from Babylon to Judea, and he immediately addressed wrongs done in the land. The people repented and recommitted to following God. After Jerusalem's walls were rebuilt, Ezra proclaimed God's law, which ignited a new spiritual hunger.

Nehemiah

Jewish Reformer. As cupbearer to the king, Nehemiah made a bold request: a leave of absence to return to his homeland, Israel, to rebuild Jerusalem's protective wall. The king obliged, and Nehemiah persevered despite opposition from his enemies. With determination, he and his people completed the wall in less than two months.

600 BC	590 BC	580 BC	570 BC	560 BC	550 BC	540 BC	530 BC	520 BC	510 BC

- ✦ 597 Zedekiah (Judah)
- ✦ 570 Confucius teaches in China
- ✦ 522 Zechariah/Haggai (prophets)
- ✦ 600 Habakkuk (prophet)
- ✦ 559 Cyrus the Great (Persia)
- ✦ 521 Darius (Persia)
- ✦ 586 Fall of Jerusalem
- ✦ 560 Aesop's fables
- ✦ 539 Darius the Mede (Babylon)

The Foundation of Spiritual Reformation	The Israelites Repent
7:1–8:18	9:1–13:31

IN EZRA, NEHEMIAH, ESTHER

Haman

Enemy of the Jews. Haman was bestowed with honor in the Persian government. Everyone was required to bow to him. A Jew named Mordecai refused. Prideful and furious, Haman planned to exterminate all Jews in the empire. His wicked plan was revealed, the Jews were saved, and Haman was killed.

Esther

Queen of Persia. Esther was a young Jewish girl who had been chosen by the king of Persia as his new queen. Evil Haman devised a plan to annihilate all Jews, but Esther risked her life to approach the king and reveal Haman's plot—thus saving her people.

500 BC	490 BC	480 BC	470 BC	460 BC	450 BC	440 BC	430 BC	420 BC	410 BC

◆ 509 Roman Republic begins   ◆ 478 Esther   ◆ 440 Malachi (prophet)

◆ 492–479 Greco-Persian Wars   ◆ 460–445 Peloponnesian War

◆ 516 Jewish temple completed   ◆ 469 Birth of Socrates   ◆ 444 Nehemiah sent to Judah

Nehemiah Arrives	Rebuilding Efforts	The Foundation of Spiritual Reformation	The Israelites Repent
1:1–3:32	4:1–6:19	7:1–8:18	9:1–13:31

NAVIGATING THE BIBLE

78

THE FOUNDATION OF SPIRITUAL REFORMATION (7:1–8:18)

Nehemiah's original task to rebuild the wall is now complete. But his work in rebuilding the city and boosting the Israelites' morale is far from over. Nehemiah's focus now is securing the city, registering the people, and delegating authority and control. Then he begins his next challenge: reviving people's spirits and their relationship with God. Ezra reads and teaches the Law of Moses to the people, who weep upon realizing how far from God they have strayed. Their tears turn to

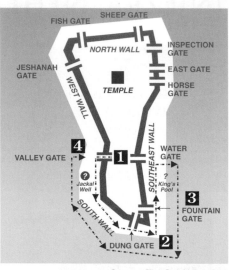

Source: The QuickView Bible

joy as they learn about the Festival of Tabernacles, and they celebrate it with great jubilation. ⌛ NEHEMIAH 7:1–5, 66–73; 8:1–18

THE ISRAELITES REPENT (9:1–13:31)

When the Israelites hear the Word of God being read, they are motivated to change. Having been away from daily worship practices, they realize an about-face on their part is necessary. In heartfelt repentance for their ongoing apostasy and infidelity, the Israelites make a new covenant with God and commit to obedience regarding intermarriage laws, the Sabbath day and year, the temple upkeep, firstfruits, the law of the firstborn, and tithes. Through a lottery, one out of ten people is chosen to dwell in Jerusalem. The wall is dedicated with great joy, and the temple's officers are appointed. ⌛ NEHEMIAH 9:1–6, 32–38; 10:28–39; 11:1–4; 12:27–30; 13:15–22

600 BC	590 BC	580 BC	570 BC	560 BC	550 BC	540 BC	530 BC	520 BC	510 BC

♦ 597 Zedekiah (Judah)   ♦ 570 Confucius teaches in China   ♦ 522 Zechariah/Haggai (prophets)

♦ 600 Habakkuk (prophet)   ♦ 559 Cyrus the Great (Persia)   ♦ 521 Darius (Persia)

          ♦ 586 Fall of Jerusalem   ♦ 560 Aesop's fables   ♦ 539 Darius the Mede (Babylon)

INTRODUCTION TO ESTHER

Author: Unknown
Date of Events: 475 BC

Esther is one of only two books in the Bible named for women, and it recounts the story of a beautiful, young Jewish girl living in Persia about one hundred years after Israel was released from Babylonian captivity. Esther, an orphan who was adopted and raised by her older cousin, Mordecai, risks her life to save her people and thus unknowingly plays a part in God's preservation of the nation of Israel.

The story of Esther's life fits between chapters 6 and 7 of Ezra, between the first return of exiles from Babylon led by Zerubbabel and the second return led by Ezra. While Ezra describes the trials and challenges of the Jewish exiles returning to the land of promise, Esther shows the plight of the Jewish people in Persia during the same period of time. The author of Esther is unknown, but the inclusion of details of Jewish customs throughout the story suggests the author is Jewish; a clear understanding of Persian etiquette and customs, the description of the palace in Susa, and details of events during Xerxes' reign indicate the author must have also lived in Persia. Written somewhere between 464 and 435 BC, Esther provides a biblical portrait of the Jews who chose to remain in Persia rather than return to the land of Israel after they were released from Babylon.

Through Esther and the wise counsel of her cousin Mordecai, the Jews experience an inexplicable deliverance. Winning the royal beauty contest, young Esther finds herself the new queen of Persia, married to King Xerxes. Mordecai, in his wisdom, instructs Esther to conceal her Jewish heritage. An evil man named Haman plots for a year to eliminate all Jews, but Esther's bravery foils his plan. God's remarkable rescue of His people that follows forms the basis of the Feast of Purim.

500 BC	490 BC	480 BC	470 BC	460 BC	450 BC	440 BC	430 BC	420 BC	410 BC

◆ 509 Roman Republic begins   ◆ 478 Esther   ◆ 440 Malachi (prophet)

◆ 492–479 Greco-Persian Wars   ◆ 460–445 Peloponnesian War

◆ 516 Jewish temple completed   ◆ 469 Birth of Socrates   ◆ 444 Nehemiah sent to Judah

A New Queen in Susa	Mordecai's Influence and Esther's Decision
1:1–2:18	2:19–4:17

Although God is never mentioned in Esther, His hand of providence is easy to see throughout the book. Prayer, Jerusalem, Judah, fasting, and worship are other themes woven throughout the narrative. The book reveals yet another threat to destroy the Jewish people and thus destroy the messianic line. Written to commemorate and memorialize God's continued faithfulness to His chosen people, Esther also shows how God uses ordinary men and women to overcome unimaginable circumstances in order to accomplish His good and gracious purposes. God will preserve His people; nothing can prevent the coming of the Messiah.

Ruins of Xerxes' palace viewed from a central hill in Persepolis, Iran

How does Esther fit into the biblical story?

Esther played a pivotal role in the biblical story. Had her nemesis Haman succeeded in his plot to annihilate the Jews, the Messiah would not have come and God's promise would have been broken. Esther's story reminds us that God always provides a way to fulfill His promises.

500 BC	490 BC	480 BC	470 BC	460 BC	450 BC	440 BC	430 BC	420 BC	410 BC

♦ 509 Roman Republic begins ♦ 478 Esther ♦ 440 Malachi (prophet)

♦ 492–479 Greco-Persian Wars ♦ 460–445 Peloponnesian War

♦ 516 Jewish temple completed ♦ 469 Birth of Socrates ♦ 444 Nehemiah sent to Judah

Two Banquets and a Death	A New Feast Is Established
5:1–7:10	8:1–10:3

Read Each 5-Minute Overview in Esther

A NEW QUEEN IN SUSA (1:1–2:18)

The Jewish people are under Persian rule. Persian King Xerxes and Queen Vashti entertain their citizens with a series of lavish banquets. When Vashti disregards her husband's request to "display her beauty," a minister convinces Xerxes that she is a threat to the country's social order and must be sent away. A search is made for a new queen, and beautiful, young Esther is among the possible choices. Mordecai, Esther's cousin, forbids her to reveal her Jewish background. Esther wins the king's favor over every other woman, and Xerxes crowns her queen. ⧗ ESTHER 1:1–22; 2:1–18

MORDECAI'S INFLUENCE AND ESTHER'S DECISION (2:19–4:17)

Mordecai now has an ally at the highest level of government. Shortly after Esther's coronation, Mordecai discovers a plot to kill the king. He tells Esther, who immediately tells Xerxes, and the two conspirators are killed. King Xerxes appoints evil Haman as his chief officer. When Mordecai refuses to bow before Haman, Haman determines to destroy Mordecai and all Jewish people along with him. Mordecai persuades Esther to approach the king and plead for her people to be spared. She instructs Mordecai to urge all the Jews in Susa to fast for three days; she fasts as well. ⧗ ESTHER 2:19–23; 3:1–15; 4:1–17

400 BC	390 BC	380 BC	370 BC	360 BC	350 BC	340 BC	330 BC	320 BC

◆ 404 Artaxerxes II (Persia)

◆ 370 Plato writes *The Republic*

◆ 336 Alexander the Great (Greece)

◆ 359 Philip (Macedonia)

◆ 312 Seleucus I

◆ 390 Aramaic begins to replace Hebrew as Jewish language

◆ 336 Birth of Aristotle

◆ 323 Ptolemy I

A New Queen in Susa	Mordecai's Influence and Esther's Decision	Two Banquets and a Death	A New Feast Is Established
1:1–2:18	2:19–4:17	5:1–7:10	8:1–10:3

TWO BANQUETS AND A DEATH (5:1–7:10)

Meanwhile, Haman has secured the king's permission to annihilate the Jews. Esther throws a party for Xerxes and Haman. Haman proudly attends but plots to have Mordecai impaled. King Xerxes remembers a good deed that Mordecai did for him and asks Haman what should be done for a man the king desires to honor. Haman thinks that Xerxes is speaking about him and suggests that the person be dressed in royal garb and led around the city. Haman is forced to parade his enemy around Susa. Esther pleads with Xerxes on behalf of her people and incriminates Haman in the process. Haman is impaled on the very pole that he had set up for Mordecai. ⌛ *ESTHER 5:1–14; 6:1–14; 7:1–10*

A NEW FEAST IS ESTABLISHED (8:1–10:3)

Haman's official message has already gone out to annihilate the Jews, so Esther and Mordecai attempt to reverse the damage. Xerxes replaces Haman with Mordecai, who issues a new decree in favor of the Jews. The Jews attack their enemies and institute the holiday of Purim to celebrate their escape and protection from Haman's evil plot. Mordecai rises to considerable power and experiences unwavering allegiance from his people. Although God is never mentioned in the book of Esther, His protective hand is clearly seen. ⌛ *ESTHER 8:1–17; 9:1–10, 23–32; 10:1–3*

Esther lived in Susa. The distance between Susa and Jerusalem was approximately 800 miles.

500 BC	490 BC	480 BC	470 BC	460 BC	450 BC	440 BC	430 BC	420 BC	410 BC

◆ 509 Roman Republic begins   ◆ 478 Esther   ◆ 440 Malachi (prophet)

◆ 492–479 Greco-Persian Wars   ◆ 460–445 Peloponnesian War

◆ 516 Jewish temple completed   ◆ 469 Birth of Socrates   ◆ 444 Nehemiah sent to Judah

Job's Life Turns Sour	Two Fair-Weather Friends Speak Out	Job Laments His Fate	Job's Second Response to Eliphaz	Continued Tongue-Lashing from Three Friends	Job's Final Response	Elihu Speaks	The Lord Speaks with Job
1.1–3:26	4:1–10:22	11:1–14:22	15:1–17:16	18:1–25:6	26:1–31:40	32:1–37:24	38:1–42:17

INTRODUCTION TO JOB

Author: *Unknown*
Dates of Events: *Unknown*

The book of Job begins in heaven, with a dispute between God and Satan. The story then moves to earth, where a detailed glimpse into the life of a man named Job is given. Overnight, this righteous man's blessed life turns into one of heartache, as he suffers the loss of his health, wealth, children, and status. Through this transforming crisis, Job wrestles with God over the question, Why? Three cycles of earthly debates between Job and his friends bring Job to a diagnosis of the problem: God is sovereign, and He does what He pleases.

Job, a book of dramatic poetry, is perhaps the earliest book of the Bible. The events in the book most likely occurred during the period of the patriarchs. It is plausible Job was Abraham's contemporary and walked

Job Mocked by His Wife *by Albrecht Dürer (1471–1528)*

400 BC	390 BC	380 BC	370 BC	360 BC	350 BC	340 BC	330 BC	320 BC

◆ 404 Artaxerxes II (Persia)   ◆ 370 Plato writes *The Republic*   ◆ 336 Alexander the Great (Greece)

◆ 359 Philip (Macedonia)   ◆ 312 Seleucus I

◆ 390 Aramaic begins to replace Hebrew as Jewish language   ◆ 336 Birth of Aristotle   ◆ 323 Ptolemy I

Job's Life Turns Sour	Two Fair-Weather Friends Speak Out	Job Laments His Fate	Job's Second Response to Eliphaz
1:1–3:26	4:1–10:22	11:1–14:22	15:1–17:16

the earth three hundred years or so after the flood, around 2000 BC. Interestingly, for as old as this text is, Job knows God to be his Redeemer and Mediator—two identifiers of Jesus. The author of Job is not known, and there are no hints in the text of who it might have been. However, there is a strong possibility the author was an Israelite, as he uses the Israelite covenant name for God: Yahweh, or the Lord. Job's story is set in Uz in the area of Edom, southeast of the Dead Sea. The first eleven chapters of Genesis predate the story of Job, but Job's story was not written down in book form until the time of Moses, around 1500 BC.

The basic question of the book, "Why do the righteous suffer?" is never really answered. What Job learns from losing everything important to him in life is the true focus of the story. God is sovereign over all creation, and He is worthy of worship in whatever He chooses to do or not do. Job's journey broadens his understanding of God and teaches him he must trust in the goodness and power of God in adversity. Though Job is a righteous man, his pride and self-righteous attitude bubbles forth and needs humbling. Job learns the greatness and majesty of the Lord, that He is supreme, full of wisdom, and good. Even though His ways are often impossible to understand, He can always be trusted. The book of Job also communicates that suffering is not always a result of sin; God uses suffering to test, teach, and draw His people near.

Making sense of suffering: What's the lesson of Job?

Job is thought to be the oldest book in the Bible. It sheds light on one man's perseverance and quest for answers in the wake of unimaginable suffering. Job suffers not because he has done something wrong but because Satan wants to test Job to see if he will renounce God. Job's friends insist he must have brought calamity on himself somehow, but Job maintains his innocence and pleads his case to God. Job never receives an explanation for his suffering—and neither do we. But God vindicates Job before his friends and restores his fortunes. The story of Job encourages us to trust God even when we do not understand everything. It's also a reminder that when we give counsel to others, we should offer it with a spirit of humility. One thing is certain: We do not know all there is to know.

3200 BC	3100 BC	3000 BC	2900 BC	2800 BC	2700 BC	2600 BC	2500 BC	2400 BC	2300 BC

◆ 3200 Sumerian alphabet

◆ 3100 King Menes (Egypt)

◆ 3000 Stonehenge erected

◆ 2700 Construction of ancient pyramids begins in Egypt

◆ 2500 Iron manufactured

◆ 2500 Egyptians use papyrus

Tongue-Lashing from Three Friends	Job's Final Response	Elihu Speaks	The Lord Speaks with Job
18:1–25:6	26:1–31:40	32:1–37:24	38:1–42:17

Read Each 5-Minute Overview in Job

JOB'S LIFE TURNS SOUR (1:1–3:26)

Job is a pious and very wealthy man, but he is tested to see if his piety is a result of his prosperity. God allows Satan to unleash horrible torment on Job: enemies steal many of his animals and kill some of his servants; fire kills his remaining animals and servants; a roof collapses and kills all ten of his children; painful sores cover his body. But Job remains faithful to God and accepts his fate with integrity. Three friends visit Job in his suffering. After seven days of silence, Job speaks from his heart and fervently curses the day he was born. He wonders why God keeps people who suffer alive. 🕱 *JOB 1:1–21; 2:1–13; 3:11–26*

2200 BC	2100 BC	2090 BC	2080 BC	2070 BC	2060 BC	2050 BC	2040 BC	2030 BC	2020 BC

◆ 2166 Birth of Abraham   ◆ ???? Life of Job   ◆ 2050 Abraham offers Isaac as a sacrifice

◆ 2100–2000? Ziggurats built in Mesopotamia

Job's Life Turns Sour	Two Fair-Weather Friends Speak Out	Job Laments His Fate	Job's Second Response to Eliphaz
1:1–3:26	4:1–10:22	11:1–14:22	15:1–17:16

TWO FAIR-WEATHER FRIENDS SPEAK OUT (4:1–10:22)

After listening to Job's monologue, Job's friend Eliphaz suggests Job has brought his troubles on himself through his own sin and recommends Job consider repenting and accept God's reprimand. Job responds by pouring out his complaints to God, longing for death. He accuses his companions of being fair-weather friends. Bildad implies Job will only be blessed again if he lives righteously. ⌛ *JOB 4:1–11; 5:17–27; 6:1–10; 8:1–7; 10:1–7*

JOB LAMENTS HIS FATE (11:1–14:22)

Job's third friend, Zophar, comes on the scene and blasts Job with stinging sarcasm. He defends God's position, degrades Job for questioning God, and tells Job to repent. Job responds by attempting to discredit his friend's arguments. Job then demands God list the sins that he has supposedly committed. He mourns over his fate as well as the fate of all humanity. ⌛ *JOB 11:13–20; 12:1–13; 13:20–28; 14:13–22*

JOB'S SECOND RESPONSE TO ELIPHAZ (15:1–17:16)

Each of Job's three friends has given his opinion, and Eliphaz speaks again, listing bad things that happen to wicked people—things that are now happening to Job. He claims Job's words are an insult to God and are themselves an indication of his guilt. Job rejects his friends' arguments and once again laments over God's treatment of him. He considers how sometimes God punishes the innocent for no reason. ⌛ *JOB 15:1–26; 17:1–16*

TONGUE-LASHING FROM THREE FRIENDS (18:1–25:6)

Bildad defends his own intelligence and once again states it is the wicked, not the innocent, who suffer. Job responds by begging his friends to treat him fairly, and he warns against their own judgment. Eliphaz tells Job if he submits to God, prosperity will come again. A third round of this three-on-one conversation begins between Job and his friends. Job still desires to debate

3200 BC	3100 BC	3000 BC	2900 BC	2800 BC	2700 BC	2600 BC	2500 BC	2400 BC	2300 BC

◆ 3200 Sumerian alphabet

◆ 3100 King Menes (Egypt)

◆ 3000 Stonehenge erected

◆ 2700 Construction of ancient pyramids begins in Egypt

◆ 2500 Iron manufactured

◆ 2500 Egyptians use papyrus

Tongue-Lashing from Three Friends	Job's Final Response	Elihu Speaks	The Lord Speaks with Job
18:1–25:6	26:1–31:40	32:1–37:24	38:1–42:17

God. Finally, Bildad says that everyone sins and nobody is perfect but God.
⌛ *JOB 18:1–21; 19:1–6; 22:21–20; 25:1–6*

Job and his three friends

JOB'S FINAL RESPONSE (26:1–31:40)
Job's three friends have little left to say; Job, on the other hand, is just getting warmed up. He praises God for dominating nature and destroying mythical creatures, and he explains that wisdom can't be found using normal methods because it comes from God alone. He recalls days past when he was respected and happy, and he wishes to prove his innocence before God. ⌛ *JOB 26:1–14; 29:1–25*

ELIHU SPEAKS (32:1-37:24)
A young man named Elihu has been listening to the confrontation between Job and his three friends, and he is ready to speak up. Elihu defends God's ability to judge fairly and criticizes wicked people for not praising God. He contends for God's righteousness and begins a hymn of praise for God's control of nature. He claims God is too great to be understood by mere humans.
⌛ *JOB 32:10–14; 34:1–20; 37:14–24*

THE LORD SPEAKS WITH JOB (38:1–42:17)
Finally, God's voice sounds. He puts Job in his place, asking him if he took part in creation, understands the world's secrets, or controls any of the wild animals. Job remains silent. God then describes two giant creatures that Job has absolutely no control over. Job sets his argument aside and acknowledges God's greatness. Job prays for his three friends who have misrepresented God, and they offer sacrifices in repentance. God restores Job's life far beyond its former glory. ⌛ *JOB 38:1–18; 42:1–17*

2200 BC	2100 BC	2090 BC	2080 BC	2070 BC	2060 BC	2050 BC	2040 BC	2030 BC	2020 BC

✦ 2166 Birth of Abraham   ✦ ???? Life of Job   ✦ 2050 Abraham offers Isaac as a sacrifice

✦ 2100–2000? Ziggurats built in Mesopotamia

Remember Your People (Lament Psalm)	True Loving-Kindness and Justice (Royal Psalm)	God Fulfills His Promises (Thanksgiving Psalm)	The Messiah as Priest, Judge, and King (Messianic Psalm)
Psalm 10	Psalm 101	Psalm 105	Psalm 110

INTRODUCTION TO PSALMS

Authors: Various
Dates Written: 1500–800 BC

The book of Psalms, the "hymnbook" of the Old Testament, is a collection of poetic songs revealing much about God and the impact of His presence during the joys and struggles of human life. Almost half of the psalms are attributed to David, and two are assigned to Solomon; a handful of other writers—some unknown—fill in the authorship for the rest. Together these psalms cover centuries of Israel's history—moments when God's people are close to Him and basking in His blessings as well as moments when the people suffer as a result of straying far from God's will.

The word *psalm* means "praises" in Hebrew, but the psalms speak to a variety of other emotions, struggles, and joys common to all humankind in all generations. They beautifully draw God's people closer to the heart of God. It is helpful to study the book of Psalms in various topical groupings.

IMPRECATORY PSALMS – These psalms invoke God's wrath and judgment against enemies. ⚱ *PSALMS 7, 35, 40, 55, 58–59, 69, 79, 109, 137, 139, 147*

WISDOM PSALMS – The Wisdom Psalms focus on God's instruction in the Pentateuch, or the Torah—the first five books of the Bible—and its central place in the life of the worshipping community. ⚱ *PSALMS 1, 19, 27, 37, 49, 73, 112, 119, 127–28, 133*

ROYAL PSALMS – These psalms focus on the Davidic king who rules the nation of Israel as God's appointed ruler, but they point toward the true heavenly King of Israel. ⚱ *PSALMS 2, 18, 20–21, 45, 72, 101, 110, 132, 144*

1110 BC	1100 BC	1090 BC	1080 BC	1070 BC	1060 BC	1050 BC	1040 BC	1030 BC	1020 BC
	◆ 1100 Life of Ruth?		◆ 1075 Elon (judge)		◆ 1060–1020 Samuel (judge/prophet)				
	◆ 1100 Eli (judge)	◆ 1087 Jephthah (judge)		◆ 1065 Abdon (judge)		◆ 1051–1011 Saul (united kingdom)			
	◆ 1100 Greece enters Dark Ages			◆ 1069 Samson (judge)?		◆ 1050 Zhou Dynasty (China)			

The Lord Is the Builder of Everything (Wisdom Psalm)	The Unity of Believers (Pilgrimage Psalm)	Reflecting on God's Omniscience (Imprecatory Psalm)	The Sustainer of the Universe (Praise Psalm)
Psalm 127	Psalm 133	Psalm 139	Psalm 147

PILGRIMAGE PSALMS – These psalms were sung by the pilgrims of ancient Israel as they made their way up to Jerusalem to celebrate the three pilgrim feasts. ⌛ *PSALMS 120–34*

PRAISE PSALMS – Psalms of praise make up about one-fifth of the book of Psalms. The primary goal of these psalms is to praise God, sometimes for no specific reason. ⌛ *PSALMS 8, 18, 21, 29–30, 33, 36, 40–41, 66, 68, 75, 93, 103–106, 111, 113–14, 116–17, 135–36, 138, 145–50*

THANKSGIVING PSALMS – Thanksgiving Psalms either begin with the call to give thanks or emphasize thanksgiving in some way. These psalms usually contain a reference to the crisis from which God delivers the psalmist or the community. ⌛ *PSALMS 9, 32, 34, 65–67, 92, 105–107, 116, 118, 136, 138*

LAMENT PSALMS – Lament Psalms are prayers for God's deliverance in moments of despair. They express the anguish, bitterness, anger, pain, disappointment, and frustration of the Israelite community of faith. ⌛ *PSALMS 3–7, 9–10, 12–14, 17, 22, 25–28, 31, 35–36, 38–44, 51–61, 64, 69–71, 74, 77, 79–80, 82–83, 85–86, 88–90, 94, 102, 108–109, 120, 123, 126, 129–30, 137, 139–43*

MESSIANIC PSALMS – Messianic Psalms speak of the person and work of the coming Anointed One, Jesus Christ. ⌛ *PSALMS 2, 8, 16, 22, 34–35, 40–41, 45, 68–69, 89, 102, 109–10, 118*

1010 BC	1000 BC	990 BC	980 BC	970 BC	960 BC	950 BC	940 BC	930 BC	920 BC

◆ 1011–971 David (united kingdom)   ◆ 971–931 Solomon (united kingdom)   ◆ 930 Kingdom divides

◆ 1000 Glazing bricks begins in Near East   ◆ 959 Temple in Jerusalem completed

◆ 1000 Mayan Empire founded (Central America)   ◆ 950 Gold vessels and jewelry popular in Europe

Remember Your People (Lament Psalm)	True Loving-Kindness and Justice (Royal Psalm)	God Fulfills His Promises (Thanksgiving Psalm)	The Messiah as Priest, Judge, and King (Messianic Psalm)
Psalm 10	Psalm 101	Psalm 105	Psalm 110

Read Each 5-Minute Overview in Psalms

PSALM 10 : REMEMBER YOUR PEOPLE (LAMENT PSALM)

In this psalm of lament, David desperately asks the Lord why He is not rescuing him from his enemies. David describes the wicked, as if God does not see the evil things they do. He pleads with God to remember him. Psalm 10 reminds readers God always hears the cries of the afflicted and needy.

1110 BC	1100 BC	1090 BC	1080 BC	1070 BC	1060 BC	1050 BC	1040 BC	1030 BC	1020 BC

◆ 1100 Life of Ruth?   ◆ 1075 Elon (judge)   ◆ 1060–1020 Samuel (judge/prophet)

◆ 1100 Eli (judge)   ◆ 1087 Jephthah (judge)   ◆ 1065 Abdon (judge)   ◆ 1051–1011 Saul (united kingdom)

◆ 1100 Greece enters Dark Ages   ◆ 1069 Samson (judge)?   ◆ 1050 Zhou Dynasty (China)

The Lord Is the Builder of Everything (Wisdom Psalm)	The Unity of Believers (Pilgrimage Psalm)	Reflecting on God's Omniscience (Imprecatory Psalm)	The Sustainer of the Universe (Praise Psalm)
Psalm 127	Psalm 133	Psalm 139	Psalm 147

Ultimately, David is confident the Lord will humble the proud, alluding to God's future just rule of the entire world. ⏳ *PSALM 10:1–18*

PSALM 101: TRUE LOVING-KINDNESS AND JUSTICE (ROYAL PSALM)

Psalm 101 states the principles on which King David will govern his house and the land when he takes the kingdom in the name of the Lord. The king's people are passive recipients of the king's loving-kindness, and his judgment extends to all the wicked people of the land—both those who commit obvious crimes and those who commit evil deeds in secret. Although speaking of himself, David is also writing of a King to come whose rule will be perfectly loving and just. ⏳ *PSALM 101:1–8*

PSALM 105: GOD FULFILLS HIS PROMISES (THANKSGIVING PSALM)

Historical in nature, Psalm 105 recounts God's deliverance of His people from bondage in Egypt. The object of this psalm is to excite God's people to gratitude by remembering His goodness, mercy, and His acts of miracles.

Prayer guide: Should we pray the psalms?

The book of Psalms is a collection of songs that were written during the history of ancient Israel. They were written as songs of worship to God during the nation's high and low points. Some of these songs declare the glory of God, while others cry out for justice or deliverance. Covering a wide range of topics, the psalms don't just show how Israel worshipped God. They also give us words that can shape our own communication with God. The psalms can deepen our understanding of God so that we can sing praise to Him, share words of comfort with others, and learn how to pray.

One important thing to remember is that the psalms are written from the real-life experiences of Israel. As a result, some of the psalms express rather unpleasant events. As you read the psalms, you will encounter the sin of kings and the rebellion of a nation. At times these songs reflect the anger of the Israelites in response to their enemies. When we read these psalms, we may not have cause to pray exactly as the Israelites did, but we can always learn from their openness and dependence on God in all their thoughts and feelings.

1010 BC	1000 BC	990 BC	980 BC	970 BC	960 BC	950 BC	940 BC	930 BC	920 BC

♦ 1011–971 David (united kingdom)   ♦ 971–931 Solomon (united kingdom)   ♦ 930 Kingdom divides

♦ 1000 Glazing bricks begins in Near East   ♦ 959 Temple in Jerusalem completed

♦ 1000 Mayan Empire founded (Central America)   ♦ 950 Gold vessels and jewelry popular in Europe

Remember Your People (Lament Psalm)	True Loving-Kindness and Justice (Royal Psalm)	God Fulfills His Promises (Thanksgiving Psalm)	The Messiah as Priest, Judge, and King (Messianic Psalm)
Psalm 10	Psalm 101	Psalm 105	Psalm 110

They should worship Him with love and thanksgiving for all His saving acts in fulfillment of His covenant with Abraham. ⏳ *PSALM 105:1–7, 16–45*

PSALM 110: THE MESSIAH AS PRIEST, JUDGE, AND KING (MESSIANIC PSALM)

This psalm clearly reveals the Messiah. Jesus Himself refers to Psalm 110 in His words found in Matthew 22:41–46. The psalmist declares the Savior's kingdom will spread out beyond the boundaries of Israel. The Messiah will serve as priest, judge, and king. His enemies will resist His rule, but this rule will be extended by force, with the Messiah at the head of a mighty army. Psalm 110 looks forward to Jesus the Messiah's final victory over His enemy. ⏳ *PSALM 110:1–7*

PSALM 127: THE LORD IS THE BUILDER OF EVERYTHING (WISDOM PSALM)

Psalm 127 is one of two psalms attributed to Solomon, and it is considered a Pilgrimage Psalm as well as a Wisdom Psalm. It addresses three of the most important of human concerns: accomplishment, security, and family. It encourages worshippers to recognize the One who is in control of these things. God is the true builder of everything; we build either in humility alongside God or with pride for our own benefit. The main principle in this psalm is that human care and toil will always be in vain without God's blessing. ⏳ *PSALM 127:1–5*

Who wrote the Psalms?
The Psalms had many different authors. Here is a listing of the authors:
- David (73 psalms)
- Asaph (12 psalms)
- Sons of Korah (11 psalms)
- Solomon (2 psalms)
- Moses (1 psalm)
- Heman (1 psalm)
- Ethan (1 psalm)
- Unknown (49 psalms)

1110 BC	1100 BC	1090 BC	1080 BC	1070 BC	1060 BC	1050 BC	1040 BC	1030 BC	1020 BC
	◆ 1100 Life of Ruth?		◆ 1075 Elon (judge)		◆ 1060–1020 Samuel (judge/prophet)				
	◆ 1100 Eli (judge)	◆ 1087 Jephthah (judge)		◆ 1065 Abdon (judge)		◆ 1051–1011 Saul (united kingdom)			
	◆ 1100 Greece enters Dark Ages			◆ 1069 Samson (judge)?		◆ 1050 Zhou Dynasty (China)			

The Lord Is the Builder of Everything (Wisdom Psalm)	The Unity of Believers (Pilgrimage Psalm)	Reflecting on God's Omniscience (Imprecatory Psalm)	The Sustainer of the Universe (Praise Psalm)
Psalm 127	Psalm 133	Psalm 139	Psalm 147

PSALM 133: THE UNITY OF BELIEVERS (PILGRIMAGE PSALM)

Another Pilgrimage Psalm, Psalm 133 portrays the perfect picture of unity—a divine unity—that shares in the blessings of God. True unity descends from above, as the anointing oil runs down Aaron's beard—a picture of the

King David Playing the Harp *by Gerard van Honthorst (1592–1656)*

1010 BC	1000 BC	990 BC	980 BC	970 BC	960 BC	950 BC	940 BC	930 BC	920 BC

◆ 1011–971 David (united kingdom)

◆ 971–931 Solomon (united kingdom)

◆ 930 Kingdom divides

◆ 1000 Glazing bricks begins in Near East

◆ 959 Temple in Jerusalem completed

◆ 1000 Mayan Empire founded (Central America)

◆ 950 Gold vessels and jewelry popular in Europe

Remember Your People (Lament Psalm)	True Loving-Kindness and Justice (Royal Psalm)	God Fulfills His Promises (Thanksgiving Psalm)	The Messiah as Priest, Judge, and King (Messianic Psalm)	The Lord Is the Builder of Everything (Wisdom Psalm)	The Unity of Believers (Pilgrimage Psalm)	Reflecting on God's Omniscience (Imprecatory Psalm)	The Sustainer of the Universe (Praise Psalm)
Psalm 10	Psalm 101	Psalm 105	Psalm 110	Psalm 127	Psalm 133	Psalm 139	Psalm 147

Holy Spirit. The goal, the focal point of unity, is Mount Zion and its King; this looks forward to King Jesus. Unity in Christ inevitably leads to righteousness, peace of mind, and freedom from things that entangle God's people. ⏳ *PSALM 133:1–3*

PSALM 139: REFLECTING ON GOD'S OMNISCIENCE (IMPRECATORY PSALM)

Psalm 139 is a prayer addressed to God and in many ways is a contemplative reflection. David considers how God knows everything about him. However, he is also bothered by the impossibility of escaping God's immense presence. David praises God for creating him, but the psalm takes an unexpected turn when David asks God to do away with wicked people. The psalm ends with a statement of commitment and innocence, followed by a short appeal for direction. ⏳ *PSALM 139:1–24*

PSALM 147: THE SUSTAINER OF THE UNIVERSE (PRAISE PSALM)

Psalm 147 praises God for being the creator, controller, and sustainer of the world and all nature. The psalmist praises God for keeping a watchful eye on Israel and Jerusalem. God is Israel's teacher, guiding and instructing the nation in His commandments and statutes. ⏳ *PSALM 147:1–20*

Poetic Devices

The writers of the book of Psalms used colorful literary devices to describe their spiritual journeys. Many of these words describe God himself while others describe their quest to find him.

- *God's law* ....used 198 times
- *Skies/Heavens* used 107 times
- *Water* .... used 94 times
- *Royalty* .... used 85 times
- *Refuge/Rock* ... used 66 times
- *Zion* .... used 51 times
- *Servant* .... used 38 times
- *Way (or Path)* ... used 36 times

1110 BC	1100 BC	1090 BC	1080 BC	1070 BC	1060 BC	1050 BC	1040 BC	1030 BC	1020 BC

- 1100 Life of Ruth?
- 1075 Elon (judge)
- 1060–1020 Samuel (judge/prophet)
- 1100 Eli (judge)
- 1087 Jephthah (judge)
- 1065 Abdon (judge)
- 1051–1011 Saul (united kingdom)
- 1100 Greece enters Dark Ages
- 1069 Samson (judge)?
- 1050 Zhou Dynasty (China)

Wisdom Praised and Personified	Solomon's Wisdom	Sayings of the Wise	More of Solomon's Wisdom	Wisdom from Solomon's Contemporaries
1:1–9:18	10:1–22:16	22:17–24:34	25:1–29:27	30:1–31:31

INTRODUCTION TO PROVERBS, ECCLESIASTES, AND SONG OF SONGS

Authors: Solomon and Others
Dates of Events: 960–920 BC

Proverbs, part of the collection of books known as Wisdom Literature, is perhaps the most practical book in the Old Testament. Proverbs teaches sensible knowledge for living a godly life. The proverbs in the book—written by various authors—reveal God's mind and heart for every kind of life situation. Wisdom is more than the ability to navigate life well. It begins with a proper attitude toward God, characterized by respect and awe for the sovereign Creator of the universe. This fear of and dependence upon the Lord is the beginning of true knowledge. Solomon, Israel's wisest king, penned thousands of proverbs during his reign, sometime before 931 BC; only some of those proverbs were collected into the first twenty-four chapters of the book of Proverbs. King Hezekiah's men compiled additional proverbs of Solomon and added chapters 25–29 to the book about 230 years later. Interestingly, Israel was at its spiritual, political, and economic summit during Solomon's reign.

Also considered part of the Wisdom Literature of the Old Testament is the book of Ecclesiastes. Within its verses are proverbs, teachings, stories, reflections, and warnings on a variety of topics that all address the futile emptiness of trying to

1010 BC	1000 BC	990 BC	980 BC	970 BC	960 BC	950 BC	940 BC	930 BC	920 BC

◆ 1011–971 David (united kingdom) ◆ 971–931 Solomon (united kingdom) ◆ 930 Kingdom divides

◆ 1000 Glazing bricks begins in Near East ◆ 959 Temple in Jerusalem completed

◆ 1000 Mayan Empire founded (Central America) ◆ 950 Gold vessels and jewelry popular in Europe

Wisdom Praised and Personified	Solomon's Wisdom	Sayings of the Wise
1:1–9:18	10:1–22:16	22:17–24:34

find happiness apart from God. Throughout the author's quest for meaning in life, he returns again and again to the meaninglessness of everything, a reality based on humanity's smallness in the face of God's great sovereignty. Most theologians agree the author of Ecclesiastes is Solomon and that Ecclesiastes was probably written later in his life, around 935 BC. Solomon recognizes humanity's purpose as God's creation is to fear Him and obey His commands—this is the only thing that brings meaning to life. Ecclesiastes convincingly points to what life looks like without a relationship with Jesus, the meaning to all the meaningless things the writer observes.

Song of Songs is a book of poems that illustrate the intense love between a shepherdess and King Solomon. Possibly written by Solomon himself early in his reign around 965 BC, the book is arranged with scenes as in a drama, with three main speakers: the bride, the king, and a chorus of friends. There is disagreement among scholars as to whether Solomon wrote Song of Songs, but he is mentioned in the book and many credit him with part of its authorship, if not all. The book celebrates sexuality in its proper context; but if taken allegorically, it pictures Israel as God's espoused bride and the church as the bride of Christ. Song of Songs is a positive endorsement by God of marital love and the physical and emotional beauty it was intended to bring to a husband and wife.

Promises or principles: How should we read Proverbs?

Proverbs show what the truth of God looks like when it's applied in the real world. Many of these sayings contain profound truths that are easily relatable to everyday life. However, some of these truths are hard to understand, let alone apply. Still, the wisdom found in Proverbs was meant to change the way we live. When reading the proverbs, we should meditate on each saying and consider its implications for our lives. Each proverb should be treated as a general principle for living. We should never read the proverbs as if they were absolute promises or formulas—as if they said, "If you do X, then Y is guaranteed to always happen." The proverbs help us to understand the general pattern of wise and foolish living. The key to applying each proverb is found in Proverbs 1:7, which commands us to fear (or respect) God. He must be the One we live for and strive to please. When we fear God first, we will gain an understanding of how to apply the truths contained in Proverbs.

1110 BC	1100 BC	1090 BC	1080 BC	1070 BC	1060 BC	1050 BC	1040 BC	1030 BC	1020 BC

- 1100 Life of Ruth? • 1075 Elon (judge) • 1060–1020 Samuel (judge/prophet)
- 1100 Eli (judge) • 1087 Jephthah (judge) • 1065 Abdon (judge) • 1051–1011 Saul (united kingdom)
- 1100 Greece enters Dark Ages • 1069 Samson (judge)? • 1050 Zhou Dynasty (China)

ISA JER LAM EZEK DAN HOS JOEL AMOS OBAD JONAH MIC NAH HAB ZEPH HAG ZECH MAL

More of Solomon's Wisdom	Wisdom from Solomon's Contemporaries
25:1–29:27	30:1–31:31

Read Each 5-Minute Overview in Proverbs

○ 1:1–9:18	Wisdom Praised and Personified	Page 97
○ 10:1–22:16	Solomon's Wisdom	Page 97
○ 22:17–24:34	Sayings of the Wise	Page 98
○ 25:1–29:27	More of Solomon's Wisdom	Page 98
○ 30:1–31:31	Wisdom from Solomon's Contemporaries	Page 98

WISDOM PRAISED AND PERSONIFIED (1:1–9:18)

King Solomon, the author of most of the book of Proverbs, focuses his writing on wisdom, justice, judgment, and equity. He desires that his readers apply their knowledge of God to their lives. True wisdom from God is more than just good advice; it is the key that unlocks the door to instruction, moral discernment, guidance, and spiritual insight. In Proverbs 1–9, wisdom is personified and seen crying in the streets and at the city gates. Solomon tells of the value of wisdom; the first step in gaining wisdom is to fear God. The blessings of wisdom include long life and prosperity. Solomon also speaks of seven things the Lord hates. ⌛ PROVERBS 1:1–7; 3:1–35; 6:16–19; 8:1–36; 9:1–10

SOLOMON'S WISDOM (10:1–22:16)

Short, pithy statements about wisdom are classic in chapters 10–22. Solomon contrasts the righteous and the unrighteous, the wise and the unwise, the diligent and the idle. He reveals the value of righteous behavior and reminds readers of the following truths: the Lord is not unaware of those who are wicked; a cheerful heart affects one's whole body; the poor should not be despised; litigations and quarrels are to be avoided; and wealth is useless to a fool. Solomon

1010 BC	1000 BC	990 BC	980 BC	970 BC	960 BC	950 BC	940 BC	930 BC	920 BC
◆ 1011–971 David (united kingdom)				◆ 971–931 Solomon (united kingdom)				◆ 930 Kingdom divides	
	◆ 1000 Glazing bricks begins in Near East				◆ 959 Temple in Jerusalem completed				
	◆ 1000 Mayan Empire founded (Central America)					◆ 950 Gold vessels and jewelry popular in Europe			

Wisdom Praised and Personified	Solomon's Wisdom	Sayings of the Wise	More of Solomon's Wis	Wisdom from Solomon's Contemporaries
1:1–9:18	10:1–22:16	22:17–24:34	25:1–29:27	30:1–31:31

also speaks against pride, gossip, lying, and injustice. ⏳ *PROVERBS 15:1–7, 13–15, 30–33; 17:14–17; 19:21–23; 20:5, 18–19; 22:1–16*

SAYINGS OF THE WISE (22:17–24:34)

Proverbs 22:17–24:34 contains "Sayings of the Wise." The unknown writers provide thirty sayings of counsel and knowledge. Like Solomon, the writers focus on the perfect wisdom of God that brings nothing but the best results for those who find it. Highlighted in these proverbs are the importance of a good reputation, the providence of God, and honesty. ⏳ *PROVERBS 22:17–29; 23:17–19; 24:23–34*

MORE OF SOLOMON'S WISDOM (25:1–29:27)

Chapter 25 begins a new section of the book of Proverbs. These are Solomon's proverbs, copied by the men of Hezekiah. Solomon contemplates God's glorious mysteriousness, doing good to enemies, avoiding contentions, and the uncertainty of what is ahead. He also refers frequently to the wicked man versus the wise man and the benefits of keeping the law. He acknowledges it is wise to accept correction. ⏳ *PROVERBS 25:1–3; 27:1–12; 29:1–27*

WISDOM FROM SOLOMON'S CONTEMPORARIES (30:1–31:31)

Chapter 30 marks the beginning of the final section of the book of Proverbs. Agur and Lemuel, the two men whose wisdom is recorded here, were contemporaries of either Solomon or Hezekiah and probably were influenced greatly by the theology of Israel. Chapter 30 speaks of things that are never satisfied, such as the grave, the barren womb, the earth that is not filled with water, and fire. The praise of a virtuous woman—due to her economy, prudence, watchfulness and assiduity in labor—is recorded in chapter 31. The virtuous woman's worth is seen to be above rubies. ⏳ *PROVERBS 30:5–14; 31:1–31*

1110 BC	1100 BC	1090 BC	1080 BC	1070 BC	1060 BC	1050 BC	1040 BC	1030 BC	1020 BC

◆ 1100 Life of Ruth?   ◆ 1075 Elon (judge)   ◆ 1060–1020 Samuel (judge/prophet)

◆ 1100 Eli (judge)   ◆ 1087 Jephthah (judge)   ◆ 1065 Abdon (judge)   ◆ 1051–1011 Saul (united kingdom)

◆ 1100 Greece enters Dark Ages   ◆ 1069 Samson (judge)?   ◆ 1050 Zhou Dynasty (China)

Everything Is Futile	God's Purpose and Timing	The Burdens of Life	The Teacher's Wise Counsel
1:1–2:23	2:24–3:22	4:1–6:9	6:10–12:14

Read Each 5-Minute Overview in Ecclesiastes

EVERYTHING IS FUTILE (1:1–2:23)

The narrator of Ecclesiastes establishes the tone and theme of the book in the prologue, but the first-person reflections of the teacher form the bulk of the book. The narrator and teacher, the son of David, is most probably Solomon. "Teacher" in the original Hebrew is the word *Koheleth* and refers to someone who gathers, leads, or speaks to a group of people. In Ecclesiastes 1:12 a shift from the narrator's voice to the voice of Koheleth occurs; the Koheleth is the speaker through 12:7. Solomon the teacher summarizes life as nothing but intense, meaningless vanity. Humankind's work, accomplishments, and searching for wisdom amount to nothing. Even the pursuit of pleasure leads to nothing; death is certain and cruel. ⧖ *ECCLESIASTES 1:1–18; 2:1–23*

GOD'S PURPOSE AND TIMING (2:24–3:22)

Solomon shifts gears slightly from reflection on life's meaninglessness to instruction. He advises how to make the best of a bad situation and reflects on how sometimes injustice seems to work in one's favor. Solomon describes the different seasons in life; he knows God has a time and purpose for all things. He understands humans have a longing for and an awareness of heaven that God has placed in their hearts. Looking at the world, Solomon sees injustice

1010 BC	1000 BC	990 BC	980 BC	970 BC	960 BC	950 BC	940 BC	930 BC	920 BC

◆ 1011–971 David (united kingdom)   ◆ 971–931 Solomon (united kingdom)   ◆ 930 Kingdom divides

    ◆ 1000 Glazing bricks begins in Near East   ◆ 959 Temple in Jerusalem completed

    ◆ 1000 Mayan Empire founded (Central America)   ◆ 950 Gold vessels and jewelry popular in Europe

Everything Is Futile	God's Purpose and Timing	The Burdens of Life	The Teacher's Wise Counsel
1:1–2:23	2:24–3:22	4:1–6:9	6:10–12:14

and evil instead of fair judgment and righteousness. ⏳ *ECCLESIASTES 2:24–26; 3:1–22*

THE BURDENS OF LIFE (4:1–6:9)

Solomon considers the burdened people he has seen around him, including the oppressed, those who labor in vain, and the friendless. For each he concludes the same thing—this too is meaningless, and humans might as well be dead. In spite of these woes, Solomon reflects on the goodness of companionship and knows it is wise to continue to worship and fear God. He also emphasizes the truth that wealth will always bring dissatisfaction. ⏳ *ECCLESIASTES 4:1–16; 5:1–7; 6:1–9*

THE TEACHER'S WISE COUNSEL (6:10–12:14)

Two brief verses express the wonder of God's sovereignty, followed by contemplation of the meaninglessness of life in a world without the hope of eternity. Solomon turns his attention from his observations to wise counsel for how others should live. People can find wisdom in adversity and suffering rather than in ease and comfort. Solomon rarely finds a person who possesses wisdom. He understands the importance of honoring government authority as a way of showing obedience to God. Joy is found only in the moment, and foolishness can't be hidden. Knowing that God and eternity exist makes everything else in life matter. ⏳ *ECCLESIASTES 6:10–12; 7:1–20; 8:1–8; 12:1–14*

1110 BC	1100 BC	1090 BC	1080 BC	1070 BC	1060 BC	1050 BC	1040 BC	1030 BC	1020 BC

◆ 1100 Life of Ruth? ◆ 1075 Elon (judge) ◆ 1060–1020 Samuel (judge/prophet)

◆ 1100 Eli (judge) ◆ 1087 Jephthah (judge) ◆ 1065 Abdon (judge) ◆ 1051–1011 Saul (united kingdom)

◆ 1100 Greece enters Dark Ages ◆ 1069 Samson (judge)? ◆ 1050 Zhou Dynasty (China)

The Transformation and Joy of Love	Love's Endurance
1:1–5:1	5:2–8:14

Read Each 5-Minute Overview in Song of Songs

○ 1:1–5:1	The Transformation and Joy of Love	Page 101
○ 5:2–8:14	Love's Endurance	Page 101

THE TRANSFORMATION AND JOY OF LOVE (1:1–5:1)

This great song, or collection of poetic songs, is unique in the Bible. Although these poems reflect the relationship between a man and his wife, they point toward the intimate relationship between Jesus and His bride. The maiden and her beloved express the joys and difficulties of their love, praise each other, and enjoy each other's presence. The maiden yearns for her beloved Solomon. Absence and longing always lead to search and discovery in the Song. A great wedding is described, and Solomon sits on his throne in splendor; he shares all that he has with his beloved, and he praises her appearance and character. ⧖ *SONG OF SONGS 1:1–17; 3:6–11; 4:1–15*

LOVE'S ENDURANCE (5:2–8:14)

The woman seems to be telling the women of Jerusalem about an actual experience. She searches for and describes her beloved as "altogether lovely." The maiden's beauty is also described; she longs for intimacy with her husband. The maiden's brothers are mentioned, and a speaker reminds the couple of their youth and family roots. The maiden recognizes her own value and, referring to the image of a seal, appeals to her husband, asking him to recognize the permanence of their commitment. The seriousness of love is something that requires self-sacrifice, needs nourishment and care, and cannot be bought or sold. ⧖ *SONG OF SONGS 5:1–16; 6:1–13; 8:1–14*

1010 BC	1000 BC	990 BC	980 BC	970 BC	960 BC	950 BC	940 BC	930 BC	920 BC
◆ 1011–971 David (united kingdom)				◆ 971–931 Solomon (united kingdom)				◆ 930 Kingdom divides	
	◆ 1000 Glazing bricks begins in Near East				◆ 959 Temple in Jerusalem completed				
	◆ 1000 Mayan Empire founded (Central America)				◆ 950 Gold vessels and jewelry popular in Europe				

An Ominous Introduction	Isaiah's Call, God's Sign, and Israel's Failure	Prophecies against Other Nations	The Fall of Babylon	The World Struggles, but God Reigns Supreme
1:1–5:30	6:1–12:6	13:1–18:7	19:1–23:18	24:1—35:10

INTRODUCTION TO ISAIAH

Author: Isaiah
Dates of Events: 760–861 BC

Because of similarities with the Old and New Testaments, the book of Isaiah is sometimes referred to as a miniature Bible. The first thirty-nine chapters of Isaiah, similar to the thirty-nine books of the Old Testament, stress the righteousness, holiness, and justice of God. The book announces Judah's impending judgment as a result of immorality and idolatry; Isaiah then broadens the scope of judgment to include Judah's neighboring nations. Finally, the prophet speaks of universal judgment, followed by blessing. The final twenty-seven chapters, not unlike the twenty-seven chapters of the New Testament, declare a message of hope: the Messiah is coming as Savior to bear sin and reign as sovereign King.

Not much is known about the author (or perhaps authors—there is some debate as to whether chapters 40–66 were written by another prophet), who speaks of the present, the near future, and the long-range future. It is believed Isaiah was from a distinguished Jewish family and probably had close contact with the royal court. Isaiah's long ministry ranged from 740 to 680 BC, as Assyria was growing in power. While the prophet's narrative can be a bit confusing at times, large portions are clear and present a merciful God who never gives up on His people, even though they repeatedly rebel and turn from Him.

The New Testament includes far more quotes from Isaiah than from any other writer. Isaiah has often been called the "evangelical prophet" because of his clear and detailed messianic prophecies. Some of these prophecies have been fulfilled, but many await future fulfillment. Chapters 1–35 include prophecies of condemnation. Chapters 36–39 look back over history into the Assyrian invasion of Judah

790 BC	780 BC	770 BC	760 BC	750 BC	740 BC	730 BC	720 BC	710 BC

◆ 792 Uzziah (Judah)   ◆ 760 Isaiah (prophet)   ◆ 722 Israel falls

◆ 798 Jehoash (Israel)   ◆ 770 Jonah (prophet)   ◆ 753 Zechariah (Israel)   ◆ 732 Ahaz (Judah)

◆ 796 Amaziah (Judah)   ◆ 755 Amos/Hosea (prophets)   ◆ 732 Hoshea (Israel)

A Dismal Future	Good News in Bad Times	God Works through a Gentile King	God's Righteous, Suffering Servant	Promise for God's People	Hope for a Bright Future
36:1–39:8	40:1–44:23	44:24–48:22	49:1–55:13	56:1–59:21	60:1–66:24

in 701 BC and also anticipate the coming Babylonian invasion. Chapters 40–66 offer comfort to Israel with prophecies of God's promises of hope and restoration.

The coming Messiah, the suffering servant who will be Israel's Savior, is revealed in chapters 49–57. He will pay for Israel's iniquities and usher in a kingdom of peace and righteousness throughout the earth. Thus, the book of Isaiah is also often called "The Book of Salvation." Not coincidentally, the very name of the prophet the book is titled after, Isaiah, means "salvation of Yahweh"; this is closely related to the name Joshua, which means "Yahweh is salvation." Joshua is the Old Testament equivalent of the name Jesus: Israel's Savior. God's sovereignty is also evident throughout Isaiah, as Isaiah tells of God maneuvering great empires to accomplish His will.

An Ominous Introduction	Isaiah's Call, God's Sign, and Israel's Failure	Prophecies against Other Nations	The Fall of Babylon	The World Struggles, but God Reigns Supreme
1:1–5:30	6:1–12:6	13:1–18:7	19:1–23:18	24:1–35:10

Read Each 5-Minute Overview in Isaiah

AN OMINOUS INTRODUCTION (1:1–5:30)

Isaiah condemns Israel and Judah for abandoning God and following the gods and customs of surrounding nations. He describes a Jerusalem that is surrounded by peace, but at the moment Israel is a powerless pawn in an international struggle. Assyria, Babylon, and Egypt are all attempting to establish or maintain empires. Isaiah prophesies that God will bring disgrace to Jerusalem and its people; He will remove its leaders, and social chaos will increase. Someday

790 BC	780 BC	770 BC	760 BC	750 BC	740 BC	730 BC	720 BC	710 BC

◆ 792 Uzziah (Judah) ◆ 760 Isaiah (prophet) ◆ 722 Israel falls

◆ 798 Jehoash (Israel) ◆ 770 Jonah (prophet) ◆ 753 Zechariah (Israel) ◆ 732 Ahaz (Judah)

◆ 796 Amaziah (Judah) ◆ 755 Amos/Hosea (prophets) ◆ 732 Hoshea (Israel)

A Dismal Future	Good News in Bad Times	God Works through a Gentile King	God's Righteous, Suffering Servant	Promise for God's People	Hope for a Bright Future
36:1–39:8	40:1–44:23	44:24–48:22	49:1–55:13	56:1–59:21	60:1–66:24

God's glory will fill Jerusalem once again; however, trouble is in the near future. Through a parable, Isaiah warns of an attack by a terrifying foreign enemy; he foretells God will cleanse Jerusalem of its sinners and reward its survivors with spiritual and material benefits. ⏳ *ISAIAH 1:18–31; 2:1–9; 3:13–26; 4:1–6*

ISAIAH'S CALL, GOD'S SIGN, AND ISRAEL'S FAILURE (6:1–12:6)

In a vision, Isaiah sees God sitting on His throne, attended by the six-winged seraphim. Isaiah is purged of his sins and then sent on a mission to rebuke rebellious Israel. Isaiah foretells how the Assyrians will destroy the land of Israel and wipe out the population, and he also predicts the fall of Samaria and Damascus. However, he speaks of a period of peace that will come with a new wise and righteous leader. These hope-inspiring prophecies about Immanuel bring needed encouragement. It is a desperate and

miserable time, so the anticipation of the hope to come—the arrival of God's Messiah as well as a time when Israel's exiles will be regathered and Judah and Samaria reunited—is especially welcome. ⏳ *ISAIAH 6:1–13; 9:1–9; 11:1–16*

PROPHECIES AGAINST OTHER NATIONS (13:1–18:7)

Isaiah presents a number of judgments concerning the surrounding nations, including Babylon and Assyria. Isaiah tells of a coming time when Babylon's men will be slaughtered, its women raped, and its children killed; the city will be reduced to ruins. Assyria will also be shattered, and the Philistines will experience a terrible famine. The Moabites will experience a nocturnal attack that will result in destroyed farmlands and a dwindling population, and Damascus will be destroyed. God will accept a tribute from Cush in Jerusalem. ⏳ *ISAIAH 13:1–22; 14:24–32; 17:1–14*

700 BC	690 BC	680 BC	670 BC	660 BC	650 BC	640 BC	630 BC	620 BC	610 BC

◆ 716 Hezekiah (Judah)   ◆ 658 Nahum (prophet)   ◆ 640 Zephaniah (prophet) ◆ 620 Daniel born

◆ 697 Manasseh (Judah)   ◆ 640 Josiah (Judah)   ◆ 620 Ezekiel (prophet)

◆ 701 Sennacherib invades   ◆ 650 Jeremiah (prophet)

NAVIGATING THE BIBLE

THE FALL OF BABYLON (19:1–23:18)

Isaiah delivers more judgments against nations surrounding Israel. He predicts a day when Egypt will be purged of its idols, afflicted by drought, and ruled by an evil tyrant. All this will cause many of Egypt's people to turn to God. Isaiah goes naked and barefoot for three years, a picture of how the Egyptians and Cushites (Ethiopians) will be sent away naked and barefoot by the Assyrians. Isaiah predicts the fall of Babylon and the siege of Jerusalem. God is very angry with His people for not trusting Him. Tyre's people lament their city's demise, but God promises it will be rebuilt in seventy years. ⌛ *ISAIAH 19:1–17; 20:1–6; 21:1–10; 22:1–4; 23:15–18*

THE WORLD STRUGGLES, BUT GOD REIGNS SUPREME (24:1–35:10)

Isaiah expands his focus next to coming world devastation. He gives

106

Detail of a Babylonian city wall

790 BC	780 BC	770 BC	760 BC	750 BC	740 BC	730 BC	720 BC	710 BC

◆ 792 Uzziah (Judah)   ◆ 760 Isaiah (prophet)   ◆ 722 Israel falls

◆ 798 Jehoash (Israel)   ◆ 770 Jonah (prophet)   ◆ 753 Zechariah (Israel)   ◆ 732 Ahaz (Judah)

◆ 796 Amaziah (Judah)   ◆ 755 Amos/Hosea (prophets)   ◆ 732 Hoshea (Israel)

A Dismal Future	Good News in Bad Times	God Works through a Gentile King	God's Righteous, Suffering Servant	Promise for God's People	Hope for a Bright Future
36:1–39:8	40:1–44:23	44:24–48:22	49:1–55:13	56:1–59:21	60:1–66:24

historical perspective through a series of woes. The land will receive punishment for the sins of the people. The people of Judah sing an allegorical song about God gathering the exiles home, and Isaiah speaks of Jerusalem outlasting its enemies; sinners will be removed, and Jerusalem's people will enjoy peace and a blissful future. Isaiah rebukes the people for rejecting God and turning to the Egyptians for help, and he points to a trying time when the land of Israel will become desolate. This will come before an era of justice and prosperity, when the righteous will prosper in the land. ⌛ *ISAIAH 24:1–23; 31:1–9; 32:1–8; 35:1–10*

A DISMAL FUTURE (36:1–39:8)

Isaiah now provides a detailed historical narrative. Sennacherib invades Judah and sends an officer to Jerusalem who tells the people to surrender; they do not respond. Hezekiah falls ill and begs God to save him. God adds fifteen years to his life and promises to protect Jerusalem from the Assyrians. Messengers from Babylon visit Jerusalem. On the surface it appears that the messengers have come to rejoice with Hezekiah over his restored health; the real reason for their visit, however, is to learn about Judah's economic resources. Isaiah again predicts Jerusalem will be invaded by Babylon; he tells Hezekiah that everything in the palace will be carried off. ⌛ *ISAIAH 36:1–22; 38:1–8; 39:1–8*

Hezekiah and Isaiah

GOOD NEWS IN BAD TIMES (40:1–44:23)

Pronouncement of judgments diminishes, and the prophet begins to focus on the Israelites' salvation, restoration, and the end of their

700 BC	690 BC	680 BC	670 BC	660 BC	650 BC	640 BC	630 BC	620 BC	610 BC

♦ 716 Hezekiah (Judah)

♦ 658 Nahum (prophet)   ♦ 640 Zephaniah (prophet)   ♦ 620 Daniel born

♦ 697 Manasseh (Judah)   ♦ 640 Josiah (Judah)   ♦ 620 Ezekiel (prophet)

♦ 701 Sennacherib invades   ♦ 650 Jeremiah (prophet)

An Ominous Introduction	Isaiah's Call, God's Sign, and Israel's Failure	Prophecies against Other Nations	The Fall of Babylon	The World Struggles, but God Reigns Supreme
1:1–5:30	6:1–12:6	13:1–18:7	19:1–23:18	24:1–35:10

captivity in Babylon. Isaiah proclaims comfort to Israel and promises a coming mighty warrior. God assures the Israelites that they are safe and that He will choose a righteous leader and perform miracles. God comforts Israel, promising Babylon's eventual destruction. He will protect His treasured possession, Israel. He reminds His people that He has redeemed them and that His presence is with them. ⏳ *ISAIAH 40:1–17; 41:8–16; 43:1–13; 44:24–28*

GOD WORKS THROUGH A GENTILE KING (44:24–48:22)

The prophet writes of the end of the Israelites' captivity, and he predicts a benefactor whom Israel might not have counted on: the Gentile king, Cyrus. Cyrus will begin the process of rebuilding the temple. God calls His people to return to Him and reminds them that His plan of redemption will come to pass. Swift judgment is prophesied against Babylon. ⏳ *ISAIAH 44:24–28; 45:1–13; 46:8–13; 47:1–15*

GOD'S RIGHTEOUS, SUFFERING SERVANT (49:1–55:13)

Isaiah describes a servant of God who will deliver not just Israel but all the nations as well. This servant will suffer, bear humanity's sin, and be crushed to the point of being unrecognizable. But this messenger will also

---

Oracles and poems: How do you get the most out of the prophets?
The prophets communicated God's will through oracles, poems, and other kinds of literature that may be less familiar to modern readers. Still, these six tips can help you get the most from the prophets.

1. Pray to God for understanding.
2. Know the background history of the book.
3. Read through the whole book to get the whole context.
4. Ask the following questions: Who is being spoken to? What is the message? Where does this book fit into the biblical timeline? Where were God's people at this time? Why was God giving these warnings?
5. Try to hear what the prophet is saying to his audience.
6. Ask how the prophet's message should change your heart, mind, and actions.

---

790 BC	780 BC	770 BC	760 BC	750 BC	740 BC	730 BC	720 BC	710 BC
✦ 792 Uzziah (Judah)		✦ 760 Isaiah (prophet)					✦ 722 Israel falls	
✦ 798 Jehoash (Israel)		✦ 770 Jonah (prophet)	✦ 753 Zechariah (Israel)		✦ 732 Ahaz (Judah)			
✦ 796 Amaziah (Judah)				✦ 755 Amos/Hosea (prophets)		✦ 732 Hoshea (Israel)		

A Dismal Future	Good News in Bad Times	God Works through a Gentile King	God's Righteous, Suffering Servant	Promise for God's People	Hope for a Bright Future
36:1–39:8	40:1–44:23	44:24–48:22	49:1–55:13	56:1–59:21	60:1–66:24

be raised up and highly exalted. God tells the nation of Israel that it will be a light to the surrounding nations. Babylon and Cyrus are no longer mentioned; the people are still in a captivity of sorts, but it is more of a spiritual bondage that only God can remedy. Isaiah speaks again of an ingathering of exiles and promises God will rebuild Jerusalem. In one of Isaiah's songs, he laments the death of God's righteous servant, who dies because of others' iniquity—a clear reference to Jesus Christ. ⏳ *ISAIAH 49:1–26; 52:13–15; 53:1–12*

PROMISE FOR GOD'S PEOPLE (56:1–59:21)

The spiritual strength of Israel's future largely depends on the people's willingness to cease their wicked living. Isaiah encourages his people to live righteously and keep the Sabbath; God's people need to look honestly at their spiritual condition and attitude. God extends the invitation of salvation to Gentiles. ⏳ *ISAIAH 56:1–12; 58:1–14; 59:12–21*

HOPE FOR A BRIGHT FUTURE (60:1–66:24)

The immediate future for the Israelites, along with the godless neighboring Gentile nations, involves God's judgment. But their long-range future is brighter. Isaiah predicts God will rebuild the land, return the exiles, defeat the nations, and bring the people great prosperity. God alone will deserve the glory, and it is His servant who will make such a future possible. God's vengeance, judgment, salvation, and redemption are themes woven throughout Isaiah's concluding thoughts. Isaiah assures God's people that they can look hopefully toward their future because God's ultimate plan is to restore them and renew close fellowship with them. ⏳ *ISAIAH 65:1–25; 66:5–24*

700 BC	690 BC	680 BC	670 BC	660 BC	650 BC	640 BC	630 BC	620 BC	610 BC

✦ 716 Hezekiah (Judah)   ✦ 658 Nahum (prophet)   ✦ 640 Zephaniah (prophet)   ✦ 620 Daniel born

✦ 697 Manasseh (Judah)   ✦ 640 Josiah (Judah)   ✦ 620 Ezekiel (prophet)

✦ 701 Sennacherib invades   ✦ 650 Jeremiah (prophet)

Jeremiah's Call	Wrong Religion	Judah's Consequences for Breaking God's Covenant	God's Warnings	A Coming King	False Prophets and a Message of Hope
1:1–6:30	7:1–10:25	11:1–13:27	14:1–20:18	21:1–25:38	26:1–29:32

INTRODUCTION TO JEREMIAH AND LAMENTATIONS

Author: Jeremiah
Dates of Events: 650–580 BC

Jeremiah is called to prophesy around 627 BC to a nation entrenched in sin. The books of Jeremiah and Lamentations are both attributed to Jeremiah. Throughout his writings, Jeremiah weaves his personal feelings and the emotional turmoil he experiences as he ministers to the people of Judah. He is deeply burdened for the spiritual state of his people, and he preaches a message of repentance until it becomes evident they have no intention of changing. A heartbroken Jeremiah then laments over the state of his nation and records in grave detail and sorrow the aftereffects of one of the lowest points in the history of the Israelites.

The book of Jeremiah is actually the prophet's autobiography, told with the backdrop of a nation caught in a web of apostasy, idolatry, perverted worship, and moral decay. God calls Jeremiah to proclaim a message of judgment for forty years and instructs him not to marry—his ministry will be too difficult to sustain a marriage and the coming judgment so severe as to preclude having a family. As a result, Jeremiah lives a life of loneliness and depression, appropriately earning the nickname "The Weeping Prophet." God's patience and holiness are evident throughout Jeremiah's writings—He delays judgment and appeals to His people to repent before it is too late. Though their opportunity for repentance will pass and Babylonian captivity is inevitable, Jeremiah proclaims God's gracious promise of hope and restoration. There will always be a remnant of faithful believers, and God will someday establish a new covenant.

700 BC	690 BC	680 BC	670 BC	660 BC	650 BC	640 BC	630 BC	620 BC	610 BC
◆ 716 Hezekiah (Judah)					◆ 658 Nahum (prophet)		◆ 640 Zephaniah (prophet)	◆ 620 Daniel born	
	◆ 697 Manasseh (Judah)					◆ 640 Josiah (Judah)		◆ 620 Ezekiel (prophet)	
	◆ 701 Sennacherib invades				◆ 650 Jeremiah (prophet)				

The God of Comfort Promises Judah's Return	Incidents Surrounding the Fall of Jerusalem	God Calls the Remnant to Remain in Judah	Prophecies about Nations	The Fall of Jerusalem Comes to Pass
30:1–33:26	34:1–39:18	40:1–45:5	46:1–51:64	52:1–34

Lamentations—a short, five-chapter, tearstained poem—immediately follows the book of Jeremiah. The book's name reveals what it is—a poem of lament. While the book of Jeremiah primarily anticipates the fall of Jerusalem, Lamentations reflects on Jerusalem's fall with deep sorrow. Jeremiah likely writes Lamentations just after the nation's destruction at the hands of the Babylonians in 586 BC. The holy city is destroyed, Israelites are exiled, and Jeremiah weeps in utter helplessness over the defeat, slaughter, and ruin of his dear nation. In addition to the clear themes of mourning, confession of sin, and acknowledgment of God's righteous and holy judgment on Judah, the strongest and unexpected theme is that of hope. Even though God has poured out His wrath, He will remain faithful to His covenant promises to restore Israel and bring His people back to the land.

The Prophet Jeremiah *by Michelangelo (1475–1564)*

600 BC	590 BC	580 BC	570 BC	560 BC	550 BC	540 BC	530 BC	520 BC	510 BC

◆ 597 Zedekiah (Judah)　　　◆ 570 Confucius teaches in China　　　◆ 522 Zechariah/Haggai (prophets)

◆ 600 Habakkuk (prophet)　　　◆ 559 Cyrus the Great (Persia)　　　◆ 521 Darius (Persia)

◆ 586 Fall of Jerusalem　　　◆ 560 Aesop's fables　　　◆ 539 Darius the Mede (Babylon)

Jeremiah's Call	Wrong Religion	Judah's Consequences for Breaking God's Covenant	God's Warnings	A Coming King	False Prophets and a Message of Hope
1:1–6:30	7:1–10:25	11:1–13:27	14:1–20:18	21:1–25:38	26:1–29:32

Read Each 5-Minute Overview in Jeremiah

JEREMIAH'S CALL (1:1–6:30)

Jeremiah is called to prophesy to his own people as well as to the nations about future events. God sends His prophet to the people of Judah with a warning of impending judgment and punishment because of their sinful lifestyle. This judgment is based on the covenant God made with the nation and the consequences that would come to them if they failed to follow God's law.

700 BC	690 BC	680 BC	670 BC	660 BC	650 BC	640 BC	630 BC	620 BC	610 BC
✦ 716 Hezekiah (Judah)				✦ 658 Nahum (prophet)		✦ 640 Zephaniah (prophet)		✦ 620 Daniel born	
	✦ 697 Manasseh (Judah)					✦ 640 Josiah (Judah)		✦ 620 Ezekiel (prophet)	
	✦ 701 Sennacherib invades				✦ 650 Jeremiah (prophet)				

The God of Comfort Promises Judah's Return	Incidents Surrounding the Fall of Jerusalem	God Calls the Remnant to Remain in Judah	Prophecies about Nations	The Fall of Jerusalem Comes to Pass
30:1–33:26	34:1–39:18	40:1–45:5	46:1–51:64	52:1–34

God's people have presumed themselves to be innocent, but Jeremiah compares them to an adulterous husband. All nations shall be gathered one day to Jerusalem. The Lord appeals for the people of Judah and Jerusalem to mourn and repent—an evil nation is coming from the north and will show no mercy. ⌛ *JEREMIAH 1:1–18; 2:1–9; 3:1–5; 6:16–26*

WRONG RELIGION (7:1–10:25)

The Lord complains that the temple has become a den of robbers, and He warns that He will destroy the temple and cast His people from His presence and into exile. These warnings are specifically geared toward the sins of hypocrisy and practicing false religion. The people will be scattered among the heathen and eat bitter food and drink poisoned water. Jeremiah proclaims any glory should be glory in the Lord. The circumcised, the Jews, and the uncircumcised, the Gentiles, will both be punished. Sin is an issue of an uncircumcised heart. The Lord's anger burns because of the people's unrepentant attitude. ⌛ *JEREMIAH 7:1–15; 9:7–16; 10:1–10, 17–22*

JUDAH'S CONSEQUENCES FOR BREAKING GOD'S COVENANT (11:1–13:27)

Judah has broken the Mosaic covenant, in which God promised to bless the Israelites if they obeyed Him. Their idolatry is a severe breach of the covenant. Twice Jeremiah laments about the gravity of the nation's sin and God's pending judgment. The people plot against Jeremiah; the Lord will punish for that as well. The Lord has left His people; the people have sown wheat but will reap thorns. Therefore, they will be scattered from their land and will not be brought back until they humbly return to Him in obedience. ⌛ *JEREMIAH 11:1–23; 12:14–17; 13:15–27*

Nebuchadnezzar's camp outside Jerusalem. Famine in the city.

600 BC	590 BC	580 BC	570 BC	560 BC	550 BC	540 BC	530 BC	520 BC	510 BC

◆ 597 Zedekiah (Judah)   ◆ 570 Confucius teaches in China   ◆ 522 Zechariah/Haggai (prophets)

◆ 600 Habakkuk (prophet)   ◆ 559 Cyrus the Great (Persia)   ◆ 521 Darius (Persia)

◆ 586 Fall of Jerusalem   ◆ 560 Aesop's fables   ◆ 539 Darius the Mede (Babylon)

Jeremiah's Call	Wrong Religion	Judah's Consequences for Breaking God's Covenant	God's Warnings	A Coming King	False Prophets and a Message of Hope
1:1–6:30	7:1–10:25	11:1–13:27	14:1–20:18	21:1–25:38	26:1–29:32

GOD'S WARNINGS (14:1–20:18)

Jeremiah gives a detailed prophecy of coming drought and famine that will accompany the coming invasions. The Lord tells Jeremiah not to pray for His people, but Jeremiah prays anyway. God is angry with false prophets. A future restoration is implied, and Jeremiah foretells the conversion of Gentiles. Jeremiah complains about his personal hardships as they relate to his ministry among the people of Judah, and he describes the nation's relationship with God metaphorically. Jeremiah faces intense persecution because of his message, but God promises to protect him. Jeremiah continues to warn against Judah's idolatry and remind the people of their need to repent to avoid the coming judgment. ⌛ *JEREMIAH 14:1–16; 15:1–9; 16:14–21; 18:18–23; 20:7–13*

Jeremiah warned of hardships to the people and the land.

A COMING KING (21:1–25:38)

Jeremiah transitions to more specific prophecies directed at Judah's kings and spiritual leaders. The priests and prophets of Judah are wicked, and divine vengeance is imminent. A righteous King will arise from the branch of David. Word comes to Jeremiah of Judah's coming punishment: The people of Judah will be taken captive in Babylon for seventy years. After seventy years, Babylon and its king will be punished. ⌛ *JEREMIAH 21:3–10; 23:1–12; 24:1–10; 25:1–12*

700 BC	690 BC	680 BC	670 BC	660 BC	650 BC	640 BC	630 BC	620 BC	610 BC

◆ 716 Hezekiah (Judah)

◆ 658 Nahum (prophet)　　◆ 640 Zephaniah (prophet)　◆ 620 Daniel born

◆ 697 Manasseh (Judah)　　　　　　　◆ 640 Josiah (Judah)　　◆ 620 Ezekiel (prophet)

◆ 701 Sennacherib invades　　　　　◆ 650 Jeremiah (prophet)

The God of Comfort Promises Judah's Return	Incidents Surrounding the Fall of Jerusalem	God Calls the Remnant to Remain in Judah	Prophecies about Nations	The Fall of Jerusalem Comes to Pass
30:1–33:26	34:1–39:18	40:1–45:5	46:1–51:64	52:1–34

FALSE PROPHETS AND A MESSAGE OF HOPE (26:1–29:32)

God deals with false prophets who continue to speak lies in His name. The focus shifts from Jeremiah's proclamation of what's to come to how the people react to his prophecies. Jeremiah represents the genuine prophet, and false prophets are contrasted to him and his message. God sends a message to the captives: build houses, have children, and settle. The people of Judah will remain in captivity for seventy long years. But Jeremiah also brings a ray of hope to Judah: after seventy years, God will fulfill His good promise and bring His people back to Jerusalem. ⌛ *JEREMIAH 26:1–15; 27:1–11; 28:1–14; 29:1–14*

THE GOD OF COMFORT PROMISES JUDAH'S RETURN (30:1–33:26)

Hundreds of years after enslavement in Egypt, the children of God are about to once again experience captivity in another land. As the people of Judah brace themselves for seventy years of anguish, the God of comfort wants them to know that there is hope. God encourages His people of a coming day when normal life will return for Judah and Israel. They will come back to their own land, build and plant, and experience peace and prosperity. While in exile, God's people can read these words and find comfort in the midst of barrenness. ⌛ *JEREMIAH 30:1–24; 31:23–38; 33:23–26*

INCIDENTS SURROUNDING THE FALL OF JERUSALEM (34:1–39:18)

The Lord rebukes the people of Jerusalem for their poor treatment of Hebrew slaves, but He commends and blesses the Rekabites who obey God. Jeremiah's scribe, Baruch, writes down Jeremiah's prophecies and has them read publicly on a day of fasting. This results in an order to have Jeremiah and his scribe seized. The Lord protects them, but eventually Jeremiah is thrown into a dungeon. In the ninth year of Zedekiah's reign, Babylonian armies attack Jerusalem. Jeremiah and Ebed-Melek are spared. ⌛ *JEREMIAH 34:8–20; 35:12–19; 36:11–26; 39:15–18*

600 BC	590 BC	580 BC	570 BC	560 BC	550 BC	540 BC	530 BC	520 BC	510 BC

◆ 597 Zedekiah (Judah) ◆ 570 Confucius teaches in China ◆ 522 Zechariah/Haggai (prophets)

◆ 600 Habakkuk (prophet) ◆ 559 Cyrus the Great (Persia) ◆ 521 Darius (Persia)

◆ 586 Fall of Jerusalem ◆ 560 Aesop's fables ◆ 539 Darius the Mede (Babylon)

The God of Comfort Promises Judah's Return	Incidents Surrounding the Fall of Jerusalem	God Calls the Remnant to Remain in Judah	Prophecies about Nations	The Fall of Jerusalem Comes to Pass
30:1–33:26	34:1–39:18	40:1–45:5	46:1–51:64	52:1–34

NAVIGATING THE BIBLE

GOD CALLS THE REMNANT TO REMAIN IN JUDAH (40:1–45:5)

Jeremiah is freed, Gedaliah is assassinated, Judah is destroyed, the people of Mizpah flee to Egypt, and Jeremiah seeks God's direction for Judah. King Nebuchadnezzar had left a remnant of God's people in Judah, and God promises He will protect His people from King Nebuchadnezzar if they remain in the land of Judah. He will save and deliver Judah from the king's hand. However, if the people of Judah disobey and flee to Egypt, God warns they will die by the sword. ⏳ *JEREMIAH 40:1–16; 42:1–22*

PROPHECIES ABOUT NATIONS (46:1–51:64)

Jeremiah prophesies concerning the nations. He pronounces God's judgment for idol worship and misplaced trust, and he warns of the punishment that will come as a consequence of such sins. He continues to encourage the people of Judah that God won't crush their nation completely. God's amazing mercy is seen in His restraint toward His people. The geographical catalog of nations moves from west to east. ⏳ *JEREMIAH 46:1–10; 47:1–7; 48:1–9; 49:1–2; 50:18–28*

THE FALL OF JERUSALEM COMES TO PASS (52:1–34)

Jeremiah's prophecies are seen from a historical point of view. The fall of Jerusalem is chronicled, and the city's destruction unfolds just as Jeremiah said it would—validating his prophecies. ⏳ *JEREMIAH 52:1–34*

Jeremiah at the fall of Jerusalem

116

700 BC	690 BC	680 BC	670 BC	660 BC	650 BC	640 BC	630 BC	620 BC	610 BC
◆ 716 Hezekiah (Judah)				◆ 658 Nahum (prophet)		◆ 640 Zephaniah (prophet)		◆ 620 Daniel born	
	◆ 697 Manasseh (Judah)					◆ 640 Josiah (Judah)		◆ 620 Ezekiel (prophet)	
	◆ 701 Sennacherib invades				◆ 650 Jeremiah (prophet)				

The Elements of Godly Grief in Suffering	Cling to Hope in God	Evidence of Jerusalem's Destruction
1:1–2:22	3:1–66	4:1–5:22

Read Each 5-Minute Overview in Lamentations

THE ELEMENTS OF GODLY GRIEF IN SUFFERING (1:1–2:22)

The author of Lamentations grieves over Jerusalem's destruction and describes God's anger toward His people's sin. The fall of the city marks the fulfillment of what had been prophesied for years—the nation's continual state of sin through idolatry would eventually lead to its downfall. ⧗ LAMENTATIONS

HOPE IN GOD (3:1–66)

the Jewish people's faithlessness, Jerusalem is destroyed.
survived the attack is taken into Babylonian captivity.
e of complete hopelessness. However, God's people vow
d, and they find encouragement and rest remembering and
hfulness. ⧗ LAMENTATIONS 3:1–43

EVIDENCE OF JERUSALEM'S DESTRUCTION (4:1–5:22)

The author responds to God's unwavering mercy, goodness, faithfulness, and control. He looks more closely at what caused God to judge Judah the way He did. Lamentations compares the state of the city of Jerusalem before and after the Babylonian attack. The author of Lamentations poetically grieves for the suffering of the nation, catalogs related tragedies, voices words of hope and a reminder of God's mercy, and prophesies an end to the suffering and the downfall of the enemy. God's swift mercy is requested. ⧗ LAMENTATIONS 4:1–22; 5:1–22

600 BC	590 BC	580 BC	570 BC	560 BC	550 BC	540 BC	530 BC	520 BC	510 BC
	✦ 597 Zedekiah (Judah)		✦ 570 Confucius teaches in China					✦ 522 Zechariah/Haggai (prophets)	
✦ 600 Habakkuk (prophet)					✦ 559 Cyrus the Great (Persia)			✦ 521 Darius (Persia)	
		✦ 586 Fall of Jerusalem		✦ 560 Aesop's fables		✦ 539 Darius the Mede (Babylon)			

Ezekiel's Call	Lessons in Judgment	Vision: Jerusalem's Temple	Ezekiel Speaks Out	Three Allegories to Describe Israel	Responsibility for Sin
1:1–3:27	4:1–7:27	8:1–11:25	12:1–14:23	15:1–17:24	18:1–24:27

INTRODUCTION TO EZEKIEL AND DANIEL

Authors: Ezekiel and Daniel
Dates of Events: 620–510 BC

E zekiel and Daniel are two prophets caught up in the unrest of their time and called by God to prophesy among the Jewish exiles in Babylon. God calls Ezekiel, whose name means "God strengthens," to communicate a hopeful message of Judah's coming restoration. Ezekiel's ministry stretches from 592 BC to at least 570 BC, overlapping the very end of Jeremiah's ministry and the beginning of Daniel's ministry. More than any other prophet, Ezekiel depicts the consummation of the kingdom of God with grandiose illustrations of a new temple and revitalized worship. He speaks to a community forced from its home, a people who had broken faith with their God. As God's spokesman, Ezekiel defends and restores Yahweh's reputation before watching nations; his oracles are full of unique parables, signs, and symbols that dramatize God's message to His people. Ezekiel often uses hard and sometimes offensive language, and he expects repentance and a longing for the restoration of God's glory in response. Ezekiel is of the priestly line; as such, he is deeply concerned with God's holiness and responds to any behavior that offends his holy God. God's supreme authority over Israel and all nations is a clear theme in Ezekiel. Even Nebuchadnezzar, king of mighty Babylon, is but a tool in God's hand used to accomplish His purposes.

Daniel serves as God's prophetic mouthpiece to the Gentile and Jewish world during Judah's entire seventy-year period of Babylonian captivity. When the Babylonians destroy Jerusalem and carry off most of the population in a series of deportations, Daniel is among the first group taken captive. He is only sixteen

700 BC	690 BC	680 BC	670 BC	660 BC	650 BC	640 BC	630 BC	620 BC	610 BC

- 716 Hezekiah (Judah)
- 697 Manasseh (Judah)
- 701 Sennacherib invades
- 658 Nahum (prophet)
- 650 Jeremiah (prophet)
- 640 Zephaniah (prophet)
- 640 Josiah (Judah)
- 620 Daniel born
- 620 Ezekiel (prophet)

Impending Judgment against the Nations	After God's Judgment of Judah	Dry Bones and New Life	A New Temple	The River Measured and the Territory Divided
25:1–32:32	33:1–36:38	37:1–39:29	40:1–46:24	47:1–48:35

and finds himself handpicked for government service because of his lineage and character. He possesses great wisdom, which brings him into a position of prominence under Babylon's rulers. Sometimes referred to as the "Apocalypse of the Old Testament," the book of Daniel sheds light on John's revelation in the New Testament. Most importantly, Daniel foretells the eventual establishment of the messianic kingdom that will overthrow the kingdoms of this world. Keeping in mind Judah's current situation, this promise of a future kingdom brings hope and comfort to a nation in bondage; God has not forgotten His chosen people, even though the circumstances look impossible. From start to finish, God's sovereignty is revealed in the book of Daniel in the way the Lord interacts with individuals, controls nations, and shares His plans for the long-range future of Israel. Thus, God's people must continue to trust in Him.

Daniel in the Lions' Den *by Sir Peter Paul Rubens (1577–1640)*

600 BC	590 BC	580 BC	570 BC	560 BC	550 BC	540 BC	530 BC	520 BC	510 BC

- 597 Zedekiah (Judah)
- 570 Confucius teaches in China
- 522 Zechariah/Haggai (prophets)
- 600 Habakkuk (prophet)
- 559 Cyrus the Great (Persia)
- 521 Darius (Persia)
- 586 Fall of Jerusalem
- 560 Aesop's fables
- 539 Darius the Mede (Babylon)

GEN EXOD LEV NUM DEUT JOSH JUDG RUTH 1 SAM 2 SAM 1 KGS 2 KGS 1 CHR 2 CHR EZRA NEH ESTH JOB PSALMS PROV ECCL SONG

Ezekiel's Call	Lessons in Judgment	Vision: Jerusalem's Temple	Ezekiel Speaks Out	Three Allegories to Describe Israel	Responsibility for Sin
1:1–3:27	4:1–7:27	8:1–11:25	12:1–14:23	15:1–17:24	18:1–24:27

Read Each 5-Minute Overview in Ezekiel

○	1:1–3:27	Ezekiel's Call	Page 120
○	4:1–7:27	Lessons in Judgment	Page 120
○	8:1–11:25	Vision: Jerusalem's Temple	Page 121
○	12:1–14:23	Ezekiel Speaks Out	Page 121
○	15:1–17:24	Three Allegories to Describe Israel	Page 122
○	18:1–24:27	Responsibility for Sin	Page 122
○	25:1–32:32	Impending Judgment against the Nations	Page 122
○	33:1–36:38	After God's Judgment of Judah	Page 123
○	37:1–39:29	Dry Bones and New Life	Page 123
○	40:1–46:24	A New Temple	Page 124
○	47:1–48:35	The River Measured and the Territory Divided	Page 124

EZEKIEL'S CALL (1:1–3:27)

Ezekiel sees God sitting on His throne. God gives Ezekiel a scroll to eat, warns him of Israel's obstinacy, and charges him to rebuke the nation. The Spirit of God brings Ezekiel to the community of exiles, and Ezekiel sees the glory of God in a nearby valley. ⌛ *EZEKIEL 1:1–28; 2:1–10; 3:22–27*

LESSONS IN JUDGMENT (4:1–7:27)

The people of Judah are being taken in large groups to Babylon, where they will live in captivity. Ezekiel is among one of the earlier groups.

700 BC	690 BC	680 BC	670 BC	660 BC	650 BC	640 BC	630 BC	620 BC	610 BC
◆ 716 Hezekiah (Judah)				◆ 658 Nahum (prophet)		◆ 640 Zephaniah (prophet)		◆ 620 Daniel born	
	◆ 697 Manasseh (Judah)					◆ 640 Josiah (Judah)		◆ 620 Ezekiel (prophet)	
	◆ 701 Sennacherib invades				◆ 650 Jeremiah (prophet)				

Impending Judgment against the Nations	After God's Judgment of Judah	Dry Bones and New Life	A New Temple	The River Measured and the Territory Divided
25:1–32:32	33:1–36:38	37:1–39:29	40:1–46:24	47:1–48:35

It is during this time that God calls him to ministry as a prophet to Israel. Initially, Ezekiel responds reluctantly to God's instructions. God commands Ezekiel to perform odd symbolic actions, such as laying siege to a brick that represents Jerusalem, sleeping on his side for 430 days, and eating bread baked over cow dung. Ezekiel is to condemn Israel and inform the people of terrible punishment to come. God will destroy Israel and wipe out its idols. Those who survive will be miserable, but they will return to the Lord in repentance. ⧗ *EZEKIEL 4:1–17; 5:7–17; 7:1–9*

VISION: JERUSALEM'S TEMPLE (8:1–11:25)

Israelites have already been deported to Babylon, and Ezekiel delivers hard-to-hear messages to the exiles. Jerusalem will soon be conquered and the temple destroyed. Ezekiel receives a vision that makes evident the source of God's displeasure regarding the temple. In the vision, God sends a man clothed in linen to mark every person in Jerusalem who denounces idolatry. Six men are sent to kill every person in Jerusalem who doesn't possess the mark. God's presence leaves the temple, but God promises to regather the exiles in the land of Israel again. ⧗ *EZEKIEL 8:1–18; 9:1–6; 10:18–19; 11:14–25*

EZEKIEL SPEAKS OUT (12:1–14:23)

Having been shown the deplorable spiritual condition of Jerusalem in a vision, Ezekiel is now told to prophesy concerning the exile of all those remaining there—or, more accurately, the exile of the few who will survive the destruction of the city. He is also told to confront other so-called prophets who are telling the exiles only what they want to hear. Although

Ezekiel's Vision, *the Zurich Bible*

◆ 597 Zedekiah (Judah)   ◆ 570 Confucius teaches in China   ◆ 522 Zechariah/Haggai (prophets)

◆ 600 Habakkuk (prophet)   ◆ 559 Cyrus the Great (Persia)   ◆ 521 Darius (Persia)

◆ 586 Fall of Jerusalem   ◆ 560 Aesop's fables   ◆ 539 Darius the Mede (Babylon)

Ezekiel's Call	Lessons in Judgment	Vision: Jerusalem's Temple	Ezekiel Speaks Out	Three Allegories to Describe Israel	Responsibility for Sin
1:1–3:27	4:1–7:27	8:1–11:25	12:1–14:23	15:1–17:24	18:1–24:27

God punishes the people of Jerusalem for their duplicity, He mercifully saves some. ⧗ *EZEKIEL 12:1–20; 13:1–9; 14:3–5, 21–23*

THREE ALLEGORIES TO DESCRIBE ISRAEL (15:1–17:24)

Ezekiel continues to address the spiritually defiant exiles in Babylon, passing along God's judgment for their recurring rejection of the Lord and pursuit of idolatry. Ezekiel is given three allegories to illustrate Israel's condition; each metaphor is clear because the interpretation is provided. ⧗ *EZEKIEL 15:1–8; 16:30–39; 17:1–24*

RESPONSIBILITY FOR SIN (18:1–24:27)

Ezekiel clarifies Gods attitude toward sin: People are judged for their own sins, not for the sins of others. Ezekiel provides two metaphors for Israel and then resumes his message of judgment on Judah and Jerusalem. God reminds the Israelites that their ancestors were punished for sinning. He vows to set fire to the land of Judah and assures He will bring His sword, in the form of a Babylonian invasion, first on the people of Jerusalem and then on the Ammonites. Finishing his message of judgment to Judah, Ezekiel begins to address other nations. God compares Jerusalem and Samaria to two sisters killed for prostitution. ⧗ *EZEKIEL 18:1–18; 20:27–31; 23:1–34*

IMPENDING JUDGMENT AGAINST THE NATIONS (25:1–32:32)

After completing his six-year ministry of preparing the exiles for the fall of Jerusalem, Ezekiel turns his attention to God's judgment on a number of surrounding nations. Babylon is not included because the Babylonians are the instrument of God's judgment during this time. God will destroy Tyre and Sidon, but He vows to return the people of Israel to their land. Egypt will be given to the king of Babylon, who will annihilate the nation and its allies. ⧗ *EZEKIEL 26:1–14; 30:1–26*

700 BC	690 BC	680 BC	670 BC	660 BC	650 BC	640 BC	630 BC	620 BC	610 BC

◆ 716 Hezekiah (Judah)　　　　　　　　　　◆ 658 Nahum (prophet)　　◆ 640 Zephaniah (prophet)　◆ 620 Daniel born

◆ 697 Manasseh (Judah)　　　　　　　　　　　　　　　◆ 640 Josiah (Judah)　　◆ 620 Ezekiel (prophet)

◆ 701 Sennacherib invades　　　　　　　　　　◆ 650 Jeremiah (prophet)

Impending Judgment against the Nations	After God's Judgment of Judah	Dry Bones and New Life	A New Temple	The River Measured and the Territory Divided
25:1–32:32	33:1–36:38	37:1—39:29	40:1–46:24	47:1–48:35

AFTER GOD'S JUDGMENT OF JUDAH (33:1–36:38)

The duty of the watchman is made clear. Ezekiel receives news of Jerusalem's destruction at the hands of the Chaldeans. The hypocrisy and abominations of the people are recounted. Ezekiel looks to the future with hope, anticipating Israel's restoration and God's renewed blessing. God asserts that individuals are responsible for their actions; the Israelites' own sins are causing their destruction. God will replace Israel's leaders, gather in the exiles, and bring prosperity to the land. God vows to destroy Edom because it supported Jerusalem's downfall. ⏳ *EZEKIEL 33:1–9; 34:1–16; 35:1–9*

DRY BONES AND NEW LIFE (37:1–39:29)

Ezekiel continues his message of God's redemption of Israel. Ezekiel is placed in the middle of a valley full of dry bones and is told to

EZEKIEL

123

The Vision of Ezekiel *by Francisco Collantes (1599–1656)*

600 BC	590 BC	580 BC	570 BC	560 BC	550 BC	540 BC	530 BC	520 BC	510 BC

◆ 597 Zedekiah (Judah)   ◆ 570 Confucius teaches in China   ◆ 522 Zechariah/Haggai (prophets)

◆ 600 Habakkuk (prophet)   ◆ 559 Cyrus the Great (Persia)   ◆ 521 Darius (Persia)

◆ 586 Fall of Jerusalem   ◆ 560 Aesop's fables   ◆ 539 Darius the Mede (Babylon)

Dry Bones and New Life	A New Temple	The River Measured and the Territory Divided
37:1–39:29	40:1–46:24	47:1–48:35

NAVIGATING THE BIBLE

prophesy to them. The bones are joined together and covered with flesh. God is showing His commitment to bring Israel back from the dead. God tells Ezekiel to take two sticks, one representing Judah and the other Israel, and join them together. This symbolizes God's promise to unite both kingdoms under a coming King, a descendant of David. Ezekiel also delivers a prophecy against the land of Gog. ⌛ *EZEKIEL 37:1–28; 38:1–6*

A NEW TEMPLE (40:1–46:24)

Ezekiel has a vision of the future of Jerusalem that includes details of a temple. The exact dimensions are given for the east, north, and south gates, the tables for the preparation of sacrifices, the chambers, and the porch. The Most Holy Place is described, and details of the priesthood are laid out. The glory of the Lord fills this temple. Of interest is the east gate of the outer court, which is to be permanently shut, for the Lord has entered through it. ⌛ *EZEKIEL 40:1–4; 41:1–26; 43:1–5; 44:1–10*

THE RIVER MEASURED AND THE TERRITORY DIVIDED (47:1–48:35)

Ezekiel's vision concludes with a description of a holy river flowing out of the temple and instructions for how the land is to be divided among the tribes. Each gate in the new city is named after a tribe. The city will be named "THE LORD IS THERE." ⌛ *EZEKIEL 47:1–23; 48:1–8, 30–35*

Making Sense of Ezekiel: Background
When Ezekiel began his prophetic work, Babylon had gained the upper hand and was holding sway over the entire ancient Near East. Judah's King Jehoiakim had first submitted to Babylon, but he later rebelled (with the encouragement of the Egyptians but against the advice of Jeremiah). As a result, the Babylonian leader, King Nebuchadnezzar, shackled him and dragged him to Babylon, where he was apparently executed. Jehoiakim's eighteen-year-old son, Jehoiachin, succeeded him as the Babylonian appointee, but he, too, was summoned to Babylon a few months later.

---

700 BC	690 BC	680 BC	670 BC	660 BC	650 BC	640 BC	630 BC	620 BC	610 BC

✦ 716 Hezekiah (Judah)

    ✦ 658 Nahum (prophet)   ✦ 640 Zephaniah (prophet) ✦ 620 Daniel born

    ✦ 697 Manasseh (Judah)   ✦ 640 Josiah (Judah)   ✦ 620 Ezekiel (prophet)

    ✦ 701 Sennacherib invades   ✦ 650 Jeremiah (prophet)

Daniel Taken to Babylon	The Fiery Furnace	Daniel, Belshazzar, and Darius	Daniel's Visions	Daniel Confesses Israel's Sin	A Prophecy Regarding the Future
1:1–2:49	3:1–4:37	5:1–6:28	7:1–8:27	9:1–27	10:1–12:13

Read Each 5-Minute Overview in Daniel

DANIEL

125

DANIEL TAKEN TO BABYLON (1:1–2:49)

Nebuchadnezzar conquers Jerusalem and King Jehoiakim. The best and the brightest of Jerusalem's young men are taken to Babylon. Young Daniel and three friends are groomed for civil service in Babylon. Daniel, who repeatedly attests to the power of the one true God at work, decides not to defile himself with the king's delicacies and wine. He trains for three years and excels. He is soon put to the test with an impossible demand. God enables Daniel to interpret Nebuchadnezzar's dream, which predicts there will be four kingdoms after Nebuchadnezzar's. The final kingdom will last forever. Nebuchadnezzar displays gratitude toward Daniel by placing him in charge over all the wise men of Babylon. ⌛ *DANIEL 1:1–21; 2:31–49*

THE FIERY FURNACE (3:1–4:37)

Nebuchadnezzar makes a huge image of gold and commands all people to worship the statue. Because Daniel's three friends would not worship Nebuchadnezzar's god, they are thrown into a fiery furnace. Miraculously, they are not burned. Nebuchadnezzar has another dream, which Daniel interprets, and one

600 BC	590 BC	580 BC	570 BC	560 BC	550 BC	540 BC	530 BC	520 BC	510 BC

• 597 Zedekiah (Judah)   • 570 Confucius teaches in China   • 522 Zechariah/Haggai (prophets)

• 600 Habakkuk (prophet)   • 559 Cyrus the Great (Persia)   • 521 Darius (Persia)

      • 586 Fall of Jerusalem   • 560 Aesop's fables   • 539 Darius the Mede (Babylon)

Daniel Taken to Babylon	The Fiery Furnace	Daniel, Belshazzar, and Darius
1:1–2:49	3:1–4:37	5:1–6:28

NAVIGATING THE BIBLE

year later, the dream is fulfilled. Nebuchadnezzar loses his sanity and his authority for a period of time until he acknowledges the one true God. Nebuchadnezzar recounts what he has learned, humbly realizing God truly is the sovereign and powerful Lord of the universe. ⏳ *DANIEL 3:1–30; 4:18–27, 29–33*

DANIEL, BELSHAZZAR, AND DARIUS (5:1–6:28)

Six years have passed. Belshazzar replaces King Nebuchadnezzar and pays no attention to Nebuchadnezzar's warnings about following God. King Belshazzar throws a wine party and uses the vessels stolen from Jerusalem's temple as his drinking cups. A hand suddenly appears and writes cryptic words on the king's wall. Daniel decodes the script and informs Belshazzar that his reign is about to end. Belshaz-zar is killed that same night. The new king, Darius, appoints Daniel to a prominent administrative position. Daniel breaks a new law that prohibits prayer to anyone except the king, and he is thrown into a lions' den as punishment. Daniel emerges unharmed, which prompts Darius to issue a decree throughout his kingdom commanding the people to worship Daniel's God. ⏳ *DANIEL 5:1–31; 6:13–28*

Belshazzar's Feast *by Rembrandt (1606–1669)*

126

700 BC	690 BC	680 BC	670 BC	660 BC	650 BC	640 BC	630 BC	620 BC	610 BC

◆ 716 Hezekiah (Judah)　　　　　　　　　　　◆ 658 Nahum (prophet)　　◆ 640 Zephaniah (prophet)　◆ 620 Daniel born

　　　◆ 697 Manasseh (Judah)　　　　　　　　　　　　　　◆ 640 Josiah (Judah)　　　◆ 620 Ezekiel (prophet)

　　◆ 701 Sennacherib invades　　　　　　　　　◆ 650 Jeremiah (prophet)

Daniel's Visions	Daniel Confesses Israel's Sin	A Prophecy Regarding the Future
7:1–8:27	9:1–27	10:1–12:13

DANIEL'S VISIONS (7:1–8:27)

Daniel has visions. Four beasts with great powers rise from the sea, but God subdues them. An angel explains the four beasts are four kingdoms that will culminate in an everlasting kingdom made up of servants of the Lord. Daniel has another vision about a two-horned ram that is trampled by a single-horned he-goat. The two-horned ram represents the Persian and Median kingdoms, the single-horned he-goat represents Greece, and the other horns represent the coming kingdoms. One of the kings from the coming kingdoms will destroy many of God's people and put an end to the temple sacrifices. Daniel learns the temple offerings will return in 2,300 days and nights. ⏳ *DANIEL 7:1–28; 8:15–27*

DANIEL CONFESSES ISRAEL'S SIN (9:1–27)

Daniel understands Jeremiah's prophecy, realizing Israel's captivity in Babylon will last seventy years. He confesses his sin and the sin of his people, acknowledging God's mercy and forgiveness in spite of the people's rebellion. During Daniel's prayer, the angel Gabriel visits him and tells Daniel what the future holds. However, the symbolism used is challenging and difficult to properly interpret and understand. ⏳ *DANIEL 9:1–27*

A PROPHECY REGARDING THE FUTURE (10:1–12:13)

Daniel fasts and mourns for three weeks after receiving another troubling vision. An angel informs him of future events: The Persian kingdom will fall after a fourth king comes to power, and a Greek kingdom will rise in its place. The Greek Empire will fragment into four regions, and eventually an evil tyrant will arise from the north. This ruler, who will come to power through deceit and political maneuvering, will attack many nations. He will enforce a treaty with Israel, ensuring the Jews they can keep their religious observances. Then suddenly, after three and a half years, he will invade Israel. Sacrifices will stop, and the temple will be desecrated. ⏳ *DANIEL 10:1–21; 11:1–10; 12:1–13*

600 BC	590 BC	580 BC	570 BC	560 BC	550 BC	540 BC	530 BC	520 BC	510 BC

◆ 597 Zedekiah (Judah)   ◆ 570 Confucius teaches in China   ◆ 522 Zechariah/Haggai (prophets)

◆ 600 Habakkuk (prophet)   ◆ 559 Cyrus the Great (Persia)   ◆ 521 Darius (Persia)

◆ 586 Fall of Jerusalem   ◆ 560 Aesop's fables   ◆ 539 Darius the Mede (Babylon)

Daniel Taken to Babylon	The Fiery Furnace	Daniel, Belshazzar, and Darius
1:1–2:49	3:1–4:37	5:1–6:28

CAST OF CHARACTERS

Isaiah

Obedient Prophet. God called Isaiah to prophesy primarily to Judah and Jerusalem and urge the people to repent from sin and return to God. Isaiah remained faithful and obedient in completing the task, despite facing rejection. Many of his prophecies foretold the Messiah, who would redeem His people from bondage.

Jeremiah

The Weeping Prophet. Jeremiah served as the last prophet God sent to preach to the southern kingdom. He preached for forty years during Israel's final days but never really saw a change in the stubborn Israelites. Broken and depressed, Jeremiah witnessed the destruction of Jerusalem after his warnings fell on deaf ears.

700 BC	690 BC	680 BC	670 BC	660 BC	650 BC	640 BC	630 BC	620 BC	610 BC

- 716 Hezekiah (Judah)
- 697 Manasseh (Judah)
- 701 Sennacherib invades
- 658 Nahum (prophet)
- 650 Jeremiah (prophet)
- 640 Zephaniah (prophet)
- 640 Josiah (Judah)
- 620 Daniel born
- 620 Ezekiel (prophet)

Daniel's Visions	Daniel Confesses Israel's Sin	A Prophecy Regarding the Future
7:1–8:27	9:1–27	10:1–12:13

IN THE MAJOR PROPHETS

Daniel

Prophet and Royal Official. Daniel was a Jewish noble, prophet, and lover of God who interceded for Israel. When the Israelites were exiled to Babylon, Daniel found himself interpreting the king's dreams. Daniel also received visions from the Lord about the future. His good reputation resulted in promotions and wealth.

Hezekiah

One Good King. Hezekiah became king of Judah after his father, evil King Ahaz. Hezekiah instituted religious reforms and improvements. He purified the temple and restored proper worship. Though one of the few good kings, he still had major flaws—materialism and pride.

600 BC	590 BC	580 BC	570 BC	560 BC	550 BC	540 BC	530 BC	520 BC	510 BC

- ◆ 597 Zedekiah (Judah)
- ◆ 570 Confucius teaches in China
- ◆ 522 Zechariah/Haggai (prophets)
- ◆ 600 Habakkuk (prophet)
- ◆ 559 Cyrus the Great (Persia)
- ◆ 521 Darius (Persia)
- ◆ 586 Fall of Jerusalem
- ◆ 560 Aesop's fables
- ◆ 539 Darius the Mede (Babylon)

An Unusual Calling	Reconciliation and God's Charge against Israel	Israel Refuses to Repent
1:1–2:23	3:1–4:19	5:1–6:11

INTRODUCTION TO HOSEA, JOEL, AND AMOS

Authors: Hosea, Joel, and Amos
Dates of Events: 790–740 BC

Hosea, Joel, and Amos are prophets called by God during the time of the divided kingdom of Israel. Amos and Hosea speak to the northern kingdom, and Joel is a prophet from the southern kingdom. Together these three prophets cover a ninety-five-year span of Israel's history. The books of Hosea, Joel, and Amos are part of the Minor Prophets, along with nine other books of prophecy. These books are no less important or less inspired than any of the five books of the Major Prophets; they are simply shorter. Though more succinct, their messages are just as powerful.

The nation of Israel is split by civil war, and God sends Hosea to prophesy to the morally corrupt northern kingdom. Through the unhappy story of Hosea and his unfaithful wife, Gomer, the truth of God's persistent and unlikely love for an unfaithful people, the Israelites, is revealed. Just as Gomer is married to Hosea, Israel is betrothed to God. In both cases, the bride plays the harlot and runs after other lovers. Hosea contrasts Israel's idolatry with God's holiness; his prophecy is meant to awaken the Israelites to their own unfaithfulness to God and call adulterous hearts back to Him.

Joel uses a recent calamity in the nation of Judah to teach a prophetic lesson. A locust plague has decimated the land, destroying every green thing. These insects are like an invading army, symbolizing a potentially greater destruction awaiting those who do not heed the prophet's call to repent. A massive army

890 BC	880 BC	870 BC	860 BC	850 BC	840 BC	830 BC	820 BC	810 BC	800 BC

◆ 886 Elah (Israel) ◆ 870 Elijah (prophet) ◆ 845 Elisha (prophet) ◆ 814 Jehoahaz (Israel)

◆ 885 Zimri & Omri (Israel) ◆ 853 Joram (Israel) ◆ 835 Joash (Judah)

◆ 874 Ahab (Israel) ◆ 841 Athaliah (Judah)

Judgment for Unfaithfulness	Punishment to Arrive	Blessing from Repentance
7:1–8:14	9:1–11:12	12:1–14:9

coming from the north will make the locusts seem mild in comparison. Through Joel, God appeals to the people to return to Him and divert the coming disaster. Joel speaks of a Day of the Lord—a time known only to God when He will exact judgment on the nations. In addition to preaching judgment and repentance, Joel encourages Israel with hopeful messages of eventual redemption and restoration.

A shepherd, gardener, and contemporary of the Old Testament prophets Hosea and Isaiah, Amos stands for justice in an era of Israel's history in which the nation is politically strong but spiritually weak, around 755 BC. Though his prophecy is directed to Israel, the northern kingdom, Amos is actually from the southern kingdom of Judah. He condemns the powerful, self-satisfied, wealthy upper class in Samaria, the capital of Israel; Israel's sins are piling up as high as heaven, and Amos warns the people of their fate if they refuse to repent. They reject God's plea, and the course of judgment cannot be altered.

Hosea and Gomer (left) and Amos (right) from Bibles that date between AD 1250–1400

790 BC	780 BC	770 BC	760 BC	750 BC	740 BC	730 BC	720 BC	710 BC

◆ 792 Uzziah (Judah)   ◆ 760 Isaiah (prophet)   ◆ 722 Israel falls

◆ 798 Jehoash (Israel)   ◆ 770 Jonah (prophet)   ◆ 753 Zechariah (Israel)   ◆ 732 Ahaz (Judah)

◆ 796 Amaziah (Judah)   ◆ 755 Amos/Hosea (prophets)   ◆ 732 Hoshea (Israel)

An Unusual Calling	Reconciliation and God's Charge against Israel	Israel Refuses to Repent
1:1–2:23	3:1–4:19	5:1–6:11

Read Each 5-Minute Overview in Hosea

132

AN UNUSUAL CALLING (1:1–2:23)

God calls Hosea to a peculiar method of ministry: Hosea is told to marry a promiscuous woman. The marriage portrays Israel's unfaithfulness to God, and the names of Hosea's children symbolize God's judgment on Israel's sin. There are three things that God promises to withdraw from the Jews: the land, His mercy, and special status as His people. However, after God testifies against Israel and promises to punish it, He also vows to renew His marriage; His saving love will restore His people, and the people of Israel will once again worship God alone. ⌛ *HOSEA 1:1–11; 2:1–23*

890 BC	880 BC	870 BC	860 BC	850 BC	840 BC	830 BC	820 BC	810 BC	800 BC

◆ 886 Elah (Israel)   ◆ 870 Elijah (prophet)   ◆ 845 Elisha (prophet)   ◆ 814 Jehoahaz (Israel)

◆ 885 Zimri & Omri (Israel)   ◆ 853 Joram (Israel)   ◆ 835 Joash (Judah)

◆ 874 Ahab (Israel)   ◆ 841 Athaliah (Judah)

Judgment for Unfaithfulness	Punishment to Arrive	Blessing from Repentance
7:1–8:14	9:1–11:12	12:1–14:9

RECONCILIATION AND GOD'S CHARGE AGAINST ISRAEL (3:1–4:19)

God commands Hosea to love his wife, Gomer, and reconcile their marriage, despite her adultery. God draws a parallel between the story of Hosea's love for his wife and God's love for unfaithful Israel. Hosea lays out God's charges against Israel: God accuses Israel of corruption, murder, harlotry, and idolatry. The children of Israel will be deprived of their cultic practices and will be destroyed. ⏳ *HOSEA 3:1–5; 4:1–19*

ISRAEL REFUSES TO REPENT (5:1–6:11)

Hosea is called to deliver the solemn message of the terrible seriousness of rebellion against God. Not only will God's people someday have to give an account for their unfaithfulness but there will also be immediate consequences for their disobedience. The Lord will be like a lion to Judah and Ephraim, tearing them away until they seek the Lord's face in their affliction. Hosea proclaims that after God is finished with His judgment, He will return to bless a future generation of His chosen people. Judah will produce a harvest. ⏳ *HOSEA 5:1–15; 6:1–11*

JUDGMENT FOR UNFAITHFULNESS (7:1–8:14)

Israel thinks the Lord has forgotten its wickedness, but Hosea dwells on Israel's complete, final, and irreversible failure of faith. The people continue to be religious and call upon the Lord, but all the while they do not really put their trust completely in Him. God longs to redeem His people, but they persist in their sin. God laments Ephraim's iniquity and vows to punish it harshly. Israel is about to reap the whirlwind of God's judgment for its unfaithfulness; fire shall be sent against its cities. God's words through Hosea are serious and somber and set the tone for the punishment to come. ⏳ *HOSEA 7:1–16; 8:1–14*

790 BC	780 BC	770 BC	760 BC	750 BC	740 BC	730 BC	720 BC	710 BC
◆ 792 Uzziah (Judah)			◆ 760 Isaiah (prophet)				◆ 722 Israel falls	
◆ 798 Jehoash (Israel)		◆ 770 Jonah (prophet)		◆ 753 Zechariah (Israel)		◆ 732 Ahaz (Judah)		
◆ 796 Amaziah (Judah)				◆ 755 Amos/Hosea (prophets)		◆ 732 Hoshea (Israel)		

An Unusual Calling	Reconciliation and God's Charge against Israel	Israel Refuses to Repent	Judgment for Unfaithfulness	Punishment to Arrive	Blessing from Repentance
1:1–2:23	3:1–4:19	5:1–6:11	7:1–8:14	9:1–11:12	12:1–14:9

PUNISHMENT TO ARRIVE (9:1–11:12)

Israel tried to be like other nations by seeking to become wealthy by the same means that the nations used: the fertility cult. But the people of Israel aren't like the other nations; they are God's children, His treasured possession, and God will not bless them when they operate with this level of harlotry. When the Israelites embrace these pagan religious practices, they are acting in a way that is inconsistent with their own identity and calling. God will put an end to Israel's monarchy, destroy its cities, and banish its idols; but He has a change of heart and promises to return His people to their land. ☧ HOSEA 9:1–17; 10:1–15; 11:1–12

BLESSING FROM REPENTANCE (12:1–14:9)

Hosea continues his meditation on the history of Israel's relationship to God—tracing the nation's sin, how it has provoked God's judgment, and how repentance restores relationship to God. Ancient Jacob is an example of Israel's present condition. A connection is made between the coming exile of Israel and the exile of Jacob when he fled

from Esau to his uncle Laban in Aram (Syria). Following a description of total disaster, Hosea ends with the blessing and hope of Israel's future restoration to God, which parallels Hosea's own story—his loving restoration to his unfaithful wife, Gomer. ☧ HOSEA 12:1–14; 13:1–16; 14:1–9

Jilted lover: Why does God compare His relationship with us to a marriage in Hosea? The people of Israel struggled to follow God. To help His people understand the importance of their relationship with Him, God used the picture of marriage. He even used the prophet Hosea's broken marriage (and reconciliation) as an object lesson. Specifically, the lesson we learn from Hosea is that God is the faithful husband who will never forsake His bride.

890 BC	880 BC	870 BC	860 BC	850 BC	840 BC	830 BC	820 BC	810 BC	800 BC

◆ 886 Elah (Israel)   ◆ 870 Elijah (prophet)   ◆ 845 Elisha (prophet)   ◆ 814 Jehoahaz (Israel)
◆ 885 Zimri & Omri (Israel)   ◆ 853 Joram (Israel)   ◆ 835 Joash (Judah)
◆ 874 Ahab (Israel)   ◆ 841 Athaliah (Judah)

Destruction: Present and Future	The Coming Judgment
1:1–2:32	3:1–21

Read Each 5-Minute Overview in Joel

DESTRUCTION: PRESENT AND FUTURE (1:1–2:32)

The arrival of a swarm of locusts is the catalyst for Joel's writing. In his opening section, he responds to the great destruction, calling on the people to mourn, fast, and pray because the Day of the Lord is near. A severe famine strikes the land, and the prophet cries out to God for help. Joel at last offers some hope to the readers and listeners. Yes, the coming Day of the Lord will be dreadful, but it is not too late. Joel begs his people to return to the Lord and declares a holy fast day for the people to repent. God takes pity on His people. He tells them He will make up for the years of the locusts and at a point in the future will pour out His Spirit on all people. Everyone who calls on the name of the Lord will be saved.
⌛ *JOEL 1:1–20; 2:12–32*

THE COMING JUDGMENT (3:1–21)

The Lord turns His attention to the judgment of other nations that have treated Israel badly throughout history. He has not overlooked their cruelty. Their judgment will be harsh indeed, and although Israel had been guilty of much wrongdoing in the past, they will experience God's great forgiveness. Joel warns that ungodly nations will be called to the Valley of Jehoshaphat to be judged. He urges the nations to prepare for war. God promises to repay the nations for taking advantage of Judah and to protect Israel on the Day of the Lord. Jerusalem is God's dwelling place. God will bring prosperity to Judah and misery to Egypt. ⌛ *JOEL 3:1–21*

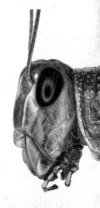

JOEL

135

The Lion Has Roared	Repentance and the Day of the Lord
1:1–3:15	4:1–5:27

Read Each 5-Minute Overview in Amos

THE LION HAS ROARED (1:1–3:15)

Amos pronounces a series of oracles of judgment against Israel's neighbors. These nations are condemned for their various crimes against humanity. They have violated principles of morality universally recognized by human beings. These oracles against the nations are embedded within Joel's sermon against Israel, and they show the progress of apostasy. Joel warns Israel that if foreign nations cannot escape God's wrath on account of their sins, Israel will not be ignored for its sins either. God is holding everyone associated with the family He delivered from Egypt responsible for their sins. ⚓ *AMOS 1:1–15; 2:6–16; 3:1–15*

REPENTANCE AND THE DAY OF THE LORD (4:1–5:27)

Amos condemns the indulgent women of Israel; God will make sure these women are judged in a humiliating manner by being dragged through the broken walls of their conquered cities. Amos warns God will exile northern Israel for its sins, and he makes a plea to the nation in hopes that some

890 BC	880 BC	870 BC	860 BC	850 BC	840 BC	830 BC	820 BC	810 BC	800 BC
	◆ 886 Elah (Israel)	◆ 870 Elijah (prophet)		◆ 845 Elisha (prophet)				◆ 814 Jehoahaz (Israel)	
	◆ 885 Zimri & Omri (Israel)			◆ 853 Joram (Israel)		◆ 835 Joash (Judah)			
		◆ 874 Ahab (Israel)			◆ 841 Athaliah (Judah)				

Measurement against God's Standard	Future Blessing
6:1–7:17	8:1–9:15

of its people will hear and respond. God is offended by Israel's corrupt religious ceremonialism; He tells the nation He hates their feasts because they are disconnected from the heart. ⏳ AMOS 4:1–13; 5:1–27

MEASUREMENT AGAINST GOD'S STANDARD (6:1–7:17)

Amos continues to focus on the northern kingdom in this section, but he condemns the influential and the rich who live and work in the capital cities of the kingdoms of both Israel and Judah. Amos describes the people's complacency and their coming judgment. He recounts a series of visions involving locusts, fire, and a plumb line. God relents in sending locusts and fire, but He will hold a measure against the people of Israel to see if they are "straight" against His standard. God will judge Israel severely with a famine from hearing the Word of the Lord. Israel will search after the Word of God to no avail. ⏳ AMOS 6:1–14; 7:1–17

AMOS

137

FUTURE BLESSING (8:1–9:15)

Amos experiences another vision of a bowl of ripe fruit, an image of Israel. As the time is short for summer fruit before it begins to rot, so the time is short for Israel. The depth of Israel's mourning will be severe; Amos describes it as like grieving the death of a firstborn son. No one can escape God's wrath; He will punish unfaithfulness. As a whole house collapses when the doorposts are damaged, so shall Israel's destruction be. However, Amos encourages Israel with the hope of the restoration of the house of David to Israel, and unexpected, quick miracles will pour from the land. ⏳ AMOS 8:1–14; 9:1–15

Figs, dates, grapes, olives, and pomegranates from Israel

790 BC	780 BC	770 BC	760 BC	750 BC	740 BC	730 BC	720 BC	710 BC

✦ 792 Uzziah (Judah)   ✦ 760 Isaiah (prophet)   ✦ 722 Israel falls

✦ 798 Jehoash (Israel)   ✦ 770 Jonah (prophet)   ✦ 753 Zechariah (Israel)   ✦ 732 Ahaz (Judah)

✦ 796 Amaziah (Judah)   ✦ 755 Amos/Hosea (prophets)   ✦ 732 Hoshea (Israel)

INTRODUCTION TO OBADIAH, JONAH, AND MICAH

Authors: Obadiah, Unknown, and Micah
Dates of Events: 770–570 BC

God calls Obadiah, Jonah, and Micah to continue speaking for Him during the time of the divided kingdom. The books bearing their names are included in the Minor Prophets. The book of Obadiah is the shortest book of the Old Testament, yet its brief message to the southern kingdom has numerous far-reaching applications. Jonah, speaking to the northern kingdom, is the most biographical of all the prophets. Micah, speaking to the southern kingdom like Obadiah, is like a miniature Isaiah—he is addressing the same people with the same problems.

Obadiah most likely writes during the exile (perhaps around 570 BC), providing a warning to anyone who mistakenly believes that sin will go unnoticed and unpunished. Not much is known about the prophet who directs his brief oracle to the nation of Edom that borders Judah on the southeast. Because Edom gloated when Jerusalem was invaded and did not protect its "brother" Judah, Obadiah warns the nation's judgment will be nothing less than total destruction. Edom's deeply rooted sense of pride will result in its certain downfall. Obadiah offers assurance of full restoration to Israel; Yahweh is faithful to His covenant promises, and His justice will ultimately prevail.

Jonah is not known for his piety but for running away from God. A prophet in the northern kingdom of Israel during the first half of the eighth century BC, during a time of great prosperity for Israel, Jonah illustrates Israel's rejection of God played out in his own life. When God calls Jonah to preach repentance to the wicked Ninevites, he turns down the assignment and heads for Tarshish

890 BC	880 BC	870 BC	860 BC	850 BC	840 BC	830 BC	820 BC	810 BC	800 BC

- 886 Elah (Israel)   • 870 Elijah (prophet)   • 845 Elisha (prophet)   • 814 Jehoahaz (Israel)
- 885 Zimri & Omri (Israel)   • 853 Joram (Israel)   • 835 Joash (Judah)
- 874 Ahab (Israel)   • 841 Athaliah (Judah)

Jonah's Sinful Heart	God Relents from Sending Calamity to Nineveh
1:1–2:10	3:1–4:11

instead. He does not want the Ninevites to benefit from God's mercy. After being swallowed by a giant fish and spit back out, Jonah realizes God is serious, and he preaches in Nineveh as commanded. Through his story, Jonah reveals God's power over nature, His mercy in human affairs, and His response to those who obey His commands.

Sometimes called the prophet to the poor, Micah speaks during a period of intense social injustice in Judah. Not much information is known about Micah, who delivers a stern message to the princes and people of Jerusalem in the form of three oracles of judgment. Rebuking anyone who uses social or political power for personal gain, Micah warns of coming punishment; he also holds out the hope of restoration once that discipline has ended. Prophesying between 735 and 710 BC, Micah emphasizes the integral relationship between true spirituality and social ethics, God's sovereignty, and the destiny of the faithful remnant.

OBADIAH

139

Jonah and the Whale *by Pieter Lastman (1583–1633)*

790 BC	780 BC	770 BC	760 BC	750 BC	740 BC	730 BC	720 BC	710 BC

◆ 792 Uzziah (Judah) ◆ 760 Isaiah (prophet) ◆ 722 Israel falls

◆ 798 Jehoash (Israel) ◆ 770 Jonah (prophet) ◆ 753 Zechariah (Israel) ◆ 732 Ahaz (Judah)

◆ 796 Amaziah (Judah) ◆ 755 Amos/Hosea (prophets) ◆ 732 Hoshea (Israel)

Joy in the Suffering of One's Enemies

1–21

Read the 5-Minute Overview in Obadiah

| o 1–21 | Joy in the Suffering of One's Enemies | Page 140 |

JOY IN THE SUFFERING OF ONE'S ENEMIES (1–21)

Obadiah announces judgment against the people of Edom and their pride against their "brother Jacob." Obadiah pointedly accuses the nation of Edom, whose people have survived while watching Judah fall to powerful enemies. More than that, Edom has taken perverse pleasure in seeing its enemies suffer, and the nation has acted aggressively against Judah during a vulnerable time. Judah's fall, however, was a result of God's judgment on His people—not because of Edom's power over Israel. Obadiah reveals God will actually use Israel to bring judgment against Edom. In the end of it all, the kingdom shall be the Lord's. ⏳ *OBADIAH 1–21*

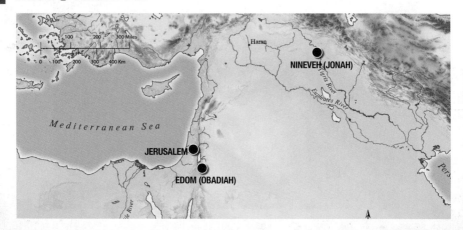

890 BC   880 BC   870 BC   860 BC   850 BC   840 BC   830 BC   820 BC   810 BC   800 BC

✦ 886 Elah (Israel)   ✦ 870 Elijah (prophet)   ✦ 845 Elisha (prophet)   ✦ 814 Jehoahaz (Israel)

✦ 885 Zimri & Omri (Israel)   ✦ 853 Joram (Israel)   ✦ 835 Joash (Judah)

✦ 874 Ahab (Israel)   ✦ 841 Athaliah (Judah)

Jonah's Sinful Heart	God Relents from Sending Calamity to Nineveh
1:1–2:10	3:1–4:11

Read Each 5-Minute Overview in Jonah

○ 1:1–2:10	Jonah's Sinful Heart	Page 141
○ 3:1–4:11	God Relents from Sending Calamity to Nineveh	Page 142

JONAH'S SINFUL HEART (1:1–2:10)

Jonah is given a divine commission to speak to the great city of Nineveh, capital city of Assyria and a potential threat to Israel. Jonah attempts to flee from God's call and hops on a ship headed for Tarshish. God prevents Jonah's escape by sending a storm; the sailors think Jonah is the cause for the horrible storm, and Jonah requests he be thrown overboard. The sea calms, and the sailors then fear the Lord. Jonah's resistance to God is the real problem. God preserves Jonah by allowing a big fish to swallow him, and he remains inside the fish for three days and three nights. From within the fish, Jonah praises God and declares salvation is of the Lord. God subsequently delivers Jonah from the fish. ✂ *JONAH 1:1–17; 2:1–10*

Jonah in the Fish
Artist unknown

Landlocked: How could Jonah have been spit up on the shores of inland Nineveh?
When Jonah was called by God to preach in Nineveh, he boarded a boat heading to Tarshish (in modern-day Spain)—in the opposite direction of Nineveh. We are told that when the great fish spit Jonah up, Jonah wound up on dry land. Afterward Jonah received another call from God, and this time the prophet went to Nineveh (Jonah 3:1–3).

790 BC	780 BC	770 BC	760 BC	750 BC	740 BC	730 BC	720 BC	710 BC
			◆ 760 Isaiah (prophet)				◆ 722 Israel falls	
◆ 792 Uzziah (Judah)								
◆ 798 Jehoash (Israel)		◆ 770 Jonah (prophet)	◆ 753 Zechariah (Israel)		◆ 732 Ahaz (Judah)			
◆ 796 Amaziah (Judah)			◆ 755 Amos/Hosea (prophets)		◆ 732 Hoshea (Israel)			

Jonah's Sinful Heart	God Relents from Sending Calamity to Nineveh
1:1–2:10	3:1–4:11

GOD RELENTS FROM SENDING CALAMITY TO NINEVEH (3:1–4:11)

God calls Jonah to speak to Nineveh a second time. Jonah obeys, and the people repent, proclaim a fast, and put on sackcloth. When God sees the people of Nineveh turn from their evil ways, He relents from the disaster He was going to send to them. Jonah is not pleased, and he blurts out his reasons for rebelling against God's commands;

this reveals Jonah's true sinfulness. God rebukes Jonah for his anger and teaches Jonah through an object lesson involving the sun, a worm, and a vine. 🗲 *JONAH 3:1–10; 4:1–11*

Fish tale: What are we to make of stories like Jonah's?

The book of Jonah tells the story of a man who was swallowed by a great fish—and survived inside for three days. Some struggle to believe such a tale. What should we make of stories like this?

First, remember that God was powerful enough to raise Jesus from the dead. By comparison, using a fish to preserve Jonah in the sea seems a relatively simple miracle.

Second, the Bible does not present stories like Jonah's as if they happen all the time. These are unique cases of supernatural intervention.

Third, when God supernaturally intervenes in the world, it is often His way of pointing to the cross. For example, Jesus once said that Jonah's sojourn in the fish was a sign pointing to the three days He would spend in the grave (Matthew 12:39–40).

---

890 BC	880 BC	870 BC	860 BC	850 BC	840 BC	830 BC	820 BC	810 BC	800 BC
	◆ 886 Elah (Israel)	◆ 870 Elijah (prophet)		◆ 845 Elisha (prophet)				◆ 814 Jehoahaz (Israel)	
	◆ 885 Zimri & Omri (Israel)			◆ 853 Joram (Israel)		◆ 835 Joash (Judah)			
		◆ 874 Ahab (Israel)			◆ 841 Athaliah (Judah)				

From Judgment and Oppression to Hope	Zion's Transformation and a Coming Champion	God's Never-Ending Mercy and Compassion
1:1–3:12	4:1–5:15	6:1–7:20

Read Each 5-Minute Overview in Micah

FROM JUDGMENT AND OPPRESSION TO HOPE (1:1–3:12)

Micah begins by announcing judgment to Israel and Judah because of sins against God and unfaithfulness to His covenant. This major theme of the prophets leads up to the destruction of the northern kingdom in 722 BC and the devastation and exile of the southern kingdom some 150 years later. God's divine justice, the ferocity of divine wrath, and the final and conclusive judgment of all people at the end of the world is revealed. Micah also pronounces judgment on the leadership of Judah. The people reject the prophets' words and listen to false prophets. Yet they cannot out-sin the grace and mercy of God. Through Micah, God announces that He will bring these false prophets into complete confusion. Because of its corrupt leadership, Jerusalem will become a pile of rubble. ⚡ *MICAH 1:1–16; 2:1–13; 3:1–12*

ZION'S TRANSFORMATION AND A COMING CHAMPION (4:1–5:15)

Micah's message shifts to one of salvation and the coming glorious transformation of the mountain of the Lord. Micah describes a new epoch that lies beyond Israel and Judah's judgment, coming in the near future. He tells of a day when there will be no wars, and Zion's people will be blessed. The people will be gathered home, and Israel will be strong among the nations. Micah begins

790 BC	780 BC	770 BC	760 BC	750 BC	740 BC	730 BC	720 BC	710 BC
◆ 792 Uzziah (Judah)			◆ 760 Isaiah (prophet)				◆ 722 Israel falls	
◆ 798 Jehoash (Israel)		◆ 770 Jonah (prophet)		◆ 753 Zechariah (Israel)		◆ 732 Ahaz (Judah)		
◆ 796 Amaziah (Judah)				◆ 755 Amos/Hosea (prophets)		◆ 732 Hoshea (Israel)		

From Judgment and Oppression to Hope	Zion's Transformation and a Coming Champion	God's Never-Ending Mercy and Compassion
1:1–3:12	4:1–5:15	6:1–7:20

a hopeful oracle regarding a champion from eternity past who will come from Bethlehem. This ruler will serve His flock and will deliver Jacob from Assyria. When God delivers Zion, it will be miraculous. However, God still has a complaint against His people. ⏳ *MICAH 4:1–13; 5:1–15*

GOD'S NEVER-ENDING MERCY AND COMPASSION (6:1–7:20)

The lawsuit God brings against the people closes with a pronouncement of Israel's sentence. Even though Micah is humbled and broken, he has complete confidence in God's salvation and Israel's vindication before its enemies. God's people know their sinful state, but they also know the greatness of God's redemption. Micah foretells that when the time comes for Israel's restoration, God will send a call out to the ends of the earth to gather and restore His people; He will shepherd them, and Israel will enjoy a close relationship with God as in ages past. Micah sees God's future work as a continuation of His past work; the same love, compassion, and mercy God showed to Israel's fathers is still available—if the people receive it by faith. ⏳ *MICAH 6:1–16; 7:1–20*

Whispers of a King: Why read the Minor Prophets?
One of the greatest contributions of the Minor Prophets is the picture they paint of Israel's Messiah. The prophets give us a vision of the work of Jesus. To better understand the mission and work of Jesus, we must read the Minor Prophets.

---

890 BC	880 BC	870 BC	860 BC	850 BC	840 BC	830 BC	820 BC	810 BC	800 BC
	◆ 886 Elah (Israel)		◆ 870 Elijah (prophet)		◆ 845 Elisha (prophet)			◆ 814 Jehoahaz (Israel)	
	◆ 885 Zimri & Omri (Israel)			◆ 853 Joram (Israel)		◆ 835 Joash (Judah)			
		◆ 874 Ahab (Israel)			◆ 841 Athaliah (Judah)				

The Doom of Nineveh Declared and Described	Nineveh Ripe for Judgment
1:1–2:13	3:1–19

INTRODUCTION TO NAHUM, HABAKKUK, AND ZEPHANIAH

Authors: Nahum, Habakkuk, and Zephaniah
Dates of Events : 660–600 BC

About 125 years after Nineveh's people repent as a result of Jonah's preaching, Nahum proclaims the downfall of this same city. Therefore, Nahum, in a sense, forms a sequel to the book of Jonah. The Ninevites are proud of their indestructible city, but Nahum establishes the fact that God will bring vengeance on those who violate His law. The people in Judah who trust in the Lord will be comforted to hear of Nineveh's doom and the demise of the mighty Assyrian Empire. Not much is known about Nahum, but most agree he is the primary author of the material that bears his name. A careful reading of this book reveals that the author has a high view of God and His Word; Nahum preaches against idolatry, immorality, injustice, and all manner of sin. In Nahum, God is seen as supreme over nature and nations, moving in just judgment against His enemies but with saving concern for those who put their trust in Him.

Like Nahum, Habakkuk refers to his message as an oracle—a message not from himself but placed on his heart by God. Unlike Nahum, however, Habakkuk does not state his message is directed at any specific individual or group of people, though he will devote a great deal of space to denouncing the Babylonians. Habakkuk asks God probing questions; he looks at his native Judah, sees the violence and injustice, and cries out to God, asking why His judgment hasn't already fallen on the nation. God assures Habakkuk He is not unaware. God is about to use the Babylonians as His chastening rod. This initially shocks Habakkuk, since Babylon is even more corrupt than Judah. However, Habakkuk praises God, knowing He is still sovereign and His plan is perfect.

790 BC	780 BC	770 BC	760 BC	750 BC	740 BC	730 BC	720 BC	710 BC

◆ 792 Uzziah (Judah) ◆ 760 Isaiah (prophet) ◆ 722 Israel falls

◆ 798 Jehoash (Israel) ◆ 770 Jonah (prophet) ◆ 753 Zechariah (Israel) ◆ 732 Ahaz (Judah)

◆ 796 Amaziah (Judah) ◆ 755 Amos/Hosea (prophets) ◆ 732 Hoshea (Israel)

The Doom of Nineveh Declared and Described

1:1–2:13

Zephaniah denounces the materialism and greed that exploit the poor in the early days of Josiah's reign, around 630 BC. Interestingly, Zephaniah is the only prophet whose lineage can be traced back to royal descent. Aware of world conditions and announcing God's judgment on the nations for their sins, this prophet has a deep concern for the Lord's reputation and for the well-being of all who humbly trust in Him. Zephaniah hammers home his message that judgment day is coming and all sin will be dealt with; Israel and its Gentile neighbors will soon experience the crushing hand of God's wrath. However, blessing will come in the person of the Messiah after the chastening process is complete.

Assyria will fall.
(Nahum)

The fig tree is barren.
(Habakkuk)

The poor go hungry.
(Zephaniah)

700 BC	690 BC	680 BC	670 BC	660 BC	650 BC	640 BC	630 BC	620 BC	610 BC

◆ 716 Hezekiah (Judah)

◆ 658 Nahum (prophet)　　◆ 640 Zephaniah (prophet)　◆ 620 Daniel born

◆ 697 Manasseh (Judah)　　　　　　　　　　◆ 640 Josiah (Judah)　　◆ 620 Ezekiel (prophet)

◆ 701 Sennacherib invades　　　　　◆ 650 Jeremiah (prophet)

Nineveh Ripe for Judgment
3:1–19

Read Each 5-Minute Overview in Nahum

THE DOOM OF NINEVEH DECLARED AND DESCRIBED (1:1–2:13)

Nahum's heavy message begins with a notice of its central focus—Nineveh's certain doom. Nineveh has slipped back into sin and is again ripe for judgment. Nahum's prophecies deal with the eventual defeat and destruction of Nineveh. The prophet sees a mighty army coming against the city, along with a fierce and bloody battle. God vows to conquer Nineveh but restore His own people. ✠ *NAHUM 1:1–15; 2:1–13*

Split personality: How can a loving God be so violent?

When we read the Old Testament, we come face-to-face with a rather unsettling aspect of God's character: His divine judgment. How can God be perfectly loving yet perfectly just? It helps to remember that love and justice are not contradictory terms. In fact, you can't have one without the other.

Love without justice allows sin to run rampant, causing pain and suffering. Earthly judges are not typically criticized for being unloving when they punish guilty criminals. To set criminals loose in society is not healthy for them or for the community. In the same way, our loving God cannot allow sin to go unpunished.

There are different dimensions to God's judgment. Sometimes He brings judgment on an individual, sometimes on a group of people, and at other times on an entire nation. Divine judgment is not driven by irrational anger but by justice. God works to restrain evil in our world; imagine how much worse things might be without His intervention! The greatest act of judgment was the cross, where God judged sin and death itself, sparing all who trust Christ from judgment.

600 BC	590 BC	580 BC	570 BC	560 BC	550 BC	540 BC	530 BC	520 BC	510 BC
	✦ 597 Zedekiah (Judah)		✦ 570 Confucius teaches in China				✦ 522 Zechariah/Haggai (prophets)		
✦ 600 Habakkuk (prophet)				✦ 559 Cyrus the Great (Persia)			✦ 521 Darius (Persia)		
	✦ 586 Fall of Jerusalem			✦ 560 Aesop's fables	✦ 539 Darius the Mede (Babylon)				

The Doom of Nineveh Declared and Described	Nineveh Ripe for Judgment
1:1–2:13	3:1–19

NINEVEH RIPE FOR JUDGMENT (3:1–19)

In his prophetic vision, Nahum tours Nineveh and observes how ripe it is for judgment. He sees a busy city, full of noise and activity, but also busy with violence, deception, and idolatry. Because of the weaknesses of the people and their leaders, Nineveh is doomed. All classes of people are ineffective and rebelling against God, from wealthy merchants to shepherds. Nahum ends his prophecy examining the righteous and their triumph over the unrighteous.

NAHUM 3:1–19

Relief created in approximately 725 BC. Image shows Assyrian archers attacking a city. One soldier holds a large shield to protect archers.

700 BC	690 BC	680 BC	670 BC	660 BC	650 BC	640 BC	630 BC	620 BC	610 BC

- ◆ 716 Hezekiah (Judah)
- ◆ 658 Nahum (prophet)
- ◆ 640 Zephaniah (prophet)
- ◆ 620 Daniel born
- ◆ 697 Manasseh (Judah)
- ◆ 640 Josiah (Judah)
- ◆ 620 Ezekiel (prophet)
- ◆ 701 Sennacherib invades
- ◆ 650 Jeremiah (prophet)

Habakkuk Questions God's Plans	The Prophet's Prayer and God's Exaltation
1:1–2:20	3:1–19

Read Each 5-Minute Overview in Habakkuk

○ 1:1–2:20	Habakkuk Questions God's Plans	Page 149
○ 3:1–19	The Prophet's Prayer and God's Exaltation	Page 149

HABAKKUK QUESTIONS GOD'S PLANS (1:1–2:20)

Habakkuk plunges into a rehearsal of his spiritual wrestling with God. Habakkuk asks God why He seems to delay judgment and why He allows people to see their own iniquity and trouble. God tells Habakkuk not to worry about those things, but to watch for the Babylonians who will come against Judah. Habakkuk also wonders why God will use a nation more evil than Judah to bring judgment on Judah. God tells Habakkuk to write down these questions and answers for the benefit of others, to edify them. Habakkuk is to make the revelation plain for others to understand. ⧗ *HABAKKUK 1:1–2:20*

THE PROPHET'S PRAYER AND GOD'S EXALTATION (3:1–19)

The perplexed prophet receives God's instructions, and in humble response, Habakkuk turns to prayer and praise to God. He begs God for revival, and he glorifies God's power, majesty, and sovereignty. The prophet knows he can trust the Lord, even when he doesn't understand or is in a crisis.
⧗ *HABAKKUK 3:1–19*

Habakkuk's Q&A

Q. God, have you left us? (1:1-4)

A. No, but sin must be dealt with. (1:5-11)

Q. But must you use the Babylonians? (1:12-2:1)

A. They aren't innocent but will serve my purpose. (2:3, 8)

Q. God, are you still there? (3:1-15)

A. Yes, and you will know my love in dark times, too. (3:16-19)

600 BC	590 BC	580 BC	570 BC	560 BC	550 BC	540 BC	530 BC	520 BC	510 BC

◆ 597 Zedekiah (Judah)   ◆ 570 Confucius teaches in China   ◆ 522 Zechariah/Haggai (prophets)

◆ 600 Habakkuk (prophet)   ◆ 559 Cyrus the Great (Persia)   ◆ 521 Darius (Persia)

◆ 586 Fall of Jerusalem   ◆ 560 Aesop's fables   ◆ 539 Darius the Mede (Babylon)

The Day of the Lord	Zephaniah's Words of Encouragement
1:1–2:15	3:1–20

Read Each 5-Minute Overview in Zephaniah

○ 1:1–2:15	The Day of the Lord	Page 150
○ 3:1–20	Zephaniah's Words of Encouragement	Page 150

THE DAY OF THE LORD (1:1–2:15)

Zephaniah, who is of royal lineage, is different from other prophets; he begins his prophecy giving timing and his own family roots. He then announces the coming of God's worldwide judgment and supplies important details concerning the devastation of that coming Day of the Lord. Judgment is promised to idolaters, royalty, merchants, and the complacent, and it will be intense. In light of the horrifying spectacle of the judgment of the Day of the Lord, Zephaniah presses his people to repent in humility before God. Judgment will come to the nations, and God will be glorified in a way that will bring the nations and their idols low. ⌛ *ZEPHANIAH 1:1–18; 2:1–15*

ZEPHANIAH'S WORDS OF ENCOURAGEMENT (3:1–20)

Despite a rather discouraging message, the prophet's report is not yet complete. The day of the Lord's judgment, however dark, is but the path to a brighter day. God will bring restoration someday. Zephaniah encourages his people to respond with joy in song. God will save and redeem them from both their enemies and their iniquities. ⌛ *ZEPHANIAH 3:1–20*

What is the Day of the Lord?
The Day of the Lord—a time, known only to God, when He will exact judgment on the nations. The concept encompasses other related themes, including the need for repentance, the certainty of coming judgment, and eventual redemption and restoration for the people of God.

700 BC	690 BC	680 BC	670 BC	660 BC	650 BC	640 BC	630 BC	620 BC	610 BC
◆ 716 Hezekiah (Judah)				◆ 658 Nahum (prophet)		◆ 640 Zephaniah (prophet)		◆ 620 Daniel born	
	◆ 697 Manasseh (Judah)					◆ 640 Josiah (Judah)		◆ 620 Ezekiel (prophet)	
	◆ 701 Sennacherib invades				◆ 650 Jeremiah (prophet)				

Rebuilding the Temple	Looking Ahead
1:1–15	2:1–23

INTRODUCTION TO HAGGAI, ZECHARIAH, AND MALACHI

Authors: Haggai, Zechariah, and Malachi
Dates of Events: 530–400 BC

B The books of Haggai, Zechariah, and Malachi are composed in the period of Israel's history after the Jews are released from captivity in Babylon. Their messages offer hope to a people whose national and personal lives are shattered. God calls three men to preach to this postexilic group of Jews from 520 to 425 BC.

Work begins on the temple in 536 BC, but construction is slowed from the land's desolation, crop failure, and opposition from the Samaritans. Work completely stops in 534 BC, and it is in this context that God calls His prophets Haggai and Zechariah in order to urge the people to complete what they have started. Haggai gives four mini-sermons, each spoken with divine authority; they are remarkably effective in shaking the Jews from their lethargy. The people are moved to finish the temple, and only twenty-three days after Haggai's first message, the people begin work for the first time in fourteen years. Haggai calls the builders to renewed courage in the Lord, repentance, obedience, and worship in the context of the temple and all it means to the Jewish community.

Zechariah magnifies Haggai's burden for the postexilic community and the temple, but he sees, through a vision and dream, the unfolding divine purpose for all of God's people and for the ages to come. With the temple still unfinished, Zechariah

600 BC	590 BC	580 BC	570 BC	560 BC	550 BC	540 BC	530 BC	520 BC	510 BC

* 597 Zedekiah (Judah)   * 570 Confucius teaches in China   * 522 Zechariah/Haggai (prophets)

* 600 Habakkuk (prophet)   * 559 Cyrus the Great (Persia)   * 521 Darius (Persia)

* 586 Fall of Jerusalem   * 560 Aesop's fables   * 539 Darius the Mede (Babylon)

Rebuilding the Temple

1:1–15

motivates the people to action, reminding them of its future importance. It must be built. Someday the Messiah's glory will inhabit it. Future blessing for Israel, as well as for the whole world, depends on the nation's present obedience. Zechariah writes using an apocalyptic format, shifting the Israelites' focus from the present to the future, from the local to the universal, and from the earthly to the cosmic and heavenly. The book outlines God's program for His people during the times of the Gentiles until the Messiah comes to deliver them and reign on the earth.

By the time Malachi arrives on the scene, enthusiasm and hopefulness for God's intervention on His people's behalf is fading. The people are discouraged spiritually, complaining, and growing indifferent to God's law. Malachi rebukes his people for keeping the best for themselves and leaving their leftovers for God. He summons his people to forsake their spiritual despondency and halfhearted commitment to the Lord and return to an active faith and devotion to God. The covenant that God made with His people in Genesis is fundamental in Malachi's message.

Traditional tomb of Zechariah

♦ 597 Zedekiah (Judah)   ♦ 570 Confucius teaches in China   ♦ 522 Zechariah/Haggai (prophets)

♦ 600 Habakkuk (prophet)   ♦ 559 Cyrus the Great (Persia)   ♦ 521 Darius (Persia)

        ♦ 586 Fall of Jerusalem   ♦ 560 Aesop's fables   ♦ 539 Darius the Mede (Babylon)

Read Each 5-Minute Overview in Haggai

HAGGAI

REBUILDING THE TEMPLE (1:1–15)

In the years after the exile, God speaks through His prophet Haggai. The work of rebuilding the temple has been at a standstill for the past fourteen years. The people make spiritual-sounding excuses for the stalled work; they claim it just wasn't God's timing. God hears their poor excuses. Haggai rebukes the people and tells them their financial problems are the result of misplaced priorities. It is time to get busy and rebuild the temple. ☧ *HAGGAI 1:1–15*

153

LOOKING AHEAD (2:1–23)

Haggai assures the temple builders that the glory of this temple should exceed the glory of Solomon's former temple. God promises to bless the people, in particular, Zerubbabel. ☧ *HAGGAI 2:1–23*

When did Haggai live?

In a day of profound discouragement and misplaced priorities after the Jews' return from Babylonian exile, the prophet Haggai sounds a call of rebuke, exhortation, and encouragement to his contemporaries. They have begun to rebuild their homes and businesses and to establish their statehood as a Jewish community but have been derelict in tending to the construction of the temple and making the Lord the central focus of all their hopes and dreams.

The prophets Haggai and Zechariah were contemporaries in Jerusalem at the end of the sixth century BC. This setting can be precisely identified; no other biblical author, with the exception of Ezekiel, ties his ministries and messages more closely to a chronological framework.

---

500 BC	490 BC	480 BC	470 BC	460 BC	450 BC	440 BC	430 BC	420 BC	410 BC

◆ 509 Roman Republic begins   ◆ 478 Esther   ◆ 440 Malachi (prophet)

◆ 492–479 Greco-Persian Wars   ◆ 460–445 Peloponnesian War

◆ 516 Jewish temple completed   ◆ 469 Birth of Socrates   ◆ 444 Nehemiah sent to Judah

God's Call for His People to Return to Him	Not by Might nor by Power but by My Spirit
1:1–2:13	3:1–4:14

Read Each 5-Minute Overview in Zechariah

GOD'S CALL FOR HIS PEOPLE TO RETURN TO HIM (1:1–2:13) Few exiles in Babylon returned to the promised land when they were allowed to come home. God pleads with His people to return to Him. Harsh circumstances in Israel make the nation feel like God is far from them. Zechariah speaks of his first of four visions. God promises to someday bring so many people to Jerusalem that the people will overflow the city walls and God will be their protection. ⌛ *ZECHARIAH 1:1–21; 2:1–13*

NOT BY MIGHT NOR BY POWER BUT BY MY SPIRIT (3:1–4:14) Zechariah sees Joshua the high priest in the presence of the Lord, clothed with filthy garments—a picture of sin. God removes Joshua's sin and admonishes him to keep His commandments. Joshua will continue to serve as high priest as long as he walks in obedience. God gives a prophetic message of the Messiah, God's servant, "the Branch." Zerubbabel will only accomplish and finish the work of rebuilding the temple by the Spirit of God, not by his own power. ⌛ *ZECHARIAH 3:1–10; 4:1–14*

600 BC	590 BC	580 BC	570 BC	560 BC	550 BC	540 BC	530 BC	520 BC	510 BC

• 597 Zedekiah (Judah)   • 570 Confucius teaches in China   • 522 Zechariah/Haggai (prophets)

• 600 Habakkuk (prophet)   • 559 Cyrus the Great (Persia)   • 521 Darius (Persia)

• 586 Fall of Jerusalem   • 560 Aesop's fables   • 539 Darius the Mede (Babylon)

Zechariah's Night Visions	The Coming of Zion's King	Israel's Redemption and Cleansing from Sin
5:1–6:15	7:1–10:12	11:1–14:21

ZECHARIAH'S NIGHT VISIONS (5:1–6:15)

Next Zechariah sees a flying scroll, followed by a vision of a woman and a basket. Zechariah condemns the exiles returning from Babylon for their materialism problem. The root of the issue, Babylon, will be destroyed. Zechariah has another vision of four horses and their chariots. Zechariah tells of a coming "Branch" who is both King and Priest and who will rebuild the temple—not the same temple Zerubbabel is working on, but the temple of His people. ⌛ *ZECHARIAH 5:1–11; 6:1–15*

THE COMING OF ZION'S KING (7:1–10:12)

Zechariah rebukes the people's hypocritical fasting based in self-pity. Israel is restored to God's favor, and He promises to rebuild Jerusalem; the people will prosper with religious fervor. God chastises Israel's leaders and promises a great redemption. Someday people will stream to glorified Jerusalem; nations will have to acknowledge God is with Israel. Zechariah also foretells of a coming King who will be lowly but full of strength and authority. ⌛ *ZECHARIAH 7:1–13; 9:9–17; 10:6–12*

ISRAEL'S REDEMPTION AND CLEANSING FROM SIN (11:1–14:21)

Zechariah laments the land's condition. God will protect Jerusalem and purge Israel of false prophets. Someday Jerusalem will become a heavy burden for all peoples. Zechariah foretells of a great outpouring of the Spirit; the people of Israel will look upon the One they have pierced and mourn for Him—a prophecy of Israel's coming Savior. Zechariah predicts a time when the Messiah will intervene for His people, and His rule will change the earth. ⌛ *ZECHARIAH 12:1–14; 13:1–9; 14:1–21*

500 BC	490 BC	480 BC	470 BC	460 BC	450 BC	440 BC	430 BC	420 BC	410 BC

◆ 509 Roman Republic begins   ◆ 478 Esther   ◆ 440 Malachi (prophet)

◆ 492–479 Greco-Persian Wars   ◆ 460–445 Peloponnesian War

◆ 516 Jewish temple completed   ◆ 469 Birth of Socrates   ◆ 444 Nehemiah sent to Judah

God's Call for His People to Return to Him	Not by Might nor by Power but by My Spirit
1:1–2:13	3:1–4:14

CAST OF CHARACTERS

Hosea/Gomer

A Picture of Israel's Unfaithfulness. God told Hosea, a prophet, to marry Gomer, a promiscuous woman. Hosea obeyed and demonstrated unrelenting love for his adulterous wife; he bought Gomer back from her lover and offered her a second chance to be faithful to him. Their marriage pictures God's faithfulness to unfaithful Israel.

Jonah

The Unwilling Prophet. God instructed Jonah to speak against the wickedness in Nineveh. But Jonah fled on a ship away from Nineveh. A storm hit, and sailors attributed it to Jonah's flight from God. Jonah was thrown overboard, and a big fish swallowed him—and later spewed him out. Jonah finally obeyed God.

400 BC	390 BC	380 BC	370 BC	360 BC	350 BC	340 BC	330 BC	320 BC

♦ 404 Artaxerxes II (Persia)

♦ 370 Plato writes *The Republic*

♦ 336 Alexander the Great (Greece)

♦ 359 Philip (Macedonia)

♦ 312 Seleucus I

♦ 390 Aramaic begins to replace Hebrew as Jewish language

♦ 336 Birth of Aristotle

♦ 323 Ptolemy I

Zechariah's Night Visions	The Coming of Zion's King	Israel's Redemption and Cleansing from Sin
5:1–6:15	7:1–10:12	11:1–14:21

IN THE MINOR PROPHETS

Amos

Shepherd and Prophet of Israel. Amos was a simple shepherd and farmer. However, the Lord called him to warn Israel of the coming "Day of the Lord" that would bring judgment against Israel and its neighbors. His prophecies reflect a deep understanding of God and the world Amos lived in.

Darius

King of Persia. Darius was the undisputed king of Persia, the greatest power the world had ever known. He assigned prestige and power to the prophet Daniel. Darius's officials became jealous of Daniel and tried to eliminate him. God spared him, and Darius made a new law that everyone should fear Daniel's God.

ZECHARIAH

157

310 BC	300 BC	290 BC	280 BC	270 BC	260 BC	250 BC	240 BC	230 BC	220 BC

◆ 264 First Punic War

◆ 255 The Septuagint translated

◆ 264–241 First Punic War

Israel, God's Treasured Possession	The Coming Messiah and a Messenger of Hope
1:1–2:9	2:10–4:6

Read Each 5-Minute Overview in Malachi

○ 1:1–2:9	Israel, God's Treasured Possession	Page 158
○ 2:10–4:6	The Coming Messiah and a Messenger of Hope	Page 158

ISRAEL, GOD'S TREASURED POSSESSION (1:1–2:9)

God shows His love for the nation of Israel through the prophet Malachi; it is now some one hundred years after the exiles have returned to Jerusalem. Malachi begins with a statement about nations rather than individuals. The people question God as to why things are the way they are if God really loves them. God assures His people that they are chosen and will remain His chosen, favored people. The Israelites, descendants of Jacob, are God's people, as opposed to the Edomites, descendants of Jacob's brother, Esau. Blemished sacrifices are exposed and condemned, as well as the unfaithful priesthood of Israel. ⚡ *MALACHI 1:1–14; 2:1–9*

THE COMING MESSIAH AND A MESSENGER OF HOPE (2:10–4:6)

Malachi resumes his rebuke of the people's sins, specifically marital unfaithfulness among God's people. The Lord asserts through His prophet that His people have violated the covenant; He will purge them of their sins and reward them for righteous behavior. God promises to set things right through His Messiah; before His arrival, a messenger will announce the Day of the Lord. Malachi tells how the people have failed to give ample offerings to God. God promises to vindicate those who have trusted Him. Malachi exhorts his people to remember the Law of Moses and turn to the God of their fathers. ⚡ *MALACHI 2:10–16; 3:1–18; 4:1–6*

210 BC	200 BC	190 BC	180 BC	170 BC	160 BC	150 BC	140 BC	130 BC	120 BC

◆ 201 Hannibal defeated

◆ 168 Antiochus IV Epiphanes occupies Jerusalem

◆ 146 Rome captures Carthage

◆ 167–142 The Maccabean Revolt

Birth: Fulfilling Prophecy	John the Baptist	The Sermon on the Mount	The Messiah's Authority	The Lord of the Sabbath
1:1–2:23	3:1–4:25	5:1–7:29	8:1–9:38	10:1–12:50

Introduction to Matthew

Author: Matthew
Date Written: AD 50–70

Matthew's Gospel provides the essential bridge between the Old and New Testaments by presenting Jesus as the Christ, Israel's messianic King. Old Testament prophets predicted and longed for the coming of the Anointed One who would enter history to bring redemption and deliverance; the very first verse in Matthew announces this long-awaited event. Matthew's Gospel emphasizes Jesus' messianic credentials: His genealogy, fulfillment of Old Testament prophecy, authority, and power.

Although Mark's Gospel appears on the scene first and is readily accepted by the early church, Matthew soon becomes the favored Gospel. It is more comprehensive than Mark, incorporating large blocks of Jesus' teaching material, such as the Sermon on the Mount. Matthew remains the most prominent of the three Synoptic Gospels (Matthew, Mark, and Luke) to this day.

Earliest records claim that the apostle Matthew wrote this Gospel, and no tradition to the contrary has ever emerged. Filled with a strong Jewish flavor, this Gospel likely speaks to Jewish-Christian church communities that had escaped Jerusalem between AD 66 and the destruction of Jerusalem in AD 70. Matthew's Gospel brings with it a strong sense of messianic expectation and fulfillment. Quoting heavily from the Old Testament, Matthew claims fifteen Old Testament prophecies are fulfilled in Jesus' ministry. Matthew also shows great interest in Jesus' teaching on the Law of Moses. Jesus teaches He came to fulfill the Law rather than abolish it—a statement found exclusively in Matthew. Finally, Matthew

90 BC	80 BC	70 BC	60 BC	50 BC	40 BC	30 BC	20 BC	10 BC	0 BC

♦ 65 Buddhism rises in China   ♦ 44 Julius Caesar assassinated   ♦ 2 Magi visit

♦ 63 Pompey conquers Jerusalem   ♦ 37 Herod the Great (Israel)

♦ 102 Chinese ships reach India   ♦ 51 Cleopatra VII reigns in Egypt   ♦ 31 Augustus (Rome)   ♦ 4 Jesus' birth

Birth: Fulfilling Prophecy	John the Baptist	The Sermon on the Mount	The Messiah's Authority	The Lord of the Sabbath	Nature of the Kingdom
1:1–2:23	3:1–4:25	5:1–7:29	8:1–9:38	10:1–12:50	13:1–15:39

NAVIGATING THE BIBLE

aptly develops the theme of the kingdom of God; a Jewish reader would wonder why Jesus did not establish the promised kingdom if indeed He was the Messiah. Matthew retells the progressive rejection of Jesus as King, shows Jesus' preparation of His disciples, and proves His kingship. Clearly, Matthew writes this Gospel to proclaim Jesus' words and works so Jewish readers can make an intelligent decision about Him. In spite of this Jewish focus, Matthew shows a genuine interest in church corporate life by viewing Christianity as reaching beyond the Jewish nation to the Gentiles.

The parables of the tares, ten virgins, and talents each contain themes relating to the final judgment. They manifest Matthew's significant interest in the final age of history—the end times. His description of the coming destruction of Jerusalem is illustrated in much greater detail and length than Mark's and Luke's.

Jesus' Trial with Pilate *by Antonio Ciseri (1821–1891)*

90 BC	80 BC	70 BC	60 BC	50 BC	40 BC	30 BC	20 BC	10 BC	0 BC

◆ 65 Buddhism rises in China   ◆ 44 Julius Caesar assassinated   ◆ 2 Magi visit

◆ 63 Pompey conquers Jerusalem   ◆ 37 Herod the Great (Israel)

◆ 102 Chinese ships reach India   ◆ 51 Cleopatra VII reigns in Egypt   ◆ 31 Augustus (Rome)   ◆ 4 Jesus' birth

Who Is This Jesus?	Living in Community	Jesus' Final Week, Part 1	Jesus' Final Week, Part 2	Signs of Jesus' Return	Betrayed and Crucified	Jesus Conquers Death
16:1–17:27	18:1–19:30	20:1–21:46	22:1–23:39	24:1–25:46	26:1–27:66	28:1–20

Read Each 5-Minute Overview in Matthew

BIRTH: FULFILLING PROPHECY (1:1–2:23)

Matthew presents Jesus as the fulfillment of prophecy and Israel's anticipated Messiah. Matthew connects Jesus' life and His lineage to both the royal line of David and the patriarch Abraham. Mary becomes pregnant as a result of a miraculous conception by the Holy Spirit. She is engaged to Joseph, who seeks a quiet divorce; but an angel comes to him in a dream and urges him not to leave Mary. The angel assures Joseph that the pregnancy is indeed from the Holy Spirit. The angel tells Joseph to name the baby Jesus, which in Hebrew means "God is salvation." Jesus is born in Bethlehem. An angel instructs Joseph to flee with his family to Egypt and remain there until the Lord tells them to return home.

✖ *MATTHEW 1:1, 17–25; 2:1–23*

AD 10	AD 20	AD 30	AD 40	AD 50	AD 60	AD 70	AD 80	AD 90	AD 100

♦ 8 Jesus visits temple ♦ 30 Jesus raised ♦ 45 James written ♦ 60 Eph–Col ♦ 68 Paul & Peter martyred ♦ 90 Revelation

♦ 5 Birth of Paul (?) ♦ 32 Stephen martyred ♦ 55 1 & 2 Corinthians ♦ 64 Rome burns ♦ 70 Temple destroyed

♦ 14 Tiberius (Rome) ♦ 37 Paul converts ♦ 57 Romans ♦ 65 1 Peter & 1 Timothy ♦ 85 1–3 John written

Birth: Fulfilling Prophecy	John the Baptist	The Sermon on the Mount	The Messiah's Authority	The Lord of the Sabbath	Nature of the Kingdom
1:1–2:23	3:1–4:25	5:1–7:29	8:1–9:38	10:1–12:50	13:1–15:39

JOHN THE BAPTIST (3:1–4:25)

John the Baptist paves the way for Jesus' ministry by calling Israel to repentance and baptizing people in the Jordan River. His ministry sparks widespread revival; many turn from their sins. John condemns two prominent religious groups for misinterpreting the Law and for their lack of repentance. John baptizes Jesus, and the sky opens; the Holy Spirit descends on Jesus and anoints Him for ministry. Shortly after, Jesus is tempted in the wilderness. Jesus begins preaching about the kingdom of God, calls His first disciples, and heals all kinds of diseases. ⏳ *MATTHEW 3:1–17; 4:1–25*

THE SERMON ON THE MOUNT (5:1–7:29)

Matthew claims Jesus is the Messiah and describes how Jesus calls His disciples to follow Him and make disciples of all nations. Matthew gives details about what a disciple's character should look like, the foundation being poverty of spirit. Those who humbly mourn over sin are meek and desire righteousness. They are merciful, pure in heart, and peacemakers. Jesus bids His disciples to display their discipleship. He also makes clear He is the correct interpretation of the Law. He warns against external works for the sake of display and discourages hypocritical giving. He also teaches the correct way to pray. Jesus warns against covetousness and exhorts His followers to keep anxiety and worry in check; they are to put God's kingdom first, and He will take care of everything else. The disciples are warned of the pitfalls of constantly judging one another hypocritically. They are encouraged to treat others as they would like to be treated. Finally, Matthew includes admonitions by Jesus to be alert to false teachers and to commit to His teachings and the will of God. ⏳ *MATTHEW 5:1–16; 6:1–14, 25–34; 7:1–6*

> **Religious leaders: Just who were the Pharisees, Sadducees, and scribes?**
> There were many different religious sects and schools of religious thought in Israel. The scribes and Pharisees focused their attention away from the temple and worshipped in the synagogues. They held fast to the Law and to their traditions. The Sadducees focused on temple worship and were more politically active.

90 BC	80 BC	70 BC	60 BC	50 BC	40 BC	30 BC	20 BC	10 BC	0 BC

• 65 Buddhism rises in China • 44 Julius Caesar assassinated • 2 Magi visit

• 63 Pompey conquers Jerusalem • 37 Herod the Great (Israel)

• 102 Chinese ships reach India • 51 Cleopatra VII reigns in Egypt • 31 Augustus (Rome) • 4 Jesus' birth

THE MESSIAH'S AUTHORITY (8:1–9:38)

Jesus performs many miracles, establishing His credentials as Israel's Messiah. He demonstrates His power over physical illnesses, the demon world, and the physical world of nature. Miracles of restoration and healing indicate the presence of the kingdom of God is at hand. This is what the prophet Isaiah had foretold; however, the scribes and religious leaders do not accept Jesus. Jesus calls Matthew, a tax collector, to follow Him. Jesus explains the difference between the old and new covenants. The disciples are commanded to pray for the harvest of believers to come. ☒ *MATTHEW 8:1–34; 9:35–38*

THE LORD OF THE SABBATH (10:1–12:50)

The twelve apostles are commissioned to reach the Jews, but they are told not to preach to the Gentiles or Samaritans. Jesus prepares the disciples to expect persecution but offers rest to anyone who comes to Him instead of living on self-sufficiency. The Pharisees condemn Jesus because His disciples had harvested grain on the Sabbath. Jesus responds by telling them He is Lord of the Sabbath. Jesus also foretells His death and compares the Messiah's upcoming time in the grave to Jonah's time in the belly of a fish. ☒ *MATTHEW 10:5–20; 12:1–21, 38–40*

NATURE OF THE KINGDOM (13:1–15:39)

Jesus teaches about the kingdom of God using parables. Many of Jesus' disciples are leaving Him; Jesus asks His closest disciples whether they will leave, too. He is rejected in His hometown, Nazareth. A great multitude of people follow Jesus. He is moved with compassion and heals the sick among them. He then challenges His disciples to feed the crowd. After more miracles, Jesus longs for time with His Father, and He leaves by Himself to pray. Jesus condemns religious leaders for appearing to be near to God but having hearts far from Him. Jesus feeds another crowd, both literally and spiritually. ☒ *MATTHEW 13:24–35; 14:13–21; 15:1–10*

AD 10	AD 20	AD 30	AD 40	AD 50	AD 60	AD 70	AD 80	AD 90	AD 100

◆ 8 Jesus visits temple ◆ 30 Jesus raised ◆ 45 James written ◆ 60 Eph–Col ◆ 68 Paul & Peter martyred ◆ 90 Revelation

◆ 5 Birth of Paul (?) ◆ 32 Stephen martyred ◆ 55 1 & 2 Corinthians ◆ 64 Rome burns ◆ 70 Temple destroyed

◆ 14 Tiberius (Rome) ◆ 37 Paul converts ◆ 57 Romans ◆ 65 1 Peter & 1 Timothy ◆ 85 1–3 John written

Birth: Fulfilling Prophecy	John the Baptist	The Sermon on the Mount	The Messiah's Authority	The Lord of the Sabbath	Nature of the Kingdom
1:1–2:23	3:1–4:25	5:1–7:29	8:1–9:38	10:1–12:50	13:1–15:39

NAVIGATING THE BIBLE

164

WHO IS THIS JESUS? (16:1–17:27)

The Sadducees and Pharisees—who hold opposing views regarding issues such as the resurrection and oral tradition—begin working together against Jesus; they clearly see Him as a grave threat. Testing Jesus, they ask Him for a sign to prove He actually is the promised Messiah. Once again, Jesus refers to the prophet Jonah. Peter speaks boldly and correctly, identifying Jesus as the Christ, the Son of the living God. A short time later, Jesus takes three of His disciples on a high mountain where He is transfigured before them. Later Jesus reminds His disciples about His future sufferings. ⌛ *MATTHEW 16:1–28; 17:1–13*

The Transfiguration *by Gerard David (ca. 1460–1523)*

LIVING IN COMMUNITY (18:1–19:30)

Jesus now prepares believers for how to live in a Christian community after He is gone. He uses a child as an example of what true greatness is. Jesus teaches that the exercise of forgiveness in the Christian community is to be extravagant and without limits. The Pharisees try to trap Jesus again, this time asking a question about divorce; Jesus' answer focuses, however, on marriage. He teaches a rich man about eternal life, referring to familiar aspects of the Mosaic Law and calling the man to put God first in all things. ⌛ *MATTHEW 18:1–20; 19:1–8, 16–26*

90 BC	80 BC	70 BC	60 BC	50 BC	40 BC	30 BC	20 BC	10 BC	0 BC

◆ 65 Buddhism rises in China ◆ 44 Julius Caesar assassinated ◆ 2 Magi visit

◆ 63 Pompey conquers Jerusalem ◆ 37 Herod the Great (Israel)

◆ 102 Chinese ships reach India ◆ 51 Cleopatra VII reigns in Egypt ◆ 31 Augustus (Rome) ◆ 4 Jesus' birth

JESUS' FINAL WEEK, PART 1 (20:1–21:46)

In the final week of Jesus' ministry, He continues to prepare His disciples for His death. He teaches on grace, greatness, and service, and He uses a parable about workers in a vineyard to describe God's fair dealings with His people. Jesus predicts His death again and heals two blind men both physically and spiritually. Jesus enters Jerusalem sitting on a colt as prophesied, and the people praise Him and address Him with messianic titles. He drives out dishonest merchants from the temple for selling approved sacrificial animals and currencies at high prices. The religious leaders question His authority. ⌛ *MATTHEW 20:1–19; 21:1–13, 22–27*

JESUS' FINAL WEEK, PART 2 (22:1–23:39)

Using a parable of a wedding feast, Jesus warns of the danger of rejecting Him. The Pharisees and the Herodians put their differences aside, and they unite against Jesus. Responding to their question about taxes, Jesus rebukes their wickedness and hypocrisy; He also scolds the Sadducees for not believing scripture about the resurrection. Jesus' opponents identify the Messiah's lineage as through David. Jesus again chastises the religious leaders for advertising their righteous deeds, and He proclaims to them seven woes of divine warning and condemnation. ⌛ *MATTHEW 22:1–22; 23:1–39*

SIGNS OF JESUS' RETURN (24:1–25:46)

Jesus now teaches on signs of His return and of the end of the age. He condemns religious leaders, predicts Jerusalem's destruction, speaks of the end of the age, and warns His people to be prepared. Terrible world conditions will become more frequent and more intense as His return

> **Déjà vu: Why are Matthew, Mark, and Luke so similar?**
> The first three books of the New Testament are often called the Synoptic Gospels. (*Synoptic* means "seen together" in Greek.) These books provide details about similar accounts in the life of Jesus. Each book, however, examines the events from a unique perspective, which helps readers more fully understand the true nature of Jesus.

MATTHEW

165

AD 10	AD 20	AD 30	AD 40	AD 50	AD 60	AD 70	AD 80	AD 90	AD 100

- ◆ 8 Jesus visits temple
- ◆ 30 Jesus raised
- ◆ 45 James written
- ◆ 60 Eph–Col
- ◆ 68 Paul & Peter martyred
- ◆ 90 Revelation
- ◆ 5 Birth of Paul (?)
- ◆ 32 Stephen martyred
- ◆ 55 1 & 2 Corinthians
- ◆ 64 Rome burns
- ◆ 70 Temple destroyed
- ◆ 14 Tiberius (Rome)
- ◆ 37 Paul converts
- ◆ 57 Romans
- ◆ 65 1 Peter & 1 Timothy
- ◆ 85 1–3 John written

Jesus' Final Week, Part 1	Jesus' Final Week, Part 2	Signs of Jesus' Return	Betrayed and Crucified	Jesus Conquers Death
20:1–21:46	22:1–23:39	24:1–25:46	26:1–27:66	28:1–20

grows closer. Believers will be persecuted, and false prophets will deceive many. Lawlessness will abound, and the love of most will grow cold. A sign spoken of by Daniel will be a specific signal that the end of the age is near. Jesus also speaks of coming judgment on the nations. ⧗ *MATTHEW 24:1–31; 25:1–13*

BETRAYED AND CRUCIFIED (26:1–27:66)

The lengthy controversy between Jesus and the religious leaders has culminated in a plot to take Jesus by trickery. A woman comes to Jesus and anoints Him with very expensive, fragrant oil, beautifully preparing Him for His death. Judas makes an evil agreement with religious leaders to betray Jesus for thirty pieces of silver. During Jesus' last meal with His disciples, He institutes the new covenant. Jesus, knowing what's ahead, cries out in deep distress to His Father in the Garden of Gethsemane. He is arrested, is tried before the Sanhedrin, and testifies He is the Christ. Peter denies his association with Jesus three times, and in repentance for his actions, he weeps bitterly. The people demand Barabbas's release and Jesus' crucifixion. Jesus is scourged, beaten, mocked, spit on, and led away to be crucified. Immediately after His death, the temple curtain that separates the Holy Place from the Most Holy Place—a vivid illustration of the separation between God and humanity—tears in two. A rich Jewish man buries Jesus in his own tomb, which is sealed and guarded. ⧗ *MATTHEW 26:6–13, 17–35, 47–51, 69–75; 27:45–51*

JESUS CONQUERS DEATH (28:1–20)

Jesus triumphs over death and sin, and He is resurrected. The tomb is found empty, and two women meet the risen Jesus themselves. The cover-up of the resurrection begins with the chief priests bribing the Roman soldiers to lie about Jesus' body being stolen. Jesus appears to the disciples in Galilee before giving the Great Commission to go out into the world and make disciples of all nations. ⧗ *MATTHEW 28:1–20*

The traditional Garden Tomb in Jerusalem

90 BC	80 BC	70 BC	60 BC	50 BC	40 BC	30 BC	20 BC	10 BC	0 BC

◆ 65 Buddhism rises in China   ◆ 44 Julius Caesar assassinated   ◆ 2 Magi visit

◆ 63 Pompey conquers Jerusalem   ◆ 37 Herod the Great (Israel)

◆ 102 Chinese ships reach India   ◆ 51 Cleopatra VII reigns in Egypt   ◆ 31 Augustus (Rome)   ◆ 4 Jesus' birth

Something New	Jesus Begins His Ministry	Jesus' Authority	Jesus Reveals Who He Is	Clarifying Twisted Laws
1:1–45	2:1–3:35	4:1–5:43	6:1–56	7:1–8:26

INTRODUCTION TO MARK

Author: John Mark
Date Written: AD 60–70

Even though 95 percent of the content of Mark is found in either Matthew or Luke, Mark's Gospel offers a fresh and immediate tone not to be missed. Mark's Gospel is a bold, concise, action-filled look at Jesus' life. It moves rapidly from story to story and focuses on two things: Jesus' service and sacrifice.

By the time Mark writes this Gospel, persecution is an ongoing concern. Therefore, he presents the life of Jesus in a way that illustrates Jesus' willingness to suffer. Mark's narrative tells the story of the Servant who is constantly on the move preaching, healing, and teaching. This Servant, who "did not come to be served," makes the ultimate sacrifice of servanthood by giving His life for many.

The shortest and simplest of the four Gospels, Mark is also considered by many to be the oldest; most agree it was written no later than AD 60 to 70. It may well have served as a source for the Gospels of Matthew and Luke. Mark is Peter's young disciple, who travels with Paul and Barnabas on their first missionary journey. It is Mark's close association with Peter that gives apostolic authority to his Gospel. In fact, the early church believed the Gospel of Mark is really the Gospel that Peter preached but that Mark wrote down.

There are a number of indications Mark is writing to a primarily Gentile Christian audience: He uses Latin words, explains Jewish traditions, leaves out Jesus' genealogy, and doesn't give geographic details. He also positions Jesus as both Son of God and Son of Man. He shows his Gentile readers how the Son of God was rejected by His own people but achieves ultimate victory through apparent defeat. The title Son of God alone, however, does not mean much to a Roman audience

AD 10	AD 20	AD 30	AD 40	AD 50	AD 60	AD 70	AD 80	AD 90	AD 100

◆ 8 Jesus visits temple   ◆ 30 Jesus raised   ◆ 45 James written   ◆ 60 Eph–Col   ◆ 68 Paul & Peter martyred   ◆ 90 Revelation

◆ 5 Birth of Paul (?)   ◆ 32 Stephen martyred   ◆ 55 1 & 2 Corinthians   ◆ 64 Rome burns   ◆ 70 Temple destroyed

◆ 14 Tiberius (Rome)   ◆ 37 Paul converts   ◆ 57 Romans   ◆ 65 1 Peter & 1 Timothy   ◆ 85 1–3 John written

Something New	Jesus Begins His Ministry	Jesus' Authority	Jesus Reveals Who He Is	Clarifying Twisted Laws	The Uniqueness of Christ
1:1–45	2:1–3:35	4:1–5:43	6:1–56	7:1–8:26	8:27–9:50

NAVIGATING THE BIBLE

unless Jesus also displays God's power, so Mark wastes no time delving into Jesus' ministry and miracles to prove He is God.

Jesus' preferred term to describe Himself, however, is Son of Man, and Mark uses this messianic title fourteen times in his Gospel. The Jewish people are still anticipating the arrival of a Messiah, but they are looking for a military figure to set them free from Roman domination. Mark shows how Jesus reinterprets the Messiah's ministry. Jesus certainly has power, yet He refuses to use this power against those in control. His arrival does indeed bring freedom—not immediate victory over Roman rule, but spiritual triumph over fear and death available only through the suffering and sacrifice of the Son of Man.

168

The Raising of the Cross *by Anthony van Dyke (1599–1641)*

90 BC	80 BC	70 BC	60 BC	50 BC	40 BC	30 BC	20 BC	10 BC	0 BC

* 65 Buddhism rises in China   * 44 Julius Caesar assassinated   * 2 Magi visit
      * 63 Pompey conquers Jerusalem   * 37 Herod the Great (Israel)
* 102 Chinese ships reach India   * 51 Cleopatra VII reigns in Egypt * 31 Augustus (Rome)   * 4 Jesus' birth

The Heart of the Matter	Temple Controversies	Watch and Wait	A Final Meal Together	Death and Resurrection
10:1–11:26	11:27–12:44	13:1–37	14:1–15:20	15:21–16:20

Read Each 5-Minute Overview in Mark

SOMETHING NEW (1:1–45)

Mark begins his Gospel with John the Baptist's ministry, recalling how a messenger and forerunner would prepare the way for the Messiah who was prophesied in the scriptures. John's message goes out with a positive response. Jesus appears and is baptized by John. Jesus sets to work calling disciples, teaching, and healing. Mark focuses on Jesus' proclamation and demonstration of the nearness of the kingdom of God. Jesus is more than a prophet—He is the Messiah and the Son of God. ⌛ *MARK 1:1–45*

JESUS BEGINS HIS MINISTRY (2:1–3:35)

At first, Jesus' public ministry is immensely popular. Now, Jesus chooses to hang around with the outcasts of society. He even selects members of this group to be included among His closest companions. Tension increases

AD 10	AD 20	AD 30	AD 40	AD 50	AD 60	AD 70	AD 80	AD 90	AD 100
✦ 8 Jesus visits temple		✦ 30 Jesus raised	✦ 45 James written		✦ 60 Eph–Col	✦ 68 Paul & Peter martyred		✦ 90 Revelation	
✦ 5 Birth of Paul (?)		✦ 32 Stephen martyred		✦ 55 1 & 2 Corinthians	✦ 64 Rome burns	✦ 70 Temple destroyed			
	✦ 14 Tiberius (Rome)		✦ 37 Paul converts	✦ 57 Romans		✦ 65 1 Peter & 1 Timothy	✦ 85 1–3 John written		

with Israel's religious leaders, who are upset about Jesus' claimed authority to forgive the sin of a paralyzed man as well as His association with tax collectors. Jesus continues to assemble a team of disciples to assist Him. As His ministry progresses, the crowd's response is unpredictable. Jesus makes a point that no one—not the religious leaders or His own family—truly understands who He is and what He came to do. ⚓ *MARK 1:1–8, 14–20; 2:1–12; 3:13–19, 31–35*

JESUS' AUTHORITY (4:1–5:43)

Jesus goes out on the sea in a boat to teach people on the shore. He tells a parable about a sower. The disciples don't understand the meaning and ask Jesus about it later. First, however, Jesus explains to the disciples why He uses parables; Jesus offers His hearers the opportunity to either dig deep and find spiritual truth or turn a blind eye to an interesting story. Jesus tells more parables, calms the Sea of Galilee during a storm, and demonstrates His authority over evil spirits, sickness, and death. His miracles are signs that the kingdom of God is near. ⚓ *MARK 4:1–20, 35–41; 5:1–13*

JESUS REVEALS WHO HE IS (6:1–56)

People struggle with their faith, and some desert Jesus. Jesus is rejected in His hometown of Nazareth. He sends the Twelve out two by two to preach. Herod hears of Jesus' ministry and fears that John the Baptist, whom he beheaded, has come back from the dead. Jesus teaches on the importance of rest, and He miraculously feeds thousands with five loaves of bread and two small fish. Later, while the disciples strain to row their boat because of a great wind, Jesus appears to them, walking on the sea. He gets into the boat, and the winds cease. ⚓ *MARK 6:1–12, 14–16, 30–56*

CLARIFYING TWISTED LAWS (7:1–8:26)

The stir concerning Jesus has led to the hope—if not outright belief—that the Messiah had arrived. But religious leaders continue to reject Him. Jesus' miracles and teachings are within the Mosaic Law, but they don't

90 BC	80 BC	70 BC	60 BC	50 BC	40 BC	30 BC	20 BC	10 BC	0 BC

◆ 65 Buddhism rises in China ◆ 44 Julius Caesar assassinated ◆ 2 Magi visit

◆ 63 Pompey conquers Jerusalem ◆ 37 Herod the Great (Israel)

◆ 102 Chinese ships reach India ◆ 51 Cleopatra VII reigns in Egypt ◆ 31 Augustus (Rome) ◆ 4 Jesus' birth

The Heart of the Matter	Temple Controversies	Watch and Wait	A Final Meal Together	Death and Resurrection
10:1–11:26	11:27–12:44	13:1–37	14:1–15:20	15:21–16:20

always conform to the traditions that had been added over the centuries to the scriptures. Jesus debates the religious leaders over issues of cleanliness and purity, and He condemns religious externalism. He heals a deaf and mute man and miraculously feeds a multitude. He warns His followers of the leaven of the Pharisees; the presence of a little sin can corrupt the whole. ⏳ *MARK 7:1–23, 31–37; 8:1–21*

THE UNIQUENESS OF CHRIST (8:27–9:50)

Jesus' disciples have witnessed, and even initiated, a number of miracles; yet they do not understand exactly who He is and what He is doing. Slowly, their eyes are opened and they begin to understand. As they do, Jesus reveals more of what they can expect ahead of them. Jesus makes His mission clear: He came to die and then rise again. Jesus leads Peter, James, and John up on a high mountain. There His whole appearance changes as He shines forth in glorious, bright light. The voice of God, thundering from a cloud, commands Jesus' disciples to listen to Him. Jesus gives the disciples authority to cast out evil spirits, but when confronted with a demon-possessed boy, they cannot. Jesus delivers the boy and tells the disciples their lack of prayer and fasting was why they could not do it themselves. Later He teaches about true greatness in the kingdom of God. Now Mark indicates that Jesus' public ministry in Galilee—the first leg of His journey to Jerusalem and the cross—is over. ⏳ *MARK 8:31–38; 9:1–32*

THE HEART OF THE MATTER (10:1–11:26)

Jesus performs many miracles, but His underlying purpose is heart transformation. Some hearts are filled with arrogance and self-interest, while others contain childlike faith and eagerness to serve God and His kingdom. Jesus dialogues with the Pharisees about legalism and love. He uses an example of a little child to teach that God will never hinder, or want us to hinder, anyone who in simple faith seeks God and His goodness. Jesus speaks about His passion, death, and resurrection again. After this, He explains that the life of a disciple is a life of a servant. Jesus begins demonstrating what kind of Messiah He is. He enters Jerusalem on a colt, just as the scriptures foretold the Messiah would do, and

AD 10	AD 20	AD 30	AD 40	AD 50	AD 60	AD 70	AD 80	AD 90	AD 100

◆ 8 Jesus visits temple ◆ 30 Jesus raised ◆ 45 James written ◆ 60 Eph–Col ◆ 68 Paul & Peter martyred ◆ 90 Revelation

◆ 5 Birth of Paul (?) ◆ 32 Stephen martyred ◆ 55 1 & 2 Corinthians ◆ 64 Rome burns ◆ 70 Temple destroyed

◆ 14 Tiberius (Rome) ◆ 37 Paul converts ◆ 57 Romans ◆ 65 1 Peter & 1 Timothy ◆ 85 1–3 John written

NAVIGATING THE BIBLE

His disciples and followers acknowledge Him as Messiah and King. He accepts the title and all the authority that goes with it. Upon entering Jerusalem, Jesus addresses wrong priorities in the temple and curses a fig tree, causing it to wither; this shows His authority over nature. The fig tree also symbolizes unfruitful and unrepentant Israel; Jesus is warning of God's displeasure when people have the appearance of fruit but lack the fruit itself. ⌛ *MARK 10:1–16; 11:1–26*

TEMPLE CONTROVERSIES (11:27–12:44)

A series of seven conflicts between Jesus and the religious authorities ensues. A parable of a landlord and evil tenants teaches a disheartening point: Israel has rejected messenger after messenger, and its people are finally rejecting the Son. Their day of reckoning will come. The religious leaders continue to try to destroy Jesus' credibility by questioning Him about Caesar and taxes. Jesus responds by reminding them that there are things that should be rendered to God alone. He teaches that what God really wants is people's love. He warns of the teachers of the Law, whose relationship with God is far more show than substance. ⌛ *MARK 11:27–33; 12:1–40*

WATCH AND WAIT (13:1–37)

Jesus foretells God's judgment, a great cataclysm in the world, and His eventual return. At this point in Mark's account, Jesus begins to reveal to the disciples some of the specifics of what will happen as the ministry of the church begins to unfold and His return grows closer. The temple will be destroyed, false messiahs will come in Jesus' name, and there will be many wars and threats of war on the earth. He warns His disciples of coming persecution but promises that before the end, the Gospel must be preached to the entire world. The biggest indicator of Jesus' return is the "abomination that causes desolation," which was prophesied by the prophet Daniel. Jesus wraps up His discourse with the lesson of the fig tree. Jesus reminds His disciples that when they see the fig tree's leaves appear, summer is near. In the same way, when these signs appear—particularly the abomination of desolation—the world can know that the triumphant return

172

90 BC	80 BC	70 BC	60 BC	50 BC	40 BC	30 BC	20 BC	10 BC	0 BC

◆ 65 Buddhism rises in China ◆ 44 Julius Caesar assassinated   ◆ 2 Magi visit

◆ 63 Pompey conquers Jerusalem   ◆ 37 Herod the Great (Israel)

◆ 102 Chinese ships reach India   ◆ 51 Cleopatra VII reigns in Egypt ◆ 31 Augustus (Rome)   ◆ 4 Jesus' birth

The Heart of the Matter	Temple Controversies	Watch and Wait	A Final Meal Together	Death and Resurrection
10:1–11:26	11:27–12:44	13:1–37	14:1–15:20	15:21–16:20

of Jesus is near. In the meantime, Jesus exhorts His followers to be alert and watch and pray for His return. ⏳ *MARK 13:1–37*

A FINAL MEAL TOGETHER (14:1–15:20)

Two days before the annual celebration of Passover, Jesus' opponents find a workable opportunity to arrest and kill Him. Jesus has made many predictions of His death and resurrection, and He has prepared His disciples accordingly. His disciples prepare a room for their last meal together. While they eat, Jesus initiates the new covenant between God and man. He is then betrayed by a friend, arrested, tried, and sentenced to death by crucifixion. Peter denies Him three times, and the rest of His friends leave Him. He is beaten, mocked, and hailed "King of the Jews." ⏳ *MARK 14:12–26, 43–51; 15:1–20*

MARK

173

The Last Supper *by Leonardo da Vinci (1452–1519)*

DEATH AND RESURRECTION (15:21–16:20)

The plot to put Jesus to death is finally implemented: Jesus is nailed to a cross. Even in His agony, He cries out to God to forgive His enemies. He declares He is fulfilling Psalm 22, and He breathes His last. Yet even in His death, there is additional evidence that Jesus is who He claimed to be—the Messiah and the Son of God. Only God controls life, and Jesus is raised from the dead. Three women find Jesus' tomb empty, and an angel tells them of the resurrected Jesus. Jesus appears to His disciples and commissions them to go into the world and preach the good news. ⏳ *MARK 15:21–47; 16:1–20*

AD 10	AD 20	AD 30	AD 40	AD 50	AD 60	AD 70	AD 80	AD 90	AD 100

◆ 8 Jesus visits temple ◆ 30 Jesus raised ◆ 45 James written ◆ 60 Eph–Col ◆ 68 Paul & Peter martyred ◆ 90 Revelation

◆ 5 Birth of Paul (?) ◆ 32 Stephen martyred ◆ 55 1 & 2 Corinthians ◆ 64 Rome burns ◆ 70 Temple destroyed

◆ 14 Tiberius (Rome) ◆ 37 Paul converts ◆ 57 Romans ◆ 65 1 Peter & 1 Timothy ◆ 85 1–3 John written

Something New	Jesus Begins His Ministry	Jesus' Authority	Jesus Reveals Who He Is	Clarifying Twisted Laws	The Uniqueness of Christ
1:1–45	2:1–3:35	4:1–5:43	6:1–56	7:1–8:26	8:27–9:50

CAST OF CHARACTERS

Jesus

Savior of the World. Born to human parents, Jesus grew up in Nazareth and became a carpenter. At age thirty, He began His three-year teaching and healing ministry, which ended when jealous Jewish leaders accused Him of treason. Romans crucified Jesus, three days later He rose from death, and later He ascended to heaven.

John the Baptist

The Baptizer. John grew up to be a prophet who prepared the way for the Messiah. He called people to repentance, and though his ministry was great and widespread, John knew his role was to point to One greater than he: Jesus. John baptized Jesus, inaugurating His earthly ministry.

90 BC	80 BC	70 BC	60 BC	50 BC	40 BC	30 BC	20 BC	10 BC	0 BC

♦ 65 Buddhism rises in China   ♦ 44 Julius Caesar assassinated   ♦ 2 Magi visit

♦ 63 Pompey conquers Jerusalem   ♦ 37 Herod the Great (Israel)

♦ 102 Chinese ships reach India   ♦ 51 Cleopatra VII reigns in Egypt   ♦ 31 Augustus (Rome)   ♦ 4 Jesus' birth

NAVIGATING THE BIBLE

174

IN THE GOSPELS (PART 1)

Mary Magdalene

Follower of Jesus. Mary Magdalene, one of Jesus' most devoted followers, was among the last to leave His side at the crucifixion. En route to anoint Jesus' body, Mary found the tomb empty. The risen Christ then entrusted Mary with the important job of spreading the news of His resurrection.

Caiaphas

High Priest. Caiaphas was a high priest and a member of the Jewish ruling council. Caiaphas offered a simple solution to Jesus' growing popularity and threat to the religious leaders' power: Kill Jesus and prevent the destruction of the nation of Israel. Caiaphas's solution eventually culminated in Jesus' crucifixion.

AD 10	AD 20	AD 30	AD 40	AD 50	AD 60	AD 70	AD 80	AD 90	AD 100

- ◆ 8 Jesus visits temple
- ◆ 30 Jesus raised
- ◆ 45 James written
- ◆ 60 Eph–Col
- ◆ 68 Paul & Peter martyred
- ◆ 90 Revelation
- ◆ 5 Birth of Paul (?)
- ◆ 32 Stephen martyred
- ◆ 55 1 & 2 Corinthians
- ◆ 64 Rome burns
- ◆ 70 Temple destroyed
- ◆ 14 Tiberius (Rome)
- ◆ 37 Paul converts
- ◆ 57 Romans
- ◆ 65 1 Peter & 1 Timothy
- ◆ 85 1–3 John written

NAVIGATING THE BIBLE

INTRODUCTION TO LUKE

Author: Luke
Date Written: AD 60–70

As author of this Gospel and its sequel, the book of Acts, Luke is responsible for over a fourth of the content of the Greek New Testament. Luke, a Gentile physician, builds his Gospel around a historical, chronological presentation of Jesus' life. Luke carefully documents Jesus' perfect humanity and portrays Him as the One who came to seek and save sinful people. Those who believe in Jesus experience opposition. Knowing this, Luke challenges believers to count the cost of discipleship. He writes with compassion and warmth, with the sophisticated style typical of Greek historians, as well as with smooth, everyday vernacular. Luke's Gospel is the longest of the four Gospels and was likely written before the destruction of Jerusalem in AD 70.

Luke was a close associate and traveling companion of Paul, who calls him a dear friend in Colossians. There is little dispute Luke is the author of both Luke and Acts. Luke knew Jesus' mother, Mary; therefore, his Gospel includes early accounts of Jesus' life: the visit of the shepherds to the manger, the story of Elizabeth and Zechariah and the birth of John the Baptist, the mention of Simeon and Anna when Jesus was presented in the temple, and the story of Jesus questioning the religious leaders in the temple at age twelve.

Evidence supports Luke's audience being Gentile, as he tends to translate Aramaic terms with Greek words and explain Jewish customs and geography to make his Gospel more intelligible to his original Greek readers. Luke writes of Jesus' unique life in order to strengthen Gentile believers' faith and stimulate saving faith among nonbelievers. There is some thought that he may have had another purpose in writing his Gospel: to show Christianity is not a politically subversive sect. Luke

90 BC	80 BC	70 BC	60 BC	50 BC	40 BC	30 BC	20 BC	10 BC	0 BC

◆ 65 Buddhism rises in China ◆ 44 Julius Caesar assassinated ◆ 2 Magi visit

◆ 63 Pompey conquers Jerusalem ◆ 37 Herod the Great (Israel)

◆ 102 Chinese ships reach India ◆ 51 Cleopatra VII reigns in Egypt ◆ 31 Augustus (Rome) ◆ 4 Jesus' birth

Warnings and Assurances	Lost and Found	Faith, Service, and Expectation	Requirements for Entering the Kingdom of God	True Worship and Coming Events	Betrayal, Denial, Arrest, and Anguish	Jesus' Third Trial and Crucifixion	Jesus, the Fulfillment of Prophecy
12:1–13:35	14:1–15:32	16:1–17:37	18:1–19:48	20:1–21:38	22:1–65	22:66–23:56	24:1–53

addresses his Gospel to Theophilus, a possible financial backer for Luke's travels and writing, and writes to confirm the authenticity and validity of the Gospel.

Luke is not an eyewitness of the events in his Gospel, but he relies on the testimony of eyewitnesses and written sources. He then personally investigates them to ensure accuracy. In his concern for Gentiles, Luke's portrayal of the Gospel is more encompassing than the other Gospel writers. He stresses an individual's privilege and ability to repent and be forgiven— and the joy that results from each such decision. Luke has a high regard for women and has much to say about money. Over half of Luke's Gospel contains content found nowhere else in scripture, including seven miracles and nineteen parables that are unique to this Gospel.

The Entombment *by Peter Paul Rubens (1577–1640)*

AD 10	AD 20	AD 30	AD 40	AD 50	AD 60	AD 70	AD 80	AD 90	AD 100
✦ 8 Jesus visits temple		✦ 30 Jesus raised		✦ 45 James written		✦ 60 Eph–Col	✦ 68 Paul & Peter martyred		✦ 90 Revelation
✦ 5 Birth of Paul (?)			✦ 32 Stephen martyred		✦ 55 1 & 2 Corinthians	✦ 64 Rome burns	✦ 70 Temple destroyed		
	✦ 14 Tiberius (Rome)		✦ 37 Paul converts		✦ 57 Romans		✦ 65 1 Peter & 1 Timothy	✦ 85 1–3 John written	

Preparing the Way	A Miracle Birth	Jesus' Ministry Begins	Defining Disciples	Legalism versus Faith	Parables, Miracles, and Greatness	Prayer, Signs, and Opposition
1:1–80	2:1–52	3:1–4:44	5:1–6:11	6:12–7:50	8:1–9:62	10:1–11:54

Read Each 5-Minute Overview in Luke

90 BC	80 BC	70 BC	60 BC	50 BC	40 BC	30 BC	20 BC	10 BC	0 BC

◆ 65 Buddhism rises in China   ◆ 44 Julius Caesar assassinated   ◆ 2 Magi visit

◆ 63 Pompey conquers Jerusalem   ◆ 37 Herod the Great (Israel)

◆ 102 Chinese ships reach India   ◆ 51 Cleopatra VII reigns in Egypt   ◆ 31 Augustus (Rome)   ◆ 4 Jesus' birth

Warnings and Assurances	Lost and Found	Faith, Service, and Expectation	Requirements for Entering the Kingdom of God	True Worship and Coming Events	Betrayal, Denial, Arrest, and Anguish	Jesus' Third Trial and Crucifixion	Jesus, the Fulfillment of Prophecy
12:1–13:35	14:1–15:32	16:1–17:37	18:1–19:48	20:1–21:38	22:1–65	22:66–23:56	24:1–53

PREPARING THE WAY (1:1–80)

Luke announces the miraculous, coming birth of John the Baptist. While the high priest Zechariah is performing his ritual temple services in the Most Holy Place of the temple, an angel appears to him proclaiming John the Baptist's birth. God makes Zechariah unable to speak because of his doubt. Elizabeth conceives, and six months later, the angel Gabriel announces to her cousin Mary that she too will conceive. Mary's son will be the Messiah foretold in the Old Testament. ⌛ *LUKE 1:5–38, 67–79*

A MIRACLE BIRTH (2:1–52)

Mary and Joseph go to Bethlehem to comply with a required census. While there, Jesus is born. Jesus is circumcised on His eighth day. Later Mary and Joseph present Him in the temple in Jerusalem. While there, a man named Simeon holds Jesus in his arms and says he can now die in peace since he has seen the Lord's salvation. He also foretells Jesus is destined for the fall and rising of many in Israel. Mary and Joseph return to Nazareth. When Jesus is twelve years old, His family travels to Jerusalem for Passover. Jesus remains at the temple while His parents return home; when they find Him, He tells His distraught parents He was about His Father's business. ⌛ *LUKE 2:1–35, 41–50*

JESUS' MINISTRY BEGINS (3:1–4:44)

The Word of God comes to John, son of Zechariah, prompting him to prepare the way for the Messiah and preach a baptism of repentance for the remission of sins. John then baptizes Jesus, inaugurating Jesus' ministry. Jesus is tempted in the desert by Satan, who challenges Jesus to display His identity as the Son of God, worship him (Satan), and test God through signs and wonders. Jesus is rejected in His hometown of Nazareth. Jesus reads from Isaiah 61:1–2 in the synagogue, teaching the people that the redeemer Isaiah was writing about is in their very presence. ⌛ *LUKE 3:1–20; 4:14–27*

The Baptism of Christ *by Piero della Francesca (ca. 1415–1492)*

AD 10	AD 20	AD 30	AD 40	AD 50	AD 60	AD 70	AD 80	AD 90	AD 100
◆ 8 Jesus visits temple		◆ 30 Jesus raised		◆ 45 James written	◆ 60 Eph–Col	◆ 68 Paul & Peter martyred		◆ 90 Revelation	
◆ 5 Birth of Paul (?)		◆ 32 Stephen martyred		◆ 55 1&2 Corinthians	◆ 64 Rome burns	◆ 70 Temple destroyed			
	◆ 14 Tiberius (Rome)		◆ 37 Paul converts	◆ 57 Romans		◆ 65 1 Peter & 1 Timothy		◆ 85 1–3 John written	

Preparing the Way	A Miracle Birth	Jesus' Ministry Begins	Defining Disciples	Legalism versus Faith	Parables, Miracles, and Greatness	Prayer, Signs, and Opposition
1:1–80	2:1–52	3:1–4:44	5:1–6:11	6:12–7:50	8:1–9:62	10:1–11:54

DEFINING DISCIPLES (5:1–6:11)

Luke focuses now on Jesus with respect to the leadership of Israel. Jesus begins to call His disciples to travel with Him in His ministry of teaching and healing. But when He and His disciples don't conform to established norms within the religious establishment, they begin to encounter opposition. *LUKE 5:1–31; 6:1–11*

LEGALISM VERSUS FAITH (6:12–7:50)

Jesus encounters the Pharisees, who show legalistic attitudes. These attitudes have twisted the intended meaning of the Gospel. Jesus provides His own outlook of how people should live; He lays out principles that should govern relationships with both friends and enemies. A Roman centurion displays faith greater than any witnessed in Israel, and a woman recognizes the significance of who Jesus is and anoints Him. Jesus gives tribute to the faithful ministry of John the Baptist. *LUKE 6:12–26; 7:1–10, 36–50*

PARABLES, MIRACLES, AND GREATNESS (8:1–9:62)

Jesus teaches crowds, trains His disciples, heals all kinds of diseases, casts out evil spirits, and performs miracles. His followers have grown in number, and women play a vital role in supporting His ministry. Jesus gives His disciples more responsibility, resulting in some successes as well as some failures. Some disciples begin to see Jesus for who He really is, yet they argue about which of them is greatest. At one point, Jesus challenges His disciples to feed a multitude of people; miraculously, with only five loaves and two fish, all eat and are filled. Jesus teaches that true greatness comes through following Him wholeheartedly with steadfast determination, mercy, and sacrifice. *LUKE 8:22–56; 9:10–17, 57–62*

Why was John the Baptist significant?

Throughout history, before a great move of God, the people were to consecrate themselves (cleansing and setting themselves apart from sin) so they would be prepared. For John the Baptist, the cleansing was accomplished through repentance. The setting apart was accomplished through baptism.

90 BC	80 BC	70 BC	60 BC	50 BC	40 BC	30 BC	20 BC	10 BC	0 BC

◆ 65 Buddhism rises in China ◆ 44 Julius Caesar assassinated ◆ 2 Magi visit

◆ 63 Pompey conquers Jerusalem ◆ 37 Herod the Great (Israel)

◆ 102 Chinese ships reach India ◆ 51 Cleopatra VII reigns in Egypt ◆ 31 Augustus (Rome) ◆ 4 Jesus' birth

Warnings and Assurances	Lost and Found	Faith, Service, and Expectation	Requirements for Entering the Kingdom of God	True Worship and Coming Events	Betrayal, Denial, Arrest, and Anguish	Jesus' Third Trial and Crucifixion	Jesus, the Fulfillment of Prophecy
12:1–13:35	14:1–15:32	16:1–17:37	18:1–19:48	20:1–21:38	22:1–65	22:66–23:56	24:1–53

PRAYER, SIGNS, AND OPPOSITION (10:1–11:54)

Jesus appoints seventy disciples and sends them out to heal and preach. Using the analogy of a ripe field of grain, Jesus explains why He feels an increased urgency about His work. Jesus answers a lawyer's question on how to obtain eternal life through a story about a kindhearted Samaritan, and He teaches two sisters an important lesson on priorities. Jesus' disciples ask how to pray, onlookers speculate as to how He casts out demons, and people are starting to expect fantastic signs from Jesus. The Pharisees' opposition increases. ⌛ *LUKE 10:1–4, 25–37; 11:1–13, 45–54*

WARNINGS AND ASSURANCES (12:1–13:35)

Jesus gives specific instructions to His apostles about the dangers of hypocrisy. He also addresses proper stewardship of the Gospel, possessions, and time. Luke describes Jesus in a number of different settings; although Jesus is still healing and teaching, the tone of His message is changing. Now, Jesus speaks of punishment, weeping and gnashing of teeth, and the coming desolation of Jerusalem. Through a parable, He calls His people to be watchful and ready, and to correctly interpret the times. ⌛ *LUKE 12:1–12, 35–48, 54–59; 13:1–8*

LOST AND FOUND (14:1–15:32)

Jesus continues to teach some difficult lessons. Much of what He says is easy to understand, even though His listeners might be reluctant to acknowledge it. His teaching often focuses on pride versus humility. Jesus debates the Pharisees, who accuse Him of receiving and eating with sinners. Jesus responds with three parables—each describes the joy and celebration that result from finding a lost item. ⌛ *LUKE 14:1–14; 15:1–31*

Jesus and the Lost Sheep

◆ 8 Jesus visits temple   ◆ 30 Jesus raised   ◆ 45 James written   ◆ 60 Eph–Col   ◆ 68 Paul & Peter martyred   ◆ 90 Revelation
◆ 5 Birth of Paul (?)   ◆ 32 Stephen martyred   ◆ 55 1 & 2 Corinthians   ◆ 64 Rome burns   ◆ 70 Temple destroyed
◆ 14 Tiberius (Rome)   ◆ 37 Paul converts   ◆ 57 Romans   ◆ 65 1 Peter & 1 Timothy   ◆ 85 1–3 John written

Preparing the Way	A Miracle Birth	Jesus' Ministry Begins	Defining Disciples	Legalism versus Faith	Parables, Miracles, and Greatness	Prayer, Signs, and Opposition
1:1–80	2:1–52	3:1–4:44	5:1–6:11	6:12–7:50	8:1–9:62	10:1–11:54

FAITH, SERVICE, AND EXPECTATION (16:1–17:37)

Jesus continues to teach His disciples, aware that the Pharisees are listening to everything He is saying. The Pharisees are lovers of money, so Jesus tells two parables about rich men. One man has a crooked employee he is about to fire, and the other finds himself suffering in hell after a lifetime of selfish luxury. Jesus teaches about not causing a brother or sister to sin, what to do when a brother or sister sins, faith and the disciple, the healing of ten lepers and the gratitude of one, and the coming kingdom of God. ⏳ *LUKE 16:1–14; 17:20–37*

REQUIREMENTS FOR ENTERING THE KINGDOM OF GOD (18:1–19:48)

Using a number of contrasts to teach about the kingdom of God, Jesus continues to pour His teaching into His disciples. He also continues to heal the sick as He approaches Jerusalem and His pending death. His focus shifts from the timing and circumstances of the coming kingdom to who would enter into it. While the rich young ruler, and those like him, would have much difficulty getting into the kingdom, those with childlike faith will possess it. ⏳ *LUKE 18:18–34; 19:1–26*

TRUE WORSHIP AND COMING EVENTS (20:1–21:38)

Jesus spends His final week of His human life in Jerusalem. Opposition to His ministry shifts from the Pharisees to the priests, scribes, and elders who question His authority and feel threatened. Knowing His time is short, He gives special attention to His followers, but many others listen to Him teach. Jesus speaks of future events; of interest is a future time of the Gentiles, and signs in the sun, moon, and stars. ⏳ *LUKE 20:1–19; 21:20–37*

BETRAYAL, DENIAL, ARREST, AND ANGUISH (22:1–65)

Jewish religious leaders have determined that Jesus must die. Jesus desires to celebrate Passover with His disciples. During this last meal with His friends, He teaches about true greatness and warns Peter of his coming

90 BC	80 BC	70 BC	60 BC	50 BC	40 BC	30 BC	20 BC	10 BC	0 BC

❖ 65 Buddhism rises in China   ❖ 44 Julius Caesar assassinated   ❖ 2 Magi visit

❖ 63 Pompey conquers Jerusalem   ❖ 37 Herod the Great (Israel)

❖ 102 Chinese ships reach India   ❖ 51 Cleopatra VII reigns in Egypt   ❖ 31 Augustus (Rome)   ❖ 4 Jesus' birth

Warnings and Assurances	Lost and Found	Faith, Service, and Expectation	Requirements for Entering the Kingdom of God	True Worship and Coming Events	Betrayal, Denial, Arrest, and Anguish	Jesus' Third Trial and Crucifixion	Jesus, the Fulfillment of Prophecy
12:1–13:35	14:1–15:32	16:1–17:37	18:1–19:48	20:1–21:38	22:1–65	22:66–23:56	24:1–53

fall. After dinner, the entourage moves to the Mount of Olives, where Jesus prays to His Father in anguish; He knows what is coming. He will drink the cup of God's fury so humankind will not have to. Jesus is betrayed and arrested, beaten and mocked. ⏳ *LUKE 22:1–65*

JESUS' THIRD TRIAL AND CRUCIFIXION (22:66–23:56)
Jesus is tried before the Sanhedrin, brought before Pilate and Herod, and found guilty of claiming to be the Son of God. The Jews have no authority to administrate the death penalty, so Jesus is brought before Pilate, the Roman governor over the region of Judea. Pilate knows Jesus is not guilty, yet he is unwilling to make an unpopular stand for Jesus. The crowd chooses to have the criminal Barabbas released instead of Jesus. Jesus is crucified. A criminal on the cross next to Jesus trusts Jesus for salvation. Jesus dies and is buried in a wealthy Jewish man's tomb. ⏳ *LUKE 22:66–71; 23:1–20, 32–43, 50–56*

JESUS, THE FULFILLMENT OF PROPHECY (24:1–53)
After the bleakness and despair of Jesus' horrid crucifixion, two women discover the empty tomb, and angelic messengers announce His resurrection. Two disciples on the road to the town of Emmaus lament the past week's events, and they end up having a heart-burning conversation with a fellow traveler who is actually the risen Christ. Jesus reveals Himself to His apostles and explains everything that has happened. Jesus is the Christ, Israel's Messiah, the fulfillment of God's promise of redemption. ⏳ *LUKE 24:13–53*

AD 10	AD 20	AD 30	AD 40	AD 50	AD 60	AD 70	AD 80	AD 90	AD 100

◆ 8 Jesus visits temple ◆ 30 Jesus raised ◆ 45 James written ◆ 60 Eph–Col ◆ 68 Paul & Peter martyred ◆ 90 Revelation

◆ 5 Birth of Paul (?) ◆ 32 Stephen martyred ◆ 55 1 & 2 Corinthians ◆ 64 Rome burns ◆ 70 Temple destroyed

◆ 14 Tiberius (Rome) ◆ 37 Paul converts ◆ 57 Romans ◆ 65 1 Peter & 1 Timothy ◆ 85 1–3 John written

Introduction to the Gospel of John	Evidence: Promised One	The Revelation of God	Jesus' Claimed Authority Causes Conflict	Jesus Reveals Himself	Messiahship Rejected	Spiritual Blindness
1:1–51	2:1–25	3:1–4:54	5:1–47	6:1–71	7:1–8:59	9:1–10:42

NAVIGATING THE BIBLE

INTRODUCTION TO JOHN

Author: John
Date Written: AD 60–90

Boasting the most quoted and preached verse in all scripture, John 3:16, John's work captures the Gospel of Jesus in its simplest form: Salvation is a gift of God, only obtained through belief in Jesus. John's Gospel is the most selective, topical, and theological of the four Gospels, written in logical units that develop unified themes with questions sprinkled throughout. Although Matthew, Mark, and Luke describe many of the same events in Jesus' life, John recounts events not found in the other Gospels. He selects only seven miracles to support the purpose for his writing: to prove Jesus is God in the flesh, and that by believing, readers would have eternal life in Jesus' name. Unlike Matthew, Mark, and Luke—who focus on Jesus' ministry in Galilee—John concentrates almost completely on Jesus' ministry in Judea.

184

As a coin has two sides, so Jesus has two natures: human and divine. Luke presents Jesus in His humanity as the Son of Man, but John displays Jesus in His deity as the Son of God. John details the last week of Jesus' life and includes the activities in the upper room as He celebrates His final meal with His disciples. John also describes Jesus' crucifixion and resurrection, proving He is the Son of God. John's Gospel is highly evangelistic; faith and belief are strong themes seen through John's accounts of those who reject Jesus versus those who believe. Those who trust Jesus as the Son of God are promised eternal life, but those who do not are under God's condemnation. John describes Jesus' life and ministry; he repeats many words that the Jewish community would have been familiar with, such as truth, light, darkness, Word, knowledge, belief, abide, love, world, witness, and judgment.

90 BC	80 BC	70 BC	60 BC	50 BC	40 BC	30 BC	20 BC	10 BC	0 BC

• 65 Buddhism rises in China   • 44 Julius Caesar assassinated   • 2 Magi visit

• 63 Pompey conquers Jerusalem   • 37 Herod the Great (Israel)

• 102 Chinese ships reach India   • 51 Cleopatra VII reigns in Egypt • 31 Augustus (Rome)   • 4 Jesus' birth

The Faithless, the Faithful	Teaching Humility	Instructions for Jesus' Disciples	A Promised Helper	Jesus' Intercession	Jesus Crucified	The Champion of Death and Lord of the Universe
11:1–12:50	13:1–38	14:1–15:27	16:1–33	17:1–19:16	19:17–20:31	21:1–25

The author's knowledge of Palestinian geography and Jewish customs makes it clear he was a Palestinian Jew, and his meticulous attention to names and numbers indicates he was an eyewitness. For these and other historical and internal reasons, including his self-identification as "the disciple whom Jesus loved," the author is understood to be John the apostle, one of the sons of Zebedee. Evidence points to the book being written sometime between AD 60 and 90; it is last of the four Gospels to be written.

Christ at the Sea of Galilee *by Tintoretto (1518–1594)*

AD 10	AD 20	AD 30	AD 40	AD 50	AD 60	AD 70	AD 80	AD 90	AD 100

• 8 Jesus visits temple   • 30 Jesus raised   • 45 James written   • 60 Eph–Col   • 68 Paul & Peter martyred   • 90 Revelation

• 5 Birth of Paul (?)   • 32 Stephen martyred   • 55 1 & 2 Corinthians   • 64 Rome burns   • 70 Temple destroyed

• 14 Tiberius (Rome)   • 37 Paul converts   • 57 Romans   • 65 1 Peter & 1 Timothy   • 85 1–3 John written

Introduction to the Gospel of John	Evidence: Promised One	The Revelation of God	Jesus' Claimed Authority Causes Conflict	Jesus Reveals Himself	Messiahship Rejected	Spiritual Blindness
1:1–51	2:1–25	3:1–4:54	5:1–47	6:1–71	7:1–8:59	9:1–10:42

Read Each 5-Minute Overview in John

INTRODUCTION TO THE GOSPEL OF JOHN (1:1–51)

John begins by summarizing the message of the entire Gospel—Jesus has come as the light of the world. John lays out an outline for his book, focusing on the deity of Christ, the forerunner of Christ, Jesus' rejection

90 BC	80 BC	70 BC	60 BC	50 BC	40 BC	30 BC	20 BC	10 BC	0 BC

♦ 65 Buddhism rises in China   ♦ 44 Julius Caesar assassinated   ♦ 2 Magi visit

♦ 63 Pompey conquers Jerusalem   ♦ 37 Herod the Great (Israel)

♦ 102 Chinese ships reach India   ♦ 51 Cleopatra VII reigns in Egypt   ♦ 31 Augustus (Rome)   ♦ 4 Jesus' birth

The Faithless, the Faithful	Teaching Humility	Instructions for Jesus' Disciples	A Promised Helper	Jesus' Intercession	Jesus Crucified	The Champion of Death and Lord of the Universe
11:1–12:50	13:1–38	14:1–15:27	16:1–33	17:1–19:16	19:17–20:31	21:1–25

and acceptance, and His incarnation. Beginning with John the Baptist and the inquisition of the religious establishment, John introduces the first of many question-and-answer times with the Jewish religious leadership. Jesus calls Philip and Nathanael, who acknowledge Jesus is the one Moses and the prophets wrote about. ⏳ *JOHN 1:1–51*

EVIDENCE: PROMISED ONE (2:1–25)

Jesus begins His public ministry, witnessing to the truth that He is the promised Messiah. He performs seven miracles, beginning by changing water in six pots into wine at a wedding. Just before the yearly Passover Festival, Jesus travels to the temple in Jerusalem, but after seeing the outer courts of the Gentiles being used as a house of merchandising, He makes a whip of cords and drives the moneychangers out. Many believe in Jesus when they see His miracles and signs. ⏳ *JOHN 2:1–25*

THE REVELATION OF GOD (3:1–4:54)

Nicodemus, a Pharisee and member of the ruling Sanhedrin, was impressed by Jesus' signs. He comes to Jesus at night, and Jesus tells him that in order to be assured of a place in God's kingdom, a person must be born again of water and the Spirit. Jesus then teaches of the nature of humankind, the need for regeneration, and the nature of the Messiah and His great love and work for humanity. Jesus meets a sinful woman at a well and tells her things about her life only God Himself could know, revealing Jesus as divine. Jesus also heals a royal official's son. ⏳ *JOHN 3:1–21; 4:7–54*

JESUS' CLAIMED AUTHORITY CAUSES CONFLICT (5:1–47)

As Jesus exercises His authority as God, religious leaders become increasingly angry and desire to kill Him. They refuse to believe He is God or that He has authority over them. Jesus works outside their legalistic system and threatens their power. They will not submit to Jesus' teaching. ⏳ *JOHN 5:1–47*

| AD 10 | AD 20 | AD 30 | AD 40 | AD 50 | AD 60 | AD 70 | AD 80 | AD 90 | AD 100 |

◆ 8 Jesus visits temple   ◆ 30 Jesus raised   ◆ 45 James written   ◆ 60 Eph–Col   ◆ 68 Paul & Peter martyred   ◆ 90 Revelation

◆ 5 Birth of Paul (?)   ◆ 32 Stephen martyred   ◆ 55 1 & 2 Corinthians   ◆ 64 Rome burns   ◆ 70 Temple destroyed

◆ 14 Tiberius (Rome)   ◆ 37 Paul converts   ◆ 57 Romans   ◆ 65 1 Peter & 1 Timothy   ◆ 85 1–3 John written

Introduction to the Gospel of John	Evidence: Promised One	The Revelation of God	Jesus' Claimed Authority Causes Conflict	Jesus Reveals Himself	Messiahship Rejected	Spiritual Blindness
1:1–51	2:1–25	3:1–4:54	5:1–47	6:1–71	7:1–8:59	9:1–10:42

JESUS REVEALS HIMSELF (6:1–71)

A crowd gathers around Jesus near the Sea of Galilee. Soliciting Philip and Andrew's help, Jesus miraculously changes five loaves of bread and two fish into enough sustenance for five thousand hungry people. Jesus is acknowledged as the prophet spoken of by Moses in the scriptures. The people desire to make Him King, but only as a political title; Jesus' mission is much bigger. Jesus identifies Himself as the bread of life, lifting their minds above earthly things to heavenly realities. Just as bread is necessary for physical survival, Jesus is all they need for spiritual survival. ⧗ *JOHN 6:1–15, 25–51*

MESSIAHSHIP REJECTED (7:1–8:59)

In spite of Jesus' signs and wonders, many people are not able to understand exactly who He is. Jesus answers religious leaders' objections to His claims of Messiahship. He declares Himself the source of life. Then Jesus shifts from presenting Himself as the Messiah to publicly condemning Israel for its rejection of the Messiah. Jesus passes a sentence of grace upon a sinful woman and proclaims His dependence on and obedience to the Father. ⧗ *JOHN 7:25–44; 8:1–30, 48–59*

SPIRITUAL BLINDNESS (9:1–10:42)

Jesus addresses the issue of sin by giving sight to a blind man who believes in Jesus. Jesus distinguishes between spiritual blindness and understanding, and He tells the Pharisees that if they would only admit their sin, they would find sight in Him. Jesus tells the Pharisees they are not the true shepherds of Israel but rather false shepherds that harm the sheep. Jesus wraps up

---

Outlier: Why is John's Gospel so different from the other three?
The Gospel of John has a narrower focus than the three Synoptic Gospels. In his Gospel, John stated that he purposefully wrote to show that Jesus is the promised Messiah and the Son of God. John wanted all who read his book to believe in Jesus and find life (John 20:31).

---

90 BC	80 BC	70 BC	60 BC	50 BC	40 BC	30 BC	20 BC	10 BC	0 BC

♦ 65 Buddhism rises in China   ♦ 44 Julius Caesar assassinated   ♦ 2 Magi visit

♦ 63 Pompey conquers Jerusalem   ♦ 37 Herod the Great (Israel)

♦ 102 Chinese ships reach India   ♦ 51 Cleopatra VII reigns in Egypt   ♦ 31 Augustus (Rome)   ♦ 4 Jesus' birth

The Faithless, the Faithful	Teaching Humility	Instructions for Jesus' Disciples	A Promised Helper	Jesus' Intercession	Jesus Crucified	The Champion of Death and Lord of the Universe
11:1–12:50	13:1–38	14:1–15:27	16:1–33	17:1–19:16	19:17–20:31	21:1–25

His public ministry to the leaders of Israel and begins His private ministry to the disciples. ⏳ *JOHN 9:1–12, 35–41; 10:1–21*

THE FAITHLESS, THE FAITHFUL (11:1–12:50)

As a group of people struggle with death, the ultimate conqueror, Jesus, performs a miracle that will attest to His divine nature. Jesus shows Himself to be champion over death when He raises His friend Lazarus to life after he had been dead four days. Many Jews believe in Him. Lazarus's sister Mary anoints Jesus' feet with oil; interestingly, Judas rejects this show of love. The chief priests, who do not believe in the resurrection, plot to put not only Jesus but also Lazarus to death. It is just before Passover, and Jesus enters Jerusalem on a colt as a coming King. Many believe, but many do not. ⏳ *JOHN 11:38–43; 12:1–19, 37–43*

TEACHING HUMILITY (13:1–38)

The Passover Festival is approaching, and Jesus knows that His hour has come. John makes it clear that Jesus is fully aware of what is about to happen. After celebrating His last meal with His disciples,

Washing of the Apostles' Feet *by Giovanni Agostino da Lodi (ca. 1495–1525)*

AD 10	AD 20	AD 30	AD 40	AD 50	AD 60	AD 70	AD 80	AD 90	AD 100

◆ 8 Jesus visits temple ◆ 30 Jesus raised ◆ 45 James written ◆ 60 Eph–Col ◆ 68 Paul & Peter martyred ◆ 90 Revelation

◆ 5 Birth of Paul (?) ◆ 32 Stephen martyred ◆ 55 1 & 2 Corinthians ◆ 64 Rome burns ◆ 70 Temple destroyed

◆ 14 Tiberius (Rome) ◆ 37 Paul converts ◆ 57 Romans ◆ 65 1 Peter & 1 Timothy ◆ 85 1–3 John written

Introduction to the Gospel of John	Evidence: Promised One	The Revelation of God	Jesus' Claimed Authority Causes Conflict	Jesus Reveals Himself	Messiahship Rejected	Spiritual Blindness
1:1–51	2:1–25	3:1–4:54	5:1–47	6:1–71	7:1–8:59	9:1–10:42

Jesus washes their feet, teaching His proud, argumentative disciples about humility. Judas departs to betray Jesus, and Jesus begins to emphasize His coming glory. ⏳ *JOHN 13:1–38*

INSTRUCTIONS FOR JESUS' DISCIPLES (14:1–15:27)

In His final address before His death, Jesus offers some very specific encouragement regarding the Spirit of God and the role He will play in the lives of the disciples. Jesus tells them how He wants them to act, and He speaks of the persecution they are to expect from this point on. Knowing it will be difficult for His disciples, He promises two gifts to help them: the Holy Spirit and peace. Jesus impresses on His disciples the importance of remaining in Him; if they remain in Him, they will produce fruit. Central to the heart of Jesus' message is His declaration that He is what the Old Testament saints looked forward to: He is the Promised One, the Redeemer of humanity. Jesus' disciples are to love others just as Jesus has loved them. With the promise of the Holy Spirit, Jesus encourages His disciples to witness to a lost and dark world. ⏳ *JOHN 14:15–31; 15:1–27*

A PROMISED HELPER (16:1–33)

To help His followers face the coming persecution He is describing, Jesus continues to teach and warn them so they will not be surprised when it happens. It should confirm their faith, and the work ahead of them should turn any sorrow they experience to joy. ⏳ *JOHN 16:1–33*

JESUS' INTERCESSION (17:1–19:16)

Jesus prays that He will be glorified. He prays for Himself, for His disciples, and for believers of every age and generation. He beautifully

---

Signs and wonders: What evidence does John provide of Jesus' divinity?
In his Gospel, John presented Jesus performing several signs that demonstrated His power over life and death. Jesus also claimed authority to do what only God can do, such as forgive sins and send the Holy Spirit.

---

90 BC	80 BC	70 BC	60 BC	50 BC	40 BC	30 BC	20 BC	10 BC	0 BC

◆ 65 Buddhism rises in China   ◆ 44 Julius Caesar assassinated   ◆ 2 Magi visit

◆ 63 Pompey conquers Jerusalem   ◆ 37 Herod the Great (Israel)

◆ 102 Chinese ships reach India   ◆ 51 Cleopatra VII reigns in Egypt   ◆ 31 Augustus (Rome)   ◆ 4 Jesus' birth

The Faithless, the Faithful	Teaching Humility	Instructions for Jesus' Disciples	A Promised Helper	Jesus' Intercession	Jesus Crucified	The Champion of Death and Lord of the Universe
11:1–12:50	13:1–38	14:1–15:27	16:1–33	17:1–19:16	19:17–20:31	21:1–25

models intercession on behalf of other believers. His prayers reveal even more about the precious relationship between Himself and His Father. Jesus finishes praying and is arrested. He is taken before Annas and then Pilate. Pilate agrees to crucify Jesus in place of another prisoner—even though he finds no basis for the charges. Pilate declares Jesus as King. ⌛ *JOHN 17:1–4, 6,17, 20–26; 18:28–40; 19:1–16*

JESUS CRUCIFIED (19:17–20:31)

Jesus is crucified, and Pilate writes a title and puts it on the cross over Jesus that says: "Jesus of Nazareth, the King of the Jews." Jesus entrusts John to care for His mother. Crying out, "It is finished," Jesus accomplishes what He came to earth to do. He gives up His life and breathes for the last time. It is the day of preparation—the day the lambs are being sacrificed for the Passover meal—and Jesus, the true Passover Lamb, is sacrificed in place of sinful humanity. Two loving disciples take Jesus' body down from the cross and bury Him before the Sabbath begins at dusk. Mary Magdalene comes to the tomb on the first day of the week and finds it empty. She meets her risen Lord, who tells her to go tell the disciples. Jesus appears to His followers and also to Thomas. ⌛ *JOHN 19:17–47; 20:1–18, 24–27*

THE CHAMPION OF DEATH AND LORD OF THE UNIVERSE (21:1–25)

Peter, sorrowful for denying his Lord three times, returns to fishing with six other disciples. They catch nothing. Jesus appears on the shore and directs them to try their nets on the other side of the boat; they catch so many fish they cannot bring them in. Jesus lovingly restores Peter and commands His disciples to follow Him. Jesus' resurrection offers His disciples a living illustration that He is their provider, sovereign Lord of the universe, and conqueror of death. Jesus is truly the manifestation of God. ⌛ *JOHN 21:1–25*

AD 10	AD 20	AD 30	AD 40	AD 50	AD 60	AD 70	AD 80	AD 90	AD 100

- 8 Jesus visits temple
- 30 Jesus raised
- 45 James written
- 60 Eph–Col
- 68 Paul & Peter martyred
- 90 Revelation
- 5 Birth of Paul (?)
- 32 Stephen martyred
- 55 1 & 2 Corinthians
- 64 Rome burns
- 70 Temple destroyed
- 14 Tiberius (Rome)
- 37 Paul converts
- 57 Romans
- 65 1 Peter & 1 Timothy
- 85 1–3 John written

Introduction to the Gospel of John	Evidence: Promised One	The Revelation of God	Jesus' Claimed Authority Causes Conflict	Jesus Reveals Himself	Messiahship Rejected	Spiritual Blindness
1:1–51	2:1–25	3:1–4:54	5:1–47	6:1–71	7:1–8:59	9:1–10:42

CAST OF CHARACTERS

Peter

Passionate Apostle. Peter emerged as the natural leader among the disciples, despite contradicting Jesus' prediction of His own death and disowning his Master three times. Jesus later restored Peter, entrusting to him the vital task of shepherding the early church. According to tradition, Peter was crucified for his faith.

Mary

Mother of Jesus. Mary, an ordinary Jewish girl, was visited by an angel and told she would be the mother of the Messiah. Mary believed and obeyed God, risking scorn. She gave birth to her baby boy, but years later she watched as her beloved son was rejected and cruelly murdered.

90 BC	80 BC	70 BC	60 BC	50 BC	40 BC	30 BC	20 BC	10 BC	0 BC

◆ 65 Buddhism rises in China ◆ 44 Julius Caesar assassinated ◆ 2 Magi visit

◆ 63 Pompey conquers Jerusalem ◆ 37 Herod the Great (Israel)

02 Chinese ships reach India ◆ 51 Cleopatra VII reigns in Egypt ◆ 31 Augustus (Rome) ◆ 4 Jesus' birth

The Faithless, the Faithful	Teaching Humility	Instructions for Jesus' Disciples	A Promised Helper	Jesus' Intercession	Jesus Crucified	The Champion of Death and Lord of the Universe
11:1–12:50	13:1–38	14:1–15:27	16:1–33	17:1–19:16	19:17–20:31	21:1–25

IN THE GOSPELS (PART 2)

Pilate

Roman Governor of Judea. Pilate, the Roman governor at the time of Christ, maintained peace through brute force and subtle negotiation. A key player in Jesus' trial, Pilate ordered Roman troops to carry out Jesus' death sentence in order to avoid problems for himself, even though he knew Jesus was innocent.

Judas

Betrayer of Jesus. Judas traveled with Jesus and studied under Him for three years as one of His twelve disciples. He was greedy, however, and sometimes stole from the group's money bag. This greed escalated to disloyalty and resulted in his betrayal of Jesus, his Messiah. Though remorseful, he did not seek God's forgiveness.

AD 10	AD 20	AD 30	AD 40	AD 50	AD 60	AD 70	AD 80	AD 90	AD 100

◆ 8 Jesus visits temple   ◆ 30 Jesus raised   ◆ 45 James written   ◆ 60 Eph–Col ◆ 68 Paul & Peter martyred   ◆ 90 Revelation

◆ 5 Birth of Paul (?)   ◆ 32 Stephen martyred   ◆ 55 1 & 2 Corinthians ◆ 64 Rome burns   ◆ 70 Temple destroyed

◆ 14 Tiberius (Rome)   ◆ 37 Paul converts   ◆ 57 Romans   ◆ 65 1 Peter & 1 Timothy   ◆ 85 1–3 John written

INTRODUCTION TO ACTS

Author: Luke
Date Written: AD 60–62

As is the case with his Gospel, Luke doesn't identify himself as the writer of Acts, though his authorship is seldom questioned. He begins the book of Acts where he leaves off in Luke, with the pouring out of the promised Holy Spirit—spoken of in the Old Testament—on the day of Pentecost. The book of Acts emphasizes the work of the Holy Spirit of Christ working in and through the apostles. It is the only book that continues recounting the story from Jesus' ascension to the period of the New Testament epistles. As such, Acts is the historical link between the Gospels and Paul's ministry.

Before ascending to the Father, Jesus commissioned His disciples to be witnesses in Jerusalem, in all Judea and Samaria, and to the ends of the earth. Acts is the evidence of this commission coming to fruition. In Acts, Luke traces the rapid expanse of the Gospel throughout both Jewish and Gentile communities, and to the entire Roman Empire. Luke records the growth, challenges, and miraculous happenings in the early Jewish church and how God's forgiveness and salvation are extended to the Gentiles through Christ. Luke seems particularly interested in seafaring, as many of his first-person accounts tell of missionary journeys by ship with his close traveling companion, Paul. These trips make Luke an eyewitness to the church's growth, giving his writing credibility.

Church expansion is clearly the dominant theme of the book. Even as the book of Acts concludes, Paul arrives in Rome to speak before the emperor there. Though beset by relentless opposition and persecution, he continues to preach the Gospel. The primarily Jewish church shifts to become predominately Gentile in membership—all part of God's perfect plan to spread the Gospel to a lost world.

A Second Journey	Two New Jewish Friends	A Forlorn Farewell	Trouble in Jerusalem	Paul before the Sanhedrin	A Trial in Caesarea	On the Way to Rome
15:36–17:34	18:1–19:41	20:1–21:26	21:27–22:29	22:30–24:26	24:27–26:32	27:1–28:31

Luke's mostly chronological account of Paul's travels is invaluable in establishing dates for and better comprehension of Paul's epistles. By combining Paul's references in his letters with Luke's in Acts, the details of Paul's ministry become much clearer. Since Luke's coverage of world events does not mention Nero's persecution of Christians from AD 64 and following, the destruction of Jerusalem in AD 70, or Paul's death in AD 68, many scholars believe Acts was written between AD 60 and 62. Through the book of Acts, readers are given a complete picture of God's plan and how He chose to include all humankind—Jew and Gentile—in His kingdom.

Saints Peter and John Healing the Lame Man *by Nicolas Poussin (1594–1665)*

AD 10	AD 20	AD 30	AD 40	AD 50	AD 60	AD 70	AD 80	AD 90	AD 100

◆ 8 Jesus visits temple   ◆ 30 Jesus raised   ◆ 45 James written   ◆ 60 Eph–Col   ◆ 68 Paul & Peter martyred   ◆ 90 Revelation

◆ 5 Birth of Paul (?)   ◆ 32 Stephen martyred   ◆ 55 1 & 2 Corinthians   ◆ 64 Rome burns   ◆ 70 Temple destroyed

◆ 14 Tiberius (Rome)   ◆ 37 Paul converts   ◆ 57 Romans   ◆ 65 1 Peter & 1 Timothy   ◆ 85 1–3 John written

The Promised Helper	The Church Is Formed	The First Casualty	The Conversion of Saul	Peter's Prison Break	First Missionary Journey and Jerusalem Council
1:1–2:47	3:1–5:42	6:1–8:40	9:1–11:30	12:1–13:52	14:1–15:35

Read Each 5-Minute Overview in Acts

THE PROMISED HELPER (1:1–2:47)

After His resurrection, and just before His ascension, Jesus instructs His disciples to go to Jerusalem and await the Holy Spirit. Fifty days after Passover, on the Jewish Feast of Pentecost when the firstfruits of the wheat harvest were brought in and presented to God, the Holy Spirit descends on the disciples in a forceful wind and with fire. This initiates the establishment of the church. Peter gives a heart-transforming message and points to Joel's prophecy hundreds of years prior to the pouring out of God's Spirit on His people. He also explains the resurrected Jesus. Multitudes respond to Peter's sermon and are baptized. ⏳ *ACTS 1:1–10; 2:1–41*

90 BC	80 BC	70 BC	60 BC	50 BC	40 BC	30 BC	20 BC	10 BC	0 BC

♦ 65 Buddhism rises in China ♦ 44 Julius Caesar assassinated ♦ 2 Magi visit

♦ 63 Pompey conquers Jerusalem ♦ 37 Herod the Great (Israel)

♦ 102 Chinese ships reach India ♦ 51 Cleopatra VII reigns in Egypt ♦ 31 Augustus (Rome) ♦ 4 Jesus' birth

A Second Journey	Two New Jewish Friends	A Forlorn Farewell	Trouble in Jerusalem	Paul before the Sanhedrin	A Trial in Caesarea	On the Way to Rome
15:36–17:34	18:1–19:41	20:1–21:26	21:27–22:29	22:30–24:26	24:27–26:32	27:1–28:31

THE CHURCH IS FORMED (3:1–5:42)

Peter quickly emerges as the prominent leader of the church. He makes an impassioned speech to a crowd and soon begins to demonstrate spiritual power similar to what Jesus had modeled. Peter heals a beggar who had been crippled from birth. The healing doesn't go unnoticed by Jewish religious leaders, who respond with persecution. The infant church is a model of unity and mutual sacrifice. The believers share all their possessions and continue to teach and heal. Their unity, however, is threatened. Opponents intensify their persecution, and the apostles are imprisoned and flogged. This, however, only strengthens Jesus' followers' faith. *ACTS 3:1–26; 4:1–22, 32–37; 5:12–42*

THE FIRST CASUALTY (6:1–8:40)

Discrimination is brewing against the followers of Jesus, which leads to the stoning of Stephen—the church's first martyr. Jesus had foretold His followers they would be His witnesses in Jerusalem, Judea, Samaria, and to the ends of the world. Until Stephen's death, the disciples had remained in Jerusalem with idyllic unity and a spirit of fellowship. Fulfilling Jesus' word, persecution drives them out of Jerusalem into the surrounding territories of Judea and Samaria. *ACTS 6:8–15; 7:44–60; 8:1–8*

THE CONVERSION OF SAUL (9:1–11:30)

The disciples speak boldly in the streets and temple courts—at the risk of arrest and imprisonment. Priests and Samaritans are among those added to the number of believers. The principal Christian persecutor, Saul, has a dramatic encounter with the risen Christ and becomes one of the foremost New Testament evangelists. Saul (Paul) begins his ministry and is chosen by God to go to the Gentiles. Peter explains to the Jewish believers that God gives the same gift of the Holy Spirit to the Gentiles and the Jews. He emphasizes that God does not show favoritism—anyone who believes in Jesus receives eternal life. *ACTS 9:1–19; 10:30–48; 11:15–18*

AD 10	AD 20	AD 30	AD 40	AD 50	AD 60	AD 70	AD 80	AD 90	AD 100
◆ 8 Jesus visits temple		◆ 30 Jesus raised	◆ 45 James written		◆ 60 Eph–Col	◆ 68 Paul & Peter martyred		◆ 90 Revelation	
◆ 5 Birth of Paul (?)		◆ 32 Stephen martyred		◆ 55 1 & 2 Corinthians	◆ 64 Rome burns	◆ 70 Temple destroyed			
	◆ 14 Tiberius (Rome)		◆ 37 Paul converts	◆ 57 Romans		◆ 65 1 Peter & 1 Timothy		◆ 85 1–3 John written	

The Promised Helper	The Church Is Formed	The First Casualty	The Conversion of Saul	Peter's Prison Break	First Missionary Journey and Jerusalem Council
1:1–2:47	3:1–5:42	6:1–8:40	9:1–11:30	12:1–13:52	14:1–15:35

PETER'S PRISON BREAK (12:1–13:52)

Problems and persecution are increasing for the church. While God continues to provide for some believers in miraculous ways, others are imprisoned and even killed for their beliefs. Herod throws Peter in prison, but an angel miraculously frees him. The church in Antioch begins to approach Gentiles with the good news of the Gospel. Its leaders commission Paul and Barnabas to travel, preach, and build up churches in various faraway places. They share the truth of the Gospel with the Gentiles throughout the entire region, despite the persecution they receive from the Jewish leaders. ⚱ ACTS 12:1–19; 13:1–3, 46–52

FIRST MISSIONARY JOURNEY AND JERUSALEM COUNCIL (14:1–15:35)

Paul and Barnabas take the Gospel into areas where it has not been heard. Resistance escalates into violent persecution in some places. Paul and Barnabas return to the church in Antioch. Believers are primarily Jewish, although Gentiles are continuing to be converted. The church makes big decisions that will affect the unity of Jews and Gentiles regarding salvation. Peter teaches that hearts are purified by faith, not by keeping the Law. Jews are saved in the same way as Gentiles: through the grace of Jesus. ⚱ ACTS 14:21–28; 15:1–35

A SECOND JOURNEY (15:36–17:34)

The church is now readily accepting Gentile believers. Paul and Barnabas, still in Antioch where many such converts live, have a heart to spread the good news about Jesus to non-Jews. When a disagreement keeps them from traveling together, they pair up with other people and double their outreach. Paul and his new traveling companion, Silas, prepare to revisit the churches previously ministered to, and the scope of their ministry widens considerably. God's Spirit directs them to travel south through Thessalonica, Berea, and Athens. Timothy and Luke join Paul and Barnabas. The disciples receive a different reception in each location. ⚱ ACTS 15:36–41; 17:1–34

90 BC	80 BC	70 BC	60 BC	50 BC	40 BC	30 BC	20 BC	10 BC	0 BC

◆ 65 Buddhism rises in China   ◆ 44 Julius Caesar assassinated   ◆ 2 Magi visit

◆ 63 Pompey conquers Jerusalem   ◆ 37 Herod the Great (Israel)

◆ 102 Chinese ships reach India   ◆ 51 Cleopatra VII reigns in Egypt   ◆ 31 Augustus (Rome)   ◆ 4 Jesus' birth

A Second Journey	Two New Jewish Friends	A Forlorn Farewell	Trouble in Jerusalem	Paul before the Sanhedrin	A Trial in Caesarea	On the Way to Rome
15:36–17:34	18:1–19:41	20:1–21:26	21:27–22:29	22:30–24:26	24:27–26:32	27:1–28:31

TWO NEW JEWISH FRIENDS (18:1–19:41)

Paul arrives in Corinth and meets a Jewish couple. Opposition rises from the Jews; in response to this, he will now preach to the Gentiles. The Lord encourages Paul in a vision, and Paul leaves Corinth with Aquila and Priscilla. He travels through Ephesus and Caesarea, then on to Antioch. As Paul works in Galatia and Phrygia, Apollos ministers in Ephesus with Aquila and Priscilla's help. Paul sends Timothy and Erastus to Macedonia while he heads to Jerusalem. Before he leaves, a riot breaks out; craftsmen whose idol sales are impacted by people's belief in Jesus are upset. ⏳ ACTS 18:1–6, 18–28; 19:8–41

A FORLORN FAREWELL (20:1–21:26)

In Ephesus, Paul desires to collect an offering for the Jerusalem church. He knows it is time to leave Ephesus, and he is sad; he may never see the Ephesians again. He leaves the Ephesians with an exhortation of the blessings of giving versus receiving. Although he has faced various hardships throughout his travels, Paul is warned specifically of trouble ahead if he continues in the direction he is going; he is not deterred. Upon arriving in Jerusalem, he is advised to join Christians and Jews in a purification rite. ⏳ ACTS 20:1–6, 13–24; 21:1–26

TROUBLE IN JERUSALEM (21:27–22:29)

In Jerusalem, Paul shares his exploits with church elders and hears how God has been active in Jerusalem. Trouble soon kicks in, however. Jews from Asia stir a riot against Paul, and he is arrested by a Roman commander. He is allowed to address the mob. He tells the people of his Jewish background and how he persecuted Christians and had a supernatural experience on the way to Damascus. The Jews are not appeased. The Romans find out Paul is a Roman citizen and refrain from flogging him. ⏳ ACTS 21:17–40; 22:1–29

PAUL BEFORE THE SANHEDRIN (22:30–24:26)

The Romans approach the Sanhedrin to help them figure out what to do about Paul; the council is divided over the situation. Jesus comforts Paul

AD 10	AD 20	AD 30	AD 40	AD 50	AD 60	AD 70	AD 80	AD 90	AD 100

◆ 8 Jesus visits temple ◆ 30 Jesus raised ◆ 45 James written ◆ 60 Eph–Col ◆ 68 Paul & Peter martyred ◆ 90 Revelation

◆ 5 Birth of Paul (?) ◆ 32 Stephen martyred ◆ 55 1 & 2 Corinthians ◆ 64 Rome burns ◆ 70 Temple destroyed

◆ 14 Tiberius (Rome) ◆ 37 Paul converts ◆ 57 Romans ◆ 65 1 Peter & 1 Timothy ◆ 85 1–3 John written

during the night in his sorrow, encouraging Paul that he will be protected. There is more work to be done in Rome. An elaborate plot is discovered that involves more than forty assassins ready to murder Paul. Roman soldiers escort Paul to Caesarea, where he is held in Herod's palace until his trial. Paul defends himself before Felix, the Roman governor of Judea. Felix keeps Paul under house arrest for two years with the hope of being offered a bribe in exchange for Paul's release. ⏳ *ACTS 22:30; 23:1–24; 24:1–16, 22–26*

A TRIAL IN CAESAREA (24:27–26:32)

Paul is still under house arrest in Caesarea. The case against him is weak, yet Felix the governor will not pardon him due to his attempt at endearing himself to his Jewish constituents. Felix loses his position, leaving his successor, Festus, with the problem of what to do with Paul. Festus asserts that Paul is crazy, but King Agrippa is almost persuaded to become a Christian. Agrippa sends Paul to Caesar. ⏳ *ACTS 24:27; 25:1–27; 26:9–32*

ON THE WAY TO ROME (27:1–28:31)

Paul is eager to go to Rome, and he begins his journey. Paul knows sailing is dangerous this time of year; it is past the Day of Atonement, or Feast of Yom Kippur, which is in late fall. Even so, the ship sets sail. Sure enough, a terrible storm forms. Paul encourages the crew, telling them of his recent visit from an angel, who promised that every person on the ship would safely make it to Rome. They experience a disastrous shipwreck, but every person reaches land. Paul lands on the island of Malta and survives a poisonous snakebite. The natives think he is some kind of god. Three months later, he sails for Rome. Paul speaks to Jewish leaders who say they have heard nothing bad about Paul. They desire to learn about Christ. Paul preaches to the Jews about the kingdom of God and Jesus. Some are convinced; others are not. Paul quotes Isaiah, saying those that don't believe have eyes that do not perceive and ears that do not understand. Paul proclaims that God's salvation has been sent to Gentiles who will listen. ⏳ *ACTS 28:1–31*

90 BC	80 BC	70 BC	60 BC	50 BC	40 BC	30 BC	20 BC	10 BC	0 BC

◆ 65 Buddhism rises in China ◆ 44 Julius Caesar assassinated ◆ 2 Magi visit

◆ 63 Pompey conquers Jerusalem ◆ 37 Herod the Great (Israel)

◆ 102 Chinese ships reach India ◆ 51 Cleopatra VII reigns in Egypt ◆ 31 Augustus (Rome) ◆ 4 Jesus' birth

The Righteousness of God	Justification by Faith Alone, before the Law	The Effect of Salvation	Life in the Spirit	Israel's Rejection	Israel's Unchanging Role in God's Plan of Redemption	The Believer's Place	Paul's Fellow Ministers
1:1–2:29	3:1–4:25	5:1–6:23	7:1–8:39	9:1–10:21	11:1–12:21	13:1–15:13	15:14–16:27

INTRODUCTION TO ROMANS

Author: Paul
Date Written: AD 57

The book of Romans is Paul's masterpiece, often called the "Constitution of the Bible." Written to Christians residing in the city of Rome, this letter describes privileges and freedoms that bring good news to the Gentiles, who come to God with little knowledge and no traditions, and also to the Jews, who have drifted away from genuine worship of God and have rejected Christ. God's love, mercy, and grace are abundant enough for everyone to experience His forgiveness. In Romans, Paul explains God's plan for salvation clearly and succinctly. Paul expresses Christian doctrine systematically but with heartfelt passion for his readers, many of whom he has never met. Chronologically, Romans is not Paul's earliest letter, but it is the first of his epistles in the New Testament.

Romans was written in AD 57, near the end of Paul's third missionary journey. Elements of the book, such as its vocabulary, style, logic, and theological development, are consistent with Paul's other writings and affirm his authorship. Traditionally, the Roman church was founded by Christians who had moved to Rome from churches Paul already established in Asia, Macedonia, and Greece; Paul had actually never been to Rome himself. He was, however, planning a visit to the Roman church on his way to Spain, and he writes this letter in anticipation of this future trip. Sadly, Paul only visits Rome as a prisoner.

The greatest and most evident theme in this epistle is the subject of the Gospel—God's sovereign plan of redemption. The book of Romans reveals the good

AD 10	AD 20	AD 30	AD 40	AD 50	AD 60	AD 70	AD 80	AD 90	AD 100

- 8 Jesus visits temple
- 30 Jesus raised
- 45 James written
- 60 Eph–Col
- 68 Paul & Peter martyred
- 90 Revelation
- 5 Birth of Paul (?)
- 32 Stephen martyred
- 55 1 & 2 Corinthians
- 64 Rome burns
- 70 Temple destroyed
- 14 Tiberius (Rome)
- 37 Paul converts
- 57 Romans
- 65 1 Peter & 1 Timothy
- 85 1–3 John written

The Righteousness of God	Justification by Faith Alone, before the Law	The Effect of Salvation	Life in the Spirit
1:1–2:29	3:1–4:25	5:1–6:23	7:1–8:39

news that both Jews and Gentiles are part of God's plan. God offers the gift of righteousness to anyone and everyone who comes to Jesus by faith. Through Romans, Paul builds believers up in the knowledge of God and in their faith, and he urges this mixed church of Jews and Gentiles to work together as one unified body. Both groups of people will be condemned by God if they choose not to believe in Christ. Conversely, both are justified, or declared righteous, by faith in Christ alone.

In Romans, Paul presents Jesus as the Second Adam, whose substitutionary death justifies all who believe. Through faith in Jesus, God's righteousness is imparted to human beings in the same way that Abraham was justified before God before the giving of the Mosaic Law. Paul teaches this is how Gentiles are able to come to God, without being required to be circumcised or observe all the Jewish dietary restrictions and feast days.

Construction for the Colosseum (Rome) began in AD 70.

90 BC	80 BC	70 BC	60 BC	50 BC	40 BC	30 BC	20 BC	10 BC	0 BC

◆ 65 Buddhism rises in China   ◆ 44 Julius Caesar assassinated   ◆ 2 Magi visit

◆ 63 Pompey conquers Jerusalem   ◆ 37 Herod the Great (Israel)

◆ 102 Chinese ships reach India   ◆ 51 Cleopatra VII reigns in Egypt ◆ 31 Augustus (Rome)   ◆ 4 Jesus' birth

Read Each 5-Minute Overview in Romans

THE RIGHTEOUSNESS OF GOD (1:1–2:29)

Paul writes his letter to the Romans before ever visiting Rome, yet his heartfelt concern for the believers there is evident throughout this epistle. Paul writes about the absence of righteousness in humankind. He later contrasts this with God's righteousness. When humans reject God, their behavior is reflected in how they respond to sinful desires and natural lusts. No law-abiding person—Jew or Gentile—is righteous enough on his or her own merit to avoid God's wrath. ⌛ ROMANS 1:18–32; 2:1–29

JUSTIFICATION BY FAITH ALONE, BEFORE THE LAW (3:1–4:25)

Paul continues his evaluation of Jewish religious beliefs. God's righteousness cannot be achieved by keeping the Law or by circumcision. Paul lays out the impossibility of achieving righteousness through works, but he follows

The Righteousness of God	Justification by Faith Alone, before the Law	The Effect of Salvation	Life in the Spirit
1:1–2:29	3:1–4:25	5:1–6:23	7:1–8:39

with the good news of God's plan that overcomes this problem. Salvation is by faith in Jesus alone; it does not require observance of the Mosaic Law or the sign of circumcision. Paul realizes many of his Jewish readers will find this hard to accept, so he uses an example of a man saved by faith alone, before the Law even existed: Abraham. ⧗ ROMANS 3:9–31; 4:1–25

THE EFFECT OF SALVATION (5:1–6:23)

A lengthy examination of the fruits of salvation—the effect salvation has on believers—is Paul's next item on his agenda. He writes of the doctrine of original sin and defines the root problem as the sinful human condition existing within everyone. Jesus died on the cross to reverse the problem of sin that Adam brought into the world, providing the possibility of new life and a right relationship with God. Paul wants to ensure his readers don't misapply what he has been saying. ⧗ ROMANS 5:1–21; 6:1–23

LIFE IN THE SPIRIT (7:1–8:39)

Paul has just taught that every person has a master. People are either slaves to sin or slaves to righteousness. Paul continues with that theme, discussing the subject of God's law and its purpose for the Christian. Once again,

90 BC	80 BC	70 BC	60 BC	50 BC	40 BC	30 BC	20 BC	10 BC	0 BC

• 65 Buddhism rises in China   • 44 Julius Caesar assassinated   • 2 Magi visit

• 63 Pompey conquers Jerusalem   • 37 Herod the Great (Israel)

• 102 Chinese ships reach India   • 51 Cleopatra VII reigns in Egypt   • 31 Augustus (Rome)   • 4 Jesus' birth

Israel's Rejection	Israel's Unchanging Role in God's Plan of Redemption	The Believer's Place	Paul's Fellow Ministers
9:1–10:21	11:1–12:21	13:1–15:13	15:14–16:27

Paul emphasizes justification by faith alone. He contrasts life in the Spirit versus life in the flesh. Life in the Spirit enables believers to live a triumphant life they would otherwise not be able to live, and Christ's glory will be revealed in them. ⌛ *ROMANS 7:1–25; 8:1–17, 28–30*

ISRAEL'S REJECTION (9:1–10:21)

Paul turns his attention to God's sovereignty concerning the salvation of Israel. The church is growing into an institution, and people are asking how God can be faithful to His promises if the majority of His chosen people—the Jews—are failing to respond to the Gospel. Paul uses familiar stories to remind believers of God's sovereign choices throughout their history. Israel missed the Messiah because it was according to God's sovereign plan. The prophets even foretold this rejection. Paul refers to the prophet Isaiah and God's right to choose a remnant from among Israel for His purpose. ⌛ *ROMANS 9:1–33; 10:16–21*

ISRAEL'S UNCHANGING ROLE IN GOD'S PLAN OF REDEMPTION (11:1–12:21)

Has God given up on the Jews for rejecting their Messiah? Paul knows the whole of Israel does not yet believe; yet a substantial remnant embraces the Gospel of Jesus Christ. God has a specific purpose to fulfill in allowing Israel to stumble: that salvation would come to the Gentiles. God's plan for Israel includes the nation's eventual restoration, but this present hardening is occurring in part until the fullness of the Gentiles comes about. Paul exhorts believers to be living sacrifices, resist conformity to the world, and embrace the transformation that comes in Jesus Christ. This is the awesome calling of their new life. ⌛ *ROMANS 11:1–36; 12:1–7*

Letters to early churches: How should we read the Epistles?
They include the books from Romans to Jude. The best way to read an epistle is to ask a few basic questions: (1) Who wrote the letter? (2) Who were the first readers? (3) Why was this letter written? (4) What did the author want the readers to do as a result of reading his letter?

AD 10	AD 20	AD 30	AD 40	AD 50	AD 60	AD 70	AD 80	AD 90	AD 100
◆ 8 Jesus visits temple		◆ 30 Jesus raised	◆ 45 James written		◆ 60 Eph–Col	◆ 68 Paul & Peter martyred		◆ 90 Revelation	
◆ 5 Birth of Paul (?)			◆ 32 Stephen martyred	◆ 55 1 & 2 Corinthians	◆ 64 Rome burns	◆ 70 Temple destroyed			
	◆ 14 Tiberius (Rome)		◆ 37 Paul converts	◆ 57 Romans	◆ 65 1 Peter & 1 Timothy		◆ 85 1–3 John written		

The Righteousness of God	Justification by Faith Alone, before the Law	The Effect of Salvation	Life in the Spirit	Israel's Rejection	Israel's Unchanging Role in God's Plan of Redemption	The Believer's Place	Paul's Fellow Ministers
1:1–2:29	3:1–4:25	5:1–6:23	7:1–8:39	9:1–10:21	11:1–12:21	13:1–15:13	15:14–16:27

THE BELIEVER'S PLACE (13:1–15:13)

Paul continues with his treatise on practical living and teaches believers to respect their governing authorities. Paul deals with conflicts that can arise between people who have different levels of spiritual maturity. What may seem completely appropriate to those in one group can appear wrong—if not outright sinful—to those in another. Paul exhorts followers of Christ to love one another, not pass judgment on others, and learn to respect one another's opinions. He quotes Isaiah, who prophesied of a day when Gentiles will hope in the Lord.
⌛ ROMANS 13:1–14; 14:13–23; 15:1–12

PAUL'S FELLOW MINISTERS (15:14–16:27)

Closing his letter, Paul shifts his attention to some personal matters, including another affirmation of his genuine concern for the believers in Rome. He acknowledges dozens of people who are working for God. Paul makes a point to affirm women who are working for the Lord. Paul warns against those who will divide or offend, and those who are internally selfish. Paul praises God and is confident everything will be done according to the Gospel and the preaching of Jesus Christ. ⌛ ROMANS 15:14–33; 16:17–25

Scaled model of ancient Rome

90 BC	80 BC	70 BC	60 BC	50 BC	40 BC	30 BC	20 BC	10 BC	0 BC

◆ 65 Buddhism rises in China   ◆ 44 Julius Caesar assassinated   ◆ 2 Magi visit

◆ 63 Pompey conquers Jerusalem   ◆ 37 Herod the Great (Israel)

◆ 102 Chinese ships reach India   ◆ 51 Cleopatra VII reigns in Egypt   ◆ 31 Augustus (Rome)   ◆ 4 Jesus' birth

True Wisdom from God	A Plea for Cooperation Rather Than Competition	Sin in the Church	Christian Freedom	Rights, Freedom, and Guidelines for Worship	The Proper Use of Spiritual Gifts—in Love	Resurrection, Expectation, Giving, and Greeting
1:1–2:16	3:1–4:21	5:1–6:20	7:1–8:13	9:1–11:34	12:1–14:40	15:1–16:24

INTRODUCTION TO
1 & 2 CORINTHIANS

Author: Paul
Date Written: AD 56

Corinth is a Roman colony and capital of the province of Achaia, with a population upwards of two hundred thousand free citizens and close to half a million slaves. The influential city, in existence since the Bronze Age, holds a less-than-stellar reputation. With the crowds and wealth come immorality, idolatry, paganism, and prostitution, and these issues are affecting the church. Paul writes two letters to the church in Corinth to address these and other problems.

In 1 Corinthians, written in AD 56, Paul confronts behavior that is destroying the Corinthian believers' testimony, and he calls the church to live with integrity. Though gifted and growing, the church faces a possibly dreadful situation if its members don't begin to apply Christian principles—as individuals and as a Christian community. Because of ongoing disputes within the church, Paul repeatedly challenges believers in 1 Corinthians to resolve conflicts, dissolve their factions, and let God's love rule in the church to unite the body. Paul emphasizes the work of the Holy Spirit in regard to spiritual gifts and the process of becoming holy as Jesus is holy. Readers should respond to what God has done through Jesus' death and resurrection by living their lives set apart for God.

Since Paul's first letter to the Corinthian church, false teachers are influencing the believers by labeling Paul as unqualified to be an apostle of Christ. They are eroding Paul's integrity and attracting followers from among the Corinthian

AD 10	AD 20	AD 30	AD 40	AD 50	AD 60	AD 70	AD 80	AD 90	AD 100

◆ 8 Jesus visits temple ◆ 30 Jesus raised ◆ 45 James written ◆ 60 Eph–Col ◆ 68 Paul & Peter martyred ◆ 90 Revelation

◆ 5 Birth of Paul (?) ◆ 32 Stephen martyred ◆ 55 1 & 2 Corinthians ◆ 64 Rome burns ◆ 70 Temple destroyed

◆ 14 Tiberius (Rome) ◆ 37 Paul converts ◆ 57 Romans ◆ 65 1 Peter & 1 Timothy ◆ 85 1–3 John written

True Wisdom from God	A Plea for Cooperation Rather Than Competition	Sin in the Church	Christian Freedom
1:1–2:16	3:1–4:21	5:1–6:20	7:1–8:13

Christians. Second Corinthians reveals the trials, tribulations, joys, and fulfillment that accompany Christian ministry through the lens of Paul's situation.

Writing from Macedonia in AD 56, Paul thanks and encourages those who have already repented of their rebellion. However, a good portion of 2 Corinthians is written to defend his ministry, credentials, and authority, and this becomes the main theme of the book. Paul shows his vulnerability and humanness; readers can identify with his personal sufferings and offense. Many regard 2 Corinthians as the most personal book in the New Testament. It is full of autobiographical material that reveals Paul's heart, character, motives, priorities, desires, and emotions more than any other letter.

In 2 Corinthians, Paul also contrasts the old and new covenants, exposes Satan's strategies, and gives a proper perspective on Christ's suffering. He describes the ministry of reconciliation and the double imputation of Christ, affirms separation from the ways of the world, and offers the most biblical perspective on Christian giving in all of scripture.

Ruins of the Temple of Apollo in ancient Corinth

90 BC	80 BC	70 BC	60 BC	50 BC	40 BC	30 BC	20 BC	10 BC	0 BC

◆ 65 Buddhism rises in China   ◆ 44 Julius Caesar assassinated

◆ 63 Pompey conquers Jerusalem   ◆ 37 Herod the Great (Israel)

◆ 102 Chinese ships reach India   ◆ 51 Cleopatra VII reigns in Egypt   ◆ 31 Augustus (Rome)

◆ 2 Magi visit

◆ 4 Jesus' birth

TRUE WISDOM FROM GOD (1:1–2:16)

Paul begins his letter to the Corinthians by addressing division among church members and wrong ways to respond to church leaders. He teaches about human wisdom versus the wisdom of God and warns against valuing one's own wisdom over the truth of the Gospel. Only the Holy Spirit knows the wisdom of God. *1 CORINTHIANS 1:10–31; 2:1–16*

A PLEA FOR COOPERATION RATHER THAN COMPETITION (3:1–4:21)

Paul appeals to the Corinthians to quit dividing into factions based on personal preference of church leadership. He speaks to the importance of individual commitment and work for God, and he challenges the Corinthians against boasting about human leaders. He also addresses church leaders, challenging them to put an end to jealousy and quarreling among church members. He gives

True Wisdom from God	A Plea for Cooperation Rather Than Competition	Sin in the Church	Christian Freedom
1:1–2:16	3:1–4:21	5:1–6:20	7:1–8:13

instruction to the church in how to properly respond to and support its leaders. ⧗ *1 CORINTHIANS 3:1–23; 4:1–21*

SIN IN THE CHURCH (5:1–6:20)

Now Paul cites a particularly offensive problem within the Corinthian church: sexual immorality. He is concerned that the sin is being taken too lightly and provides instructions for how to deal with it. Paul warns the congregation that a little sin influences the entire group; he is concerned about the purity of members of the church, especially leadership. He also addresses the issue of lawsuits. ⧗ *1 CORINTHIANS 5:1–13; 6:1–20*

CHRISTIAN FREEDOM (7:1–8:13)

Next Paul discusses the Corinthian believers' questions on marriage and singleness, rebuking improper attitudes and prescribing positive behavior. Another divisive problem in the church in Corinth is eating meat sacrificed to idols. Idols are nothing of substance, so Paul concludes it doesn't matter if believers eat meat sacrificed to them. However, what is most important is love toward those in God's family. Paul instructs believers to willingly forgo their Christian rights if by doing so they can prevent more immature believers from stumbling. ⧗ *1 CORINTHIANS 7:1–16, 39–40; 8:1–13*

RIGHTS, FREEDOM, AND GUIDELINES FOR WORSHIP (9:1–11:34)

Paul gives a personal example of how he has sacrificed his rights for the good of others, addressing some underlying resentment from a portion of the Corinthian church. He follows up on the issue of eating food sacrificed to idols,

---

Stumbling block: What can we learn from Paul's advice concerning meat sacrificed to idols?

When Paul advised the church in Corinth about meat sacrificed to idols, he shared an important lesson: Different people will be at different places with respect to their faith. Our freedom in Christ does not give us license to pursue what we want; it provides a way for us to serve others wherever they are in the cultivation of their conscience.

---

90 BC	80 BC	70 BC	60 BC	50 BC	40 BC	30 BC	20 BC	10 BC	0 BC

◆ 65 Buddhism rises in China   ◆ 44 Julius Caesar assassinated   ◆ 2 Magi visit

◆ 63 Pompey conquers Jerusalem   ◆ 37 Herod the Great (Israel)

◆ 102 Chinese ships reach India   ◆ 51 Cleopatra VII reigns in Egypt   ◆ 31 Augustus (Rome)   ◆ 4 Jesus' birth

Rights, Freedom, and Guidelines for Worship	The Proper Use of Spiritual Gifts—in Love	Resurrection, Expectation, Giving, and Greeting
9:1–11:34	12:1–14:40	15:1–16:24

encouraging believers to avoid anything that might create spiritual difficulties for immature and growing Christians. He provides an extensive argument for voluntarily suspending the exercise of Christian freedom for the good of others, but he warns against taking too much pride in that freedom. He next addresses gender issues and also provides clear instructions for how to observe the Lord's Supper.
⧗ *1 CORINTHIANS 9:1–23; 10:23–33; 11:23–32*

THE PROPER USE OF SPIRITUAL GIFTS— IN LOVE (12:1–14:40)

Paul addresses some women who are disrupting worship services with the way they pray and prophesy. He also deals with abominable ways church members are demeaning the Lord's Supper. He turns his attention to the topic of spiritual gifts. Paul scolds the Corinthians for arguing over spiritual gifts, which are meant to bring people closer together instead of dividing the church. He offers a definition of love and challenges believers to exercise the gifts given to them out of love for the benefit of the church as a whole. He also provides some specific guidelines for how spiritual gifts should be properly used in a church context.
⧗ *1 CORINTHIANS 12:1–11; 13:1–13; 14:26–40*

RESURRECTION, EXPECTATION, GIVING, AND GREETING (15:1–16:24)

Paul turns the Corinthians' attention to the future. Some Corinthian believers were claiming that there would be no resurrection of the body. Paul responds by affirming both the certainty of Christ's bodily resurrection and the centrality of the resurrection. He also discusses the nature of believers' glorified bodies and gives guidelines concerning the collection of money. Paul wraps up his lengthy letter to the Corinthians with personal greetings and a few final requests. ⧗ *1 CORINTHIANS 15:12–58; 16:1–3*

AD 10	AD 20	AD 30	AD 40	AD 50	AD 60	AD 70	AD 80	AD 90	AD 100
		✦ 8 Jesus visits temple	✦ 30 Jesus raised	✦ 45 James written	✦ 60 Eph–Col	✦ 68 Paul & Peter martyred		✦ 90 Revelation	
✦ 5 Birth of Paul (?)		✦ 32 Stephen martyred	✦ 55 1 & 2 Corinthians	✦ 64 Rome burns	✦ 70 Temple destroyed				
	✦ 14 Tiberius (Rome)	✦ 37 Paul converts	✦ 57 Romans	✦ 65 1 Peter & 1 Timothy		✦ 85 1–3 John written			

MATT	MARK	LUKE

(spines shown: MATT, MARK, LUKE, JOHN, ACTS, ROM, 1 COR, 2 COR, GAL, EPH, PHIL, COL, 1 THESS, 2 THESS)

Setting the Record Straight	New Creations, New Attitudes, and Generous Giving
1:1–4:18	5:1–9:15

Read Each 5-Minute Overview in 2 Corinthians

○ 1:1–4:18	Setting the Record Straight	Page 212
○ 5:1–9:15	New Creations, New Attitudes, and Generous Giving	Page 212
○ 10:1–13:14	Inexpressible Glory and Unavoidable Thorns	Page 213

SETTING THE RECORD STRAIGHT (1:1–4:18)

Paul writes this second letter to the Corinthians out of trials and suffering, but with a heart filled with joy. He describes his reconnection with Titus after sending his first letter to the church. He learns the Corinthian believers have repented, and he breaks into joyful praise to God. Paul launches into an extended discussion of the joys and victory of the Christian ministry, reminding the believers they are ministers of a new covenant: The Holy Spirit completes and fulfills the work of the written Law in their hearts. Paul also makes reference to those who do not respond to the Gospel. ⌛ *2 CORINTHIANS 1:3–7; 3:4–18; 4:1–18*

NEW CREATIONS, NEW ATTITUDES, AND GENEROUS GIVING (5:1–9:15)

Some Corinthians actively oppose Paul's authority. He defends himself and his ministry while addressing his concerns for genuine believers. Human life is fleeting, and Paul turns his readers' attention to eternal things yet to come. Trials are hard on earth, but God has given the Holy Spirit as a guarantee of the hope to come in heaven. Jesus' resurrection gives new life. Paul is concerned at how his first letter was received, but he takes comfort in knowing that the sorrow he produced in the Corinthians' hearts led to repentance. Therefore, he does not regret sending the letter. Titus is refreshed after visiting the Corinthians and seeing

NAVIGATING THE BIBLE

212

90 BC	80 BC	70 BC	60 BC	50 BC	40 BC	30 BC	20 BC	10 BC	0 BC

◆ 65 Buddhism rises in China ◆ 44 Julius Caesar assassinated ◆ 2 Magi visit

◆ 63 Pompey conquers Jerusalem ◆ 37 Herod the Great (Israel)

◆ 102 Chinese ships reach India ◆ 51 Cleopatra VII reigns in Egypt ◆ 31 Augustus (Rome) ◆ 4 Jesus' birth

their changed hearts and attitudes. Paul encourages believers to get rid of and continually cleanse themselves of evil. He encourages generous giving motivated from the heart, and he lists the benefits of giving. ⧖ *2 CORINTHIANS 5:11–21; 6:1–18, 7:1; 9:6–15*

 INEXPRESSIBLE GLORY AND UNAVOIDABLE THORNS (10:1–13:14)

Paul exhorts believers to battle carnal thinking and allow the Spirit to renew their minds. He defends himself more emphatically against his critics, letting his readers know he feels no shame or regret for his methods or other aspects of his ministry. Paul turns up the heat in his defense against the accusations of his critics, coming on stronger as he boasts in what God has done through him. As he closes the letter, he provides some additional proof of the authenticity of his ministry. He expresses his credentials and compares himself to the friend of the bridegroom, who presents the bride, pure and chaste, to her husband on her wedding day. He tells of a chronic "thorn," or ailment, he has, and he points out God's sufficiency in meeting his every need in spite of it. ⧖ *2 CORINTHIANS 10:1–18; 11:1–16; 12:1–10*

Ruins in Corinth

2 CORINTHIANS

213

◆ 8 Jesus visits temple   ◆ 30 Jesus raised   ◆ 45 James written   ◆ 60 Eph–Col ◆ 68 Paul & Peter martyred ◆ 90 Revelation

◆ 5 Birth of Paul (?)   ◆ 32 Stephen martyred   ◆ 55 1 & 2 Corinthians ◆ 64 Rome burns   ◆ 70 Temple destroyed

◆ 14 Tiberius (Rome)   ◆ 37 Paul converts   ◆ 57 Romans   ◆ 65 1 Peter & 1 Timothy   ◆ 85 1–3 John written

INTRODUCTION TO GALATIANS AND EPHESIANS

Author: Paul
Date Written: AD 52–62

Galatians and Ephesians are powerful letters written by Paul and much-loved contributions to the Bible.

After establishing a number of churches in Galatia and leaving them standing firm and healthy, Paul receives word that Gentile believers are being taught to add traditional Jewish beliefs and practices, such as circumcision, to their newfound faith. Paul writes this letter to circulate through the churches and call the believers back to the truth of the Gospel of Christ.

Paul declares blessing comes from God not on the basis of the Law but through faith. The Law declares people guilty, bringing them to a place of bondage; faith sets people free, bringing liberty. Faith alone brings justification before God—the clear theme of this urgent and corrective book. New liberty, however, is not a license to keep sinning; the power of the Holy Spirit enables the Christian to live a changed, Spirit-led life that produces the fruits of righteousness.

Paul's letter to the Ephesians, which he addresses primarily to Gentile believers, does not rebuke a specific false doctrine or conflict within the church, as most of Paul's other epistles do. Instead, it seems Paul thinks his readers need to receive exhortation to pursue unity and a distinctively Christian ethic.

Ephesians speaks of Paul as in prison, which is usually taken to refer to his imprisonment in Rome toward the end of his life. This would date the letter in the early 60s. If this is so, Paul would have experienced a long, strenuous journey, including

90 BC	80 BC	70 BC	60 BC	50 BC	40 BC	30 BC	20 BC	10 BC	0 BC
			✦ 65 Buddhism rises in China		✦ 44 Julius Caesar assassinated				✦ 2 Magi visit
			✦ 63 Pompey conquers Jerusalem		✦ 37 Herod the Great (Israel)				
✦ 102 Chinese ships reach India			✦ 51 Cleopatra VII reigns in Egypt		✦ 31 Augustus (Rome)				✦ 4 Jesus' birth

True Freedom and Fruit	Doing Good without Becoming Weary
5:1–26	6:1–18

a false arrest in Jerusalem, a series of trials and imprisonment for more than two years, a traumatic shipwreck on the way to Rome, and the current uncertainty of what would happen to him as he awaits trial. Yet his letter is filled with enthusiasm, faith, and confidence. His letter makes it clear that all believers—Jew or Gentile—are fully reconciled to God and are entitled to every spiritual blessing God offers.

Paul focuses on the Trinity—of God the Father, Jesus Christ the Son, and the Holy Spirit—and also speaks of the "mystery of Christ," a mystery long hidden that can now be understood: Jews and Gentiles are one in Christ. Paul also regularly shifts his readers' attention from their personal, earthly concerns to the spiritual conflict they are involved in. Providing both a theological basis for how to live and practical applications for what to do, Paul's overall intent is to build up the body of Christ.

Ruins of the library in Ephesus

AD 10	AD 20	AD 30	AD 40	AD 50	AD 60	AD 70	AD 80	AD 90	AD 100
✦ 8 Jesus visits temple		✦ 30 Jesus raised	✦ 45 James written		✦ 60 Eph–Col	✦ 68 Paul & Peter martyred		✦ 90 Revelation	
✦ 5 Birth of Paul (?)		✦ 32 Stephen martyred		✦ 55 1 & 2 Corinthians	✦ 64 Rome burns	✦ 70 Temple destroyed			
✦ 14 Tiberius (Rome)		✦ 37 Paul converts		✦ 57 Romans		✦ 65 1 Peter & 1 Timothy	✦ 85 1–3 John written		

The Counterfeit Threat	A Closer Look at the Law
1:1–2:21	3:1–4:31

Read Each 5-Minute Overview in Galatians

○ 1:1–2:21	The Counterfeit Threat	Page 216
○ 3:1–4:31	A Closer Look at the Law	Page 216
○ 5:1–26	True Freedom and Fruit	Page 217
○ 6:1–18	Doing Good without Becoming Weary	Page 217

THE COUNTERFEIT THREAT (1:1–2:21)

Paul's letter to the Galatian churches contains a sense of urgency; they are turning to a gospel other than the Gospel of Christ. Paul's critics are accusing him of being out of step with the Jerusalem apostles. However, Paul refutes these claims; he has had enough contact with the apostles in Jerusalem to be in perfect agreement. He describes a second trip to Jerusalem and claims God told him to go. Paul explains his confrontation with Peter concerning Peter's hypocritical, inconsistent attitude in relationship to the Law and the Gentiles. ⌛ GALATIANS 1:1–24; 2:1–21

A CLOSER LOOK AT THE LAW (3:1–4:31)

Salvation is by grace through faith alone and the only true gospel; Paul demonstrates this truth using a biblical, theological argument. Paul teaches that these concepts are not new; they would be evident to anyone who was familiar with the Law and the Prophets. The Gospel has always been the promise of righteousness before God through faith in Christ—Abraham's seed. Justification has never been about good works or obedience to the Law. Paul contrasts slavery to the Law versus freedom, using two well-known figures from the Old Testament scriptures as examples. ⌛ GALATIANS 3:1–25; 4:21–31

90 BC	80 BC	70 BC	60 BC	50 BC	40 BC	30 BC	20 BC	10 BC	0 BC

◆ 65 Buddhism rises in China   ◆ 44 Julius Caesar assassinated   ◆ 2 Magi visit

◆ 63 Pompey conquers Jerusalem   ◆ 37 Herod the Great (Israel)

◆ 102 Chinese ships reach India   ◆ 51 Cleopatra VII reigns in Egypt   ◆ 31 Augustus (Rome)   ◆ 4 Jesus' birth

True Freedom and Fruit	Doing Good without Becoming Weary
5:1–26	6:1–18

TRUE FREEDOM AND FRUIT (5:1–26)

Paul continues refuting the restrictive and destructive philosophies of the Judaizers, calling believers to a freedom only Christ can provide. He warns against the dangers of legalism that can corrupt the whole body of Christ, like yeast in a lump of dough. He also explains how the Holy Spirit influences lives of believers to produce fruit—something no law can possibly countermand or contradict. Believers should use their liberty in Christ to live holy lives, love others, and overcome works of the flesh. ⌛ *GALATIANS 5:1–26*

DOING GOOD WITHOUT BECOMING WEARY (6:1–18)

The power of sin and the grip it can have on people is a sobering reality. Paul provides practical advice for how to deal with sin existing in the church. Believers are personally responsible in helping restore other believers in the church, fulfilling the law of Christ to love one another by bearing each other's burdens. Believers also need to examine their hearts to make sure they are not falling into pride. Using the imagery of sowing and reaping, Paul encourages his readers to carefully manage the resources God has given and patiently wait for results. ⌛ *GALATIANS 6:1–18*

GALATIANS

The All–Sufficiency of Christ	Revealed Mystery
1:1–2:22	3:1–21

Read Each 5-Minute Overview in Ephesians

THE ALL-SUFFICIENCY OF CHRIST (1:1–2:22)

In this letter to the Ephesian church, Paul does not address specific problem areas but rather directs his readers toward the things God has done for them and how they should respond. After a magnificent opening section reminding his readers of the work of God the Father, Jesus Christ, and the Holy Spirit, Paul assesses the Ephesian believers, explaining how they came to connect with such a holy God. He speaks of redemption, which implies a price being paid for the freedom that is purchased. He also describes their salvation and transformation in terms of a move from death to life, with a resulting warm and confident relationship with the Father. ⚒ *EPHESIANS 1:3–23; 2:1–22*

REVEALED MYSTERY (3:1–21)

Through Jesus, God has brought Jews and Gentiles together into one body. Paul's thoughts turn to the mystery of God that had become much clearer in light of the life, death, and resurrection of Jesus. Paul turns from theological issues to ethics and the Christian walk. His hope is to make plain and understandable to everyone this mystery that was once hidden but is now revealed. Paul prays for the Ephesians, for power to grasp the magnitude of Christ, and to know His love. ⚒ *EPHESIANS 3:1–21*

90 BC	80 BC	70 BC	60 BC	50 BC	40 BC	30 BC	20 BC	10 BC	0 BC

◆ 65 Buddhism rises in China   ◆ 44 Julius Caesar assassinated   ◆ 2 Magi visit

◆ 63 Pompey conquers Jerusalem   ◆ 37 Herod the Great (Israel)

◆ 102 Chinese ships reach India   ◆ 51 Cleopatra VII reigns in Egypt ◆ 31 Augustus (Rome)   ◆ 4 Jesus' birth

Unity in the Faith	Living Carefully and Standing Firm
4:1–32	5:1–6:24

UNITY IN THE FAITH (4:1–32)

Now that he has shown what God has done on behalf of believers, Paul addresses practical ways in which believers should respond. He describes the character of a follower of Christ and what unity in the church should look like. He also describes how to live as children of the light. Believers are to speak truth, be guarded against sinning out of anger, and control their speech. In the same way Christ forgave and showed compassion to them, they are to forgive and show compassion to others. ⏳ *EPHESIANS 4:1–32*

LIVING CAREFULLY AND STANDING FIRM (5:1–6:24)

Paul continues his instruction concerning daily living and includes guidelines for sexual propriety, speech, drinking, and marriage, as well as instructions for parents and children, slaves and masters. The perfect model for all these relationships is Christ. Spirit-filled believers should imitate Jesus and walk in the light, with worshipful, grateful, and submissive hearts. All Christians are engaged in spiritual warfare; Paul exhorts them to stand firm and emerge victoriously. ⏳ *EPHESIANS 5:1–6:24*

A statue of the goddess Nike found in Ephesus

AD 10	AD 20	AD 30	AD 40	AD 50	AD 60	AD 70	AD 80	AD 90	AD 100
✦ 8 Jesus visits temple		✦ 30 Jesus raised		✦ 45 James written		✦ 60 Eph–Col	✦ 68 Paul & Peter martyred		✦ 90 Revelation
✦ 5 Birth of Paul (?)			✦ 32 Stephen martyred		✦ 55 1 & 2 Corinthians	✦ 64 Rome burns		✦ 70 Temple destroyed	
	✦ 14 Tiberius (Rome)		✦ 37 Paul converts		✦ 57 Romans		✦ 65 1 Peter & 1 Timothy		✦ 85 1–3 John written

INTRODUCTION TO PHILIPPIANS AND COLOSSIANS

Author: Paul
Date Written: AD 60–62

The apostle Paul is the author of both letters to the Philippian and the Colossian churches, but some scholars speculate that Paul's very warm and tender relationship with the Philippian church indicates it was perhaps his favorite. In his letter to the church in Philippi, he expresses joyful gratitude against the striking background of the prison he is writing from. Paul writes about the peace, joy, and contentment he finds in Christ, no matter what his situation or circumstances.

The church at Philippi is the first church Paul begins in Macedonia, making Philippi the birthplace of European Christianity. Paul reminds the Philippians they are partners in ministry and fellow sufferers in Christ. He urges them to live a lifestyle of unity, holiness, and joy; living this way is only possible in Christ. Paul recognizes a growing problem of disunity in the Philippian church and through this letter seeks to correct it before it becomes worse.

Paul's letter to the Colossian church has been called the most Christ-centered book of the Bible, presenting Jesus as the Savior, the Creator, and the Sustainer of the universe—the total solution for humanity's needs, both for time and eternity. Paul's purpose in Colossians is to show that Christ is first and foremost in everything—He is sufficient for every spiritual and practical need the Christian will ever have.

90 BC	80 BC	70 BC	60 BC	50 BC	40 BC	30 BC	20 BC	10 BC	0 BC

◆ 65 Buddhism rises in China ◆ 44 Julius Caesar assassinated ◆ 2 Magi visit

◆ 63 Pompey conquers Jerusalem ◆ 37 Herod the Great (Israel)

◆ 102 Chinese ships reach India ◆ 51 Cleopatra VII reigns in Egypt ◆ 31 Augustus (Rome) ◆ 4 Jesus' birth

	Walking the Christian Walk
	4:1–23

Though small, Colossae in Paul's day is a cosmopolitan city with many different cultural and religious elements. Though the population is significantly Jewish, the epistle suggests the church is primarily Gentile; Colossians does not reference the Old Testament often, and there is almost no reference to the reconciliation of Jews and Gentiles.

Several years after the church in Colossae is established, around AD 61–62, Epaphras visits Paul and brings good news regarding the Colossian congregation. His primary purpose, however, is to solicit Paul's help against a certain heresy affecting the Colossian church: a religious system that combined elements from Greek speculation, Jewish legalism, and Oriental mysticism. Paul writes this letter to counter this false teaching. He expresses his personal interest in the people and warns them against reverting to their old pagan ways.

The overriding themes throughout the book of Colossians are the supremacy of Christ and the power of the Gospel message. Christ has all the treasures of wisdom and knowledge; there is no need for speculation, mystical visions, or ritualistic regulations as though faith in Christ is not enough.

PHILIPPIANS

Archaeological area of ancient Philippi, Greece

AD 10	AD 20	AD 30	AD 40	AD 50	AD 60	AD 70	AD 80	AD 90	AD 100
		♦ 8 Jesus visits temple	♦ 30 Jesus raised	♦ 45 James written	♦ 60 Eph–Col	♦ 68 Paul & Peter martyred		♦ 90 Revelation	
♦ 5 Birth of Paul (?)			♦ 32 Stephen martyred	♦ 55 1 & 2 Corinthians	♦ 64 Rome burns	♦ 70 Temple destroyed			
	♦ 14 Tiberius (Rome)		♦ 37 Paul converts	♦ 57 Romans	♦ 65 1 Peter & 1 Timothy		♦ 85 1–3 John written		

| MATT | MARK | LUKE | JOHN | ACTS | ROM | 1 COR | 2 COR | GAL | EPH | PHIL | COL | 1 THESS | 2 THESS |

Opening Words and Family Business	Knowing Christ, the Goal of Life
1:1–2:30	3:1–21

Read Each 5-Minute Overview in Philippians

○ 1:1–2:30	Opening Words and Family Business	Page 222
○ 3:1–21	Knowing Christ, the Goal of Life	Page 222
○ 4:1–23	Walking the Christian Walk	Page 223

OPENING WORDS AND FAMILY BUSINESS (1:1–2:30)

Paul opens his letter to the Philippian church with heartfelt words of gratitude and rich blessings. He introduces the main theme of Philippians: joy and partnership in the Gospel. Even though Paul is in prison, the Gospel is being furthered. He provides encouragement, acknowledging their special relationship, and prays for them. He is thankful for them, confident in them, and affirms his genuine love for them as co-laborers for Christ. He asks God to give the Philippians discernment and enduring righteousness. It is important to be one in spirit and purpose, to esteem others better than themselves, and to live humble lives as Christ humbled Himself in obedience to God—even to death. Paul looks forward to the day when Jesus will be exalted and every person on earth will confess His lordship. Paul then gives practical ways the Philippians can live out his exhortation. ⌛ *PHILIPPIANS 1:1–18; 2:1–18*

KNOWING CHRIST, THE GOAL OF LIFE (3:1–21)

Paul calls the Philippians to watch out for Jews who are seeking to add requirements to salvation. Those with circumcised hearts do not put their confidence in anything they can do in an effort to achieve salvation. Paul lists his credentials as a Jewish man but tells how they are worthless to him—he counts them as loss for the sake of knowing Christ, his ultimate goal in life.

90 BC	80 BC	70 BC	60 BC	50 BC	40 BC	30 BC	20 BC	10 BC	0 BC

◆ 65 Buddhism rises in China   ◆ 44 Julius Caesar assassinated   ◆ 2 Magi visit

◆ 63 Pompey conquers Jerusalem   ◆ 37 Herod the Great (Israel)

◆ 102 Chinese ships reach India   ◆ 51 Cleopatra VII reigns in Egypt ◆ 31 Augustus (Rome)   ◆ 4 Jesus' birth

Paul realizes that he has not fully arrived, and he encourages the Philippians to press on, too, as they move toward the goal of Christ. Paul looks forward to a time when Jesus will transform his and all believers' bodies to be like His glorious body. Paul gives examples of what the Christian walk should look like; Christians should be so marked by their heavenly citizenship that their lives look distinctly different from the world. ⌛ *PHILIPPIANS 3:1–21*

WALKING THE CHRISTIAN WALK (4:1–23)

Paul repeats the theme of rejoicing in the Lord in spite of hard circumstances, and he gives more instruction on walking the Christian walk. He encourages a prayerful and thankful life, and describes unexplainable peace for those who trust God. Paul is thankful for the gifts the Philippians have given him, referring to them as "an acceptable sacrifice, pleasing to God." Paul prays that God will provide everything the Philippians need. ⌛ *PHILIPPIANS 4:1–23*

PHILIPPIANS

The amphitheater of Philippi was home to races and competitions familiar to Paul's readers.

AD 10	AD 20	AD 30	AD 40	AD 50	AD 60	AD 70	AD 80	AD 90	AD 100
		✦ 8 Jesus visits temple		✦ 30 Jesus raised	✦ 45 James written	✦ 60 Eph–Col	✦ 68 Paul & Peter martyred	✦ 90 Revelation	
✦ 5 Birth of Paul (?)			✦ 32 Stephen martyred	✦ 55 1&2 Corinthians	✦ 64 Rome burns	✦ 70 Temple destroyed			
	✦ 14 Tiberius (Rome)		✦ 37 Paul converts	✦ 57 Romans	✦ 65 1 Peter & 1 Timothy	✦ 85 1–3 John written			

The Person and Work of Jesus	Standing Firm against False Teachers and Legalism
1:1–2:3	2:4–23

Read Each 5-Minute Overview in Colossians

THE PERSON AND WORK OF JESUS (1:1–2:3)

The apostle Paul identifies himself as the author of Colossians, along with his associate Timothy. He identifies his recipients and follows with a brief greeting. Paul is preparing the Colossian readers for words of warning and the exhortations that will follow. He encourages the Colossian believers with his love for them and constant prayer. He also expresses heartfelt thankfulness for their faith and love for the saints, which has resulted in the spread of the Gospel throughout the Roman Empire. Paul reflects on the person of Christ and how Jesus has changed the Colossian believers' lives. ⏳ *COLOSSIANS 1:1–29; 2:1–3*

STANDING FIRM AGAINST FALSE TEACHERS AND LEGALISM (2:4–23)

Dangerous false teachers are deceiving believers with hollow philosophies and traditions. Paul encourages the believers in Colossae to stand firm, and he reminds them of the person and work of Christ. Followers of Jesus are complete in Him. They don't need to add anything to their faith or be circum-

90 BC	80 BC	70 BC	60 BC	50 BC	40 BC	30 BC	20 BC	10 BC	0 BC

• 65 Buddhism rises in China • 44 Julius Caesar assassinated • 2 Magi visit

• 63 Pompey conquers Jerusalem • 37 Herod the Great (Israel)

• 102 Chinese ships reach India • 51 Cleopatra VII reigns in Egypt • 31 Augustus (Rome) • 4 Jesus' birth

Dead to Sin and Alive in Christ	Make Jesus Known to the World
3:1–4:1	4:2–18

cised, as this falls into legalism. However, Paul encourages the Colossians to progress in their faith. He sets forth the means of their protection: living in Christ. ⌛ *COLOSSIANS 2:4–23*

DEAD TO SIN AND ALIVE IN CHRIST (3:1–4:1)

Paul shifts gears from the negative to the positive. He tells the Colossian believers how they are to experience true spirituality in this world. Rather than subjecting themselves to the bondage of false teachers, they are to understand who they are in Christ and experience true freedom with that knowledge. Instead of thinking that the flesh must be contained by human philosophy, religious legalism, or spiritual mysticism, they are to understand that in Christ, their human tendency to sin has been killed on the cross. They must think of themselves as dead to sin and alive in Christ. ⌛ *COLOSSIANS 3:1–25; 4:1*

MAKE JESUS KNOWN TO THE WORLD (4:2–18)

Encouraging the believers in Colossae about being raised up in Christ, Paul draws their attention outward to their responsibility to make Christ known to the world—by praying for those who are actively involved in sharing the Gospel and living out the life of Christ and sharing the Gospel in love. They are to be witnesses within the church and outside the church as well. Paul desires to see the Colossians as active participants in the progress of the Gospel through responding to the issues and questions of the world. He gives instruction for passing along the message of the letter, and he asks them to remember him, as he is still in prison. ⌛ *COLOSSIANS 4:2–18*

Anatomy of an epistle: How are the New Testament letters structured?
When you read the Epistles, you may notice they often follow a similar pattern. This pattern was fairly typical for letters written in this day. Observing their structure can help you understand their meaning better. Typically an epistle will have five main sections: (1) a greeting to the people; (2) a prayer or word of praise about what God is doing or has done; (3) the body of the letter—where teaching is given, actions are corrected, or advice is offered; (4) a summary of the main point of the letter; (5) personal greetings and a word of conclusion.

AD 10	AD 20	AD 30	AD 40	AD 50	AD 60	AD 70	AD 80	AD 90	AD 100

◆ 8 Jesus visits temple ◆ 30 Jesus raised ◆ 45 James written ◆ 60 Eph–Col ◆ 68 Paul & Peter martyred ◆ 90 Revelation

◆ 5 Birth of Paul (?) ◆ 32 Stephen martyred ◆ 55 1 & 2 Corinthians ◆ 64 Rome burns ◆ 70 Temple destroyed

◆ 14 Tiberius (Rome) ◆ 37 Paul converts ◆ 57 Romans ◆ 65 1 Peter & 1 Timothy ◆ 85 1–3 John written

Faith That Inspires Others	Encouragement in Suffering
1:1–2:20	3:1–13

INTRODUCTION TO
1 & 2 THESSALONIANS

Author: Paul
Date Written: AD 51–52

These two letters written by Paul to the Thessalonian church, Jesus' Olivet discourse in Matthew 24 and 25, and the book of Revelation form the three major prophetic texts of the New Testament. They affirm doctrine that seems to have already become settled truth in Paul's day. The return of Christ is mentioned more times in these writings than any other doctrine.

Written to a predominantly Gentile church of new converts, 1 Thessalonians provides all the basic requirements for holy living. The theme of the epistle is the salvation and sanctification of the Thessalonian believers. Paul expresses his thanksgiving for their faith and love, defends himself against slanderous attacks originating from Jewish opposition, reminds the believers of his conduct and motive while he was with them, and exhorts them to resist the temptations of moral impurity and lazy behavior. He also addresses a big doctrinal issue: the second coming of Christ. He comforts the Thessalonian believers with the revelation that those who trust Jesus and are alive when He returns will have no advantage over those who have already died, since both groups will meet the Lord in the air.

The shortest of Paul's nine letters to various churches, 2 Thessalonians picks up where 1 Thessalonians leaves off, in AD 51. As such, it deals with many of the same concerns as 1 Thessalonians. Some Christians are not responding to Paul's corrections in the first epistle, so the tone of 2 Thessalonians is more urgent.

90 BC	80 BC	70 BC	60 BC	50 BC	40 BC	30 BC	20 BC	10 BC	0 BC

◆ 65 Buddhism rises in China   ◆ 44 Julius Caesar assassinated   ◆ 2 Magi visit

◆ 63 Pompey conquers Jerusalem   ◆ 37 Herod the Great (Israel)

◆ 102 Chinese ships reach India   ◆ 51 Cleopatra VII reigns in Egypt ◆ 31 Augustus (Rome)   ◆ 4 Jesus' birth

Holy Living	Living in Expectation of Christ's Return
4:1–18	5:1–28

One of Paul's primary purposes in this letter is to encourage the Thessalonian believers to press on in the midst of intense persecution. Paul applauds their continued growth in faith and love, and he urges them to endure persecution in the knowledge that one day God will vindicate His name. This second letter also corrects false teachings about the return of the Lord. Some are claiming the second coming of Christ has already occurred, causing dissention among Thessalonian believers who are confused as to when the "day of the Lord" will take place. Assuming the end is at hand, some believers are abandoning their work and living off others. Paul makes it very clear that this day has not occurred yet, and he recounts events that must first take place. Paul rebukes their idleness and sternly tells the Thessalonian believers to continue contending for the faith until the Lord returns.

Thessalonica is a port city in modern-day Turkey.

AD 10	AD 20	AD 30	AD 40	AD 50	AD 60	AD 70	AD 80	AD 90	AD 100

◆ 8 Jesus visits temple ◆ 30 Jesus raised ◆ 45 James written ◆ 60 Eph–Col ◆ 68 Paul & Peter martyred ◆ 90 Revelation

◆ 5 Birth of Paul (?) ◆ 32 Stephen martyred ◆ 55 1 & 2 Corinthians ◆ 64 Rome burns ◆ 70 Temple destroyed

◆ 14 Tiberius (Rome) ◆ 37 Paul converts ◆ 57 Romans ◆ 65 1 Peter & 1 Timothy ◆ 85 1–3 John written

Faith that Inspires Others	Encouragement in Suffering
1:1–2:20	3:1–13

Read Each 5-Minute Overview in 1 Thessalonians

FAITH THAT INSPIRES OTHERS (1:1–2:20)

Hearing of persecution and suffering in the church in Thessalonica, Paul writes to encourage believers. He is full of genuine praise for the Thessalonians, who through enduring difficult times are setting an example that other churches are noticing. Theirs is a faith that is helping others grow stronger. Paul recalls his personal experiences in Thessalonica, comparing himself to both a loving mother and a concerned father. Paul is thankful for how the Thessalonians welcomed the Gospel as God's message, not man's, and commends the church for remaining steadfast in suffering. ⏳ *1 THESSALONIANS 1:1–10; 2:1–20*

ENCOURAGEMENT IN SUFFERING (3:1–13)

Setting straight the false insinuations of his opponents, Paul continues to express personal concern for the Thessalonian believers. He cares so much for their spiritual health that he sends Timothy to establish and encourage them, knowing Satan would tempt them in their suffering to give up on God. As their spiritual parent, he wants to see their faith continue to develop. Paul rejoices over Timothy's message affirming the ongoing faithfulness of the Thessalonian believers, and he expresses deep thanksgiving for the church. He encourages the believers to increase and abound in love. ⏳ *1 THESSALONIANS 3:1–13*

90 BC	80 BC	70 BC	60 BC	50 BC	40 BC	30 BC	20 BC	10 BC	0 BC

◆ 65 Buddhism rises in China   ◆ 44 Julius Caesar assassinated   ◆ 2 Magi visit

◆ 63 Pompey conquers Jerusalem   ◆ 37 Herod the Great (Israel)

◆ 102 Chinese ships reach India   ◆ 51 Cleopatra VII reigns in Egypt ◆ 31 Augustus (Rome)   ◆ 4 Jesus' birth

Holy Living	Living in Expectation of Christ's Return
4:1–18	5:1–28

HOLY LIVING (4:1–18)

Paul begins a series of exhortations regarding appropriate Christian living. He writes about remaining sexually pure, leading a quiet life, increasing in love, and living in a way that earns the respect of unbelievers. The Thessalonians are concerned about believers who have died, and Paul encourages them by explaining that death for the believer is like moving, not dying. He gives them full assurance that those who have died in Christ yet live. Those who have died before Christ returns are actually at an advantage; they will be raised first when Christ returns for His bride, the church. ⧗ *1 THESSALONIANS 4:1–18*

LIVING IN EXPECTATION OF CHRIST'S RETURN (5:1–28)

In light of Jesus' return, Paul turns his full attention to what the Thessalonian believers can expect when that happens. They are a church under persecution, and the anticipated return of the One to whom they are faithful is an ongoing comfort for them. Paul gives insight into signs of the nearness of Jesus' coming, encouraging the Thessalonians that because they are in the light of Christ, they will not be caught unaware. However, they are to live in expectation of His return, and they are to be watchful and ready at all times. While they wait, they are to comfort, exhort, and love one another, and turn from every kind of evil. ⧗ *1 THESSALONIANS 5:1–28*

Ancient Byzantine fresco of the last judgment

AD 10	AD 20	AD 30	AD 40	AD 50	AD 60	AD 70	AD 80	AD 90	AD 100

- ✦ 8 Jesus visits temple
- ✦ 30 Jesus raised
- ✦ 45 James written
- ✦ 60 Eph–Col
- ✦ 68 Paul & Peter martyred
- ✦ 90 Revelation
- ✦ 5 Birth of Paul (?)
- ✦ 32 Stephen martyred
- ✦ 55 1 & 2 Corinthians
- ✦ 64 Rome burns
- ✦ 70 Temple destroyed
- ✦ 14 Tiberius (Rome)
- ✦ 37 Paul converts
- ✦ 57 Romans
- ✦ 65 1 Peter & 1 Timothy
- ✦ 85 1–3 John written

Responding to Persecution	Hold to Reliable Teaching and Remain Faithful
1:1–12	2:1–17

RESPONDING TO PERSECUTION (1:1–12)

Paul had written 1 Thessalonians largely to encourage the believers in Thessalonica to remain faithful as they encountered persecution from various sources. Not long after sending the first letter, he hears of increasing opposition. Paul acknowledges what the Thessalonians are facing. He spurs them on with the hope of a better day ahead, when God will deal with those mistreating His people in Thessalonica. This coming day of judgment will be like a flaming fire. For the persecutors, those who do not know God, and those who do not obey the Gospel of the Lord Jesus, it will be a day of vengeance and everlasting destruction. Paul comforts the Thessalonian believers, reminding them that he is in constant prayer for them, that they would be found worthy of the calling of seeing Jesus glorified in them at His coming. This can only happen by the Holy Spirit's power, favor, and acceptance at work in believers. ⌛ *2 THESSALONIANS 1:1–12*

Be ready: What lesson does 2 Thessalonians have for us?
Second Thessalonians is a very relevant book for today. Since the beginning of the church, there have been some people who have claimed to know the timing of Jesus' return. This throws some believers into a panic. Paul helped the church in Thessalonica to realize that the real issue is not when Jesus is going to return but the importance of being ready for His return. Our job is not to predict the date of Jesus' return but to be faithful to the mission He has given us—so that when He does return, we'll be ready.

90 BC	80 BC	70 BC	60 BC	50 BC	40 BC	30 BC	20 BC	10 BC	0 BC

• 65 Buddhism rises in China • 44 Julius Caesar assassinated • 2 Magi visit

• 63 Pompey conquers Jerusalem • 37 Herod the Great (Israel)

• 102 Chinese ships reach India • 51 Cleopatra VII reigns in Egypt • 31 Augustus (Rome) • 4 Jesus' birth

A Warning against Becoming Idle
3:1–18

HOLD TO RELIABLE TEACHING AND REMAIN FAITHFUL (2:1–17)

In addition to intense persecution of believers, false teachings are circulating regarding the return of Christ, creating more stress on those who are trying to remain faithful. Paul sets the record straight, differentiating between Jesus' return and the believers being gathered to Him. Paul gives insight to signs that will occur before the coming of Christ, including the surfacing of a man who will oppose and exalt himself above God. This man will demand worship that is for God alone. Paul gives encouragement to these last days' believers, exhorting them to stand firm, and he prays for Jesus to strengthen his friends.
⌛ *2 THESSALONIANS 2:1–17*

A WARNING AGAINST BECOMING IDLE (3:1–18)

Closing his letter, Paul emphasizes how his and his associates' confidence should not be placed in human plans or promotions, but in God alone. They should model right behavior and steer away from idle brothers who do work hard for their keep. It is important for the Thessalonian believers to follow Jesus' pattern of teaching and living. Paul gives instruction on how to deal with those who disobey, and then he bestows the peace, presence, and grace of the Lord Himself on the believers. ⌛ *2 THESSALONIANS 3:1–18*

2 THESSALONIANS

231

The Last Judgment *by Hans Memling (1430–1494)*

* 8 Jesus visits temple * 30 Jesus raised * 45 James written * 60 Eph–Col * 68 Paul & Peter martyred * 90 Revelation

* 5 Birth of Paul (?) * 32 Stephen martyred * 55 1&2 Corinthians * 64 Rome burns * 70 Temple destroyed

* 14 Tiberius (Rome) * 37 Paul converts * 57 Romans * 65 1 Peter & 1 Timothy * 85 1–3 John written

The Purpose of the Law	The Local Church and Its Leaders
1:1–2:15	3:1–4:16

INTRODUCTION TO
1 & 2 TIMOTHY

Author: Paul
Date Written: AD 63–67

Of all of Paul's letters, the Pastoral Epistles—1 Timothy, 2 Timothy, and Titus—are by far the most disputed in terms of authorship. Differences of language, style, and theology have caused some scholars to doubt that Paul is the original author. However, there are many features of these letters consistent with Paul's language and style, and most scholars continue to assert that these letters come from the apostle's hand.

Sometimes referred to as a "leadership manual," 1 Timothy is a letter from Paul to one of his dearest disciples, Timothy. Paul writes 1 Timothy from Macedonia, sometime after being released from his first Roman imprisonment—around AD 63–64. He has left his young protégé to minister at the church in Ephesus, a church plagued with false teachers and dissension. Paul writes to Timothy, offering instruction on how to choose and strengthen leaders in the church and how to train them to preserve godliness and reject false teaching. Timothy is challenged to be aware of his youthfulness; his personal and public life must be beyond reproach.

If 1 Timothy is a leadership manual, 2 Timothy can be viewed as more of a "combat manual" for use in spiritual warfare. Paul's instructions in this second letter give Timothy further guidance in leading the church and battling false teachers. Paul begins by assuring Timothy of his continued prayer, deep love, and concern. He reminds Timothy of his spiritual heritage and responsibilities as a leader. Paul then urges Timothy to continue to press on through hardships, overcome timidity, and boldly spread the Gospel.

90 BC	80 BC	70 BC	60 BC	50 BC	40 BC	30 BC	20 BC	10 BC	0 BC

• 65 Buddhism rises in China   • 44 Julius Caesar assassinated   • 2 Magi visit

• 63 Pompey conquers Jerusalem   • 37 Herod the Great (Israel)

• 102 Chinese ships reach India   • 51 Cleopatra VII reigns in Egypt • 31 Augustus (Rome)   • 4 Jesus' birth

Instructions For Specific Groups	Closing Thoughts
5:1–25	6:1–21

Paul writes this second letter from a cold prison cell in Rome in AD 67 hoping Timothy and Mark will visit him before the approaching winter; he asks them to bring his scrolls and parchment, along with his cloak. Perhaps Paul has some sense of passing on the torch of leadership. This letter is, in one way, Paul's last will and testament. In spite of Paul's dark circumstances, he encourages Timothy to remain steadfast in the fulfillment of his divinely appointed assignment.

Together 1 and 2 Timothy offer a real-life look at the church, its conflicts, and its leadership in the first century. As Paul reviews the past, analyzes the present, and looks forward to his future with Christ in His heavenly kingdom, he provides comfort, encouragement, and motivation not only to Timothy but also to all worn-out Christian workers.

AD 10	AD 20	AD 30	AD 40	AD 50	AD 60	AD 70	AD 80	AD 90	AD 100
		◆ 8 Jesus visits temple		◆ 30 Jesus raised		◆ 45 James written		◆ 60 Eph–Col	◆ 68 Paul & Peter martyred		◆ 90 Revelation
◆ 5 Birth of Paul (?)			◆ 32 Stephen martyred		◆ 55 1 & 2 Corinthians	◆ 64 Rome burns		◆ 70 Temple destroyed	
	◆ 14 Tiberius (Rome)		◆ 37 Paul converts		◆ 57 Romans		◆ 65 1 Peter & 1 Timothy		◆ 85 1–3 John written

The Purpose of the Law	The Local Church and Its Leaders
1:1–2:15	3:1–4:16

Read Each 5-Minute Overview in 1 Timothy

○ 1:1–2:15	The Purpose of the Law	Page 234
○ 3:1–4:16	The Local Church and Its Leaders	Page 234
○ 5:1–25	Instructions for Specific Groups	Page 235
○ 6:1–21	Closing Thoughts	Page 235

THE PURPOSE OF THE LAW (1:1–2:15)

The opening of Paul's letter to his young friend Timothy charges Timothy to stay in Ephesus and make sure correct doctrine continues to be taught. Fables and genealogies are distracting believers from the purity of the Gospel. Paul clarifies that the purpose of the Law is heart transformation, not outward observance. He calls God's people to love from a pure heart—not because they are following legalistic rules. Paul begins describing the kind of people Timothy should appoint as leaders in the church. Of utmost importance is prayer for the salvation of all people through Jesus Christ. Paul also gives instruction for men and women in church leadership, and he gives reasons for male authority in the church. ⏳ *1 TIMOTHY 1:1–20; 2:1–15*

THE LOCAL CHURCH AND ITS LEADERS (3:1–4:16)

Paul continues shepherding Timothy in the organization and character of the church, and in understanding the principles of its leadership. He spends more time discussing the kind of people Timothy should choose to help him lead the church. Paul lists characteristics that offer a glimpse into the kind of mature person that would be able to effectively rise to leadership in the local church. Paul takes the logical next step, moving from the responsibility and role of the church leaders to obstacles that prevent fellowship from being all that God

90 BC	80 BC	70 BC	60 BC	50 BC	40 BC	30 BC	20 BC	10 BC	0 BC

◆ 65 Buddhism rises in China ◆ 44 Julius Caesar assassinated ◆ 2 Magi visit

◆ 63 Pompey conquers Jerusalem ◆ 37 Herod the Great (Israel)

◆ 102 Chinese ships reach India ◆ 51 Cleopatra VII reigns in Egypt ◆ 31 Augustus (Rome) ◆ 4 Jesus' birth

Instructions for Specific Groups	Closing Thoughts
5:1–25	6:1–21

intends it to be. Once again, Paul warns against false teachers and gives specific instructions for Timothy in his leadership role. ⏳ *1 TIMOTHY 3:1–16; 4:1–16*

INSTRUCTIONS FOR SPECIFIC GROUPS (5:1–25)

Now Paul teaches Timothy how to deal with a variety of different groups within the church. Using his gift of exhortation in varying contexts, Timothy is to exhort older men respectfully as fathers, younger men relationally as brothers, older women tenderly as mothers, and younger women with dignity as sisters. The majority of these instructions relate to widows and the church's care for them. Paul instructs against favoritism, warns against appointing a person too quickly to ministry, and reminds Timothy of the importance of keeping his own life pure. ⏳ *1 TIMOTHY 5:1–25*

CLOSING THOUGHTS (6:1–21)

Paul addresses the relationships slaves are to have with their masters, and he discusses godly contentment versus greed. Those who desire riches will always fall into a snare. Finally, Paul stresses to Timothy the utmost importance of guarding the gospel entrusted to him. ⏳ *1 TIMOTHY 6:1–21*

AD 10   AD 20   AD 30   AD 40   AD 50   AD 60   AD 70   AD 80   AD 90   AD 100

♦ 8 Jesus visits temple   ♦ 30 Jesus raised   ♦ 45 James written   ♦ 60 Eph–Col   ♦ 68 Paul & Peter martyred   ♦ 90 Revelation

♦ 5 Birth of Paul (?)   ♦ 32 Stephen martyred   ♦ 55 1 & 2 Corinthians   ♦ 64 Rome burns   ♦ 70 Temple destroyed

♦ 14 Tiberius (Rome)   ♦ 37 Paul converts   ♦ 57 Romans   ♦ 65 1 Peter & 1 Timothy   ♦ 85 1–3 John written

Greetings for Steadfast Friends	Press On for the Sake of the Gospel
1:1–18	2:1–26

Read Each 5-Minute Overview in 2 Timothy

GREETINGS FOR STEADFAST FRIENDS (1:1–18)

Writing from prison, Paul remembers his fellow Jewish brothers from generations past who sincerely followed God with pure hearts and were not puffed up like the Pharisees. Paul acknowledges the impact that the faith of Timothy's mother and grandmother had on Timothy. Paul charges Timothy to be bold, reminding him of the power, love, and sound mind he has in Christ. Timothy is not to be ashamed of the Gospel and needs to hold on to it for dear life. ⌛ *2 TIMOTHY 1:1–18*

PRESS ON FOR THE SAKE OF THE GOSPEL (2:1–26)

Using the example of a soldier, Paul tells Timothy he must expect hardship as one who does not give up just because something is difficult. Using the example of an athlete, Paul urges Timothy to press on according to the rules to receive the prize. And using the example of a farmer, Paul encourages

> **Pastoral challenge: Are Paul's words to Timothy relevant to us today?**
> In Ephesians 3:7–10, we read that Paul's job was to help establish the local church. It is clear from 2 Timothy 2:2 that Paul intended for the church to continue far beyond his and Timothy's lifetimes. Therefore, much of Paul's advice to the young pastor can be taken to heart today.

90 BC	80 BC	70 BC	60 BC	50 BC	40 BC	30 BC	20 BC	10 BC	0 BC

◆ 65 Buddhism rises in China ◆ 44 Julius Caesar assassinated ◆ 2 Magi visit

◆ 63 Pompey conquers Jerusalem ◆ 37 Herod the Great (Israel)

◆ 102 Chinese ships reach India ◆ 51 Cleopatra VII reigns in Egypt ◆ 31 Augustus (Rome) ◆ 4 Jesus' birth

Perilous Times in the Last Days	Do the Work of an Evangelist—at All Times
3:1–17	4:1–22

Timothy to work hard to correctly teach his congregation. In addition, he must seek the Lord for understanding and endure everything, good and bad, for the sake of the Gospel. God will always be faithful; His solid foundation will stand. Timothy's goal should be to present himself approved to God and to keep himself pure by pursuing righteousness, peace, love, and faith. ⏳ *2 TIMOTHY 2:1–26*

PERILOUS TIMES IN THE LAST DAYS (3:1–17)

There are difficult days ahead, and Paul predicts the uphill battle against sin will only grow steeper over time. The human condition before the return of Christ will be marked with distinct characteristics, according to Paul, most notably selfishness and pride. Men will despise the power of godliness that comes from acknowledging the authority of Christ, a power that should guide their lives. Paul reminds Timothy that all scripture is from God and profits those who believe it as truth; it has the power to transform lives. ⏳ *2 TIMOTHY 3:1–17*

DO THE WORK OF AN EVANGELIST—AT ALL TIMES (4:1–22)

Writing from prison, Paul solemnly shares his mission with young Timothy: to proclaim Jesus. He charges Timothy to preach the Word of God at all times, knowing many will not want to hear what he is proclaiming. Knowing his time is short and needing companionship, Paul begs Timothy to visit him in prison. Penning his last words of the letter, he prays for the Lord Jesus to be with Timothy's spirit. ⏳ *2 TIMOTHY 4:1–22*

The Martyrdom of St. Paul. *Artist unknown.*

2 TIMOTHY

237

A Call for Authentic Beliefs and Leadership	A Call for Authentic Behavior and Relationships
1:1–16	2:1–3:15

INTRODUCTION TO TITUS AND PHILEMON

Author: Paul
Date Written: AD 60–65

Paul's ministry had initiated Titus's conversion to Christianity, and the Gentile believer is soon given the responsibility of traveling and ministering, sometimes with Paul and sometimes on his own. This letter to Titus highlights one of the latter cases. Paul leaves Titus in Crete, while the apostle is elsewhere. Crete is an island in the Mediterranean. In Greek mythology, it's the birthplace of Zeus. The citizens of Crete have a poor reputation, but this is where Titus is entrusted to oversee new converts. Paul writes to encourage Titus and give him some practical instructions for how to organize new believers into local churches. A proper understanding of the Gospel of Christ is especially needed in the hedonistic and idolatrous culture of Crete. Paul desires to stay in touch with Titus, and he writes to call Titus to firmly exercise his authority as a representative of the Lord. These new churches need order, false teachers need to be rebuked, and immoral behavior needs to be invalidated.

Paul addresses how leaders should be chosen and what leaders should do with false teachers. Church members of all ages are encouraged to live lives worthy of the

90 BC	80 BC	70 BC	60 BC	50 BC	40 BC	30 BC	20 BC	10 BC	0 BC

♦ 65 Buddhism rises in China   ♦ 44 Julius Caesar assassinated   ♦ 2 Magi visit

♦ 63 Pompey conquers Jerusalem   ♦ 37 Herod the Great (Israel)

♦ 102 Chinese ships reach India   ♦ 51 Cleopatra VII reigns in Egypt   ♦ 31 Augustus (Rome)   ♦ 4 Jesus' birth

Forgiveness and Second Chances
1–25

Gospel they claim they believe and should demonstrate their faith by maintaining good works.

Of the thirteen epistles traditionally attributed to Paul in scripture, his letter to Philemon is the shortest and most personal. Some say it is a masterpiece of diplomacy and tact, as it deals with human slavery and was written to be proclaimed aloud in public. Philemon's situation is very specific, yet Paul's advice, as usual, contains wisdom appropriate for all believers.

In the book of Philemon, Paul addresses the issue of Christian brotherly love and whether it truly works in all situations, especially tense or difficult circumstances. Paul had come upon a runaway slave named Onesimus, who had stolen from his master, Philemon, and then deserted him. Onesimus had since put his faith in Jesus for his salvation. Paul has convinced Onesimus to return to Philemon, and he asks Philemon, a fellow believer in Jesus, to receive Onesimus back with love and gentleness; they are now brothers in Christ. Paul promises to pay back any debt Onesimus owes Philemon.

It appears Paul is in prison as he writes this letter, probably during his first imprisonment under house arrest in Rome. The book is not so much about proclaiming doctrine as it is about applying doctrine in such a way that the life-changing effects of Christianity would impact social conditions.

TITUS

239

AD 10	AD 20	AD 30	AD 40	AD 50	AD 60	AD 70	AD 80	AD 90	AD 100

- 8 Jesus visits temple   • 30 Jesus raised   • 45 James written   • 60 Eph–Col   • 68 Paul & Peter martyred   • 90 Revelation
- 5 Birth of Paul (?)   • 32 Stephen martyred   • 55 1 & 2 Corinthians   • 64 Rome burns   • 70 Temple destroyed
- 14 Tiberius (Rome)   • 37 Paul converts   • 57 Romans   • 65 1 Peter & 1 Timothy   • 85 1–3 John written

A Call for Authentic Beliefs and Leadership	A Call for Authentic Behavior and Relationships
1:1–16	2:1–3:15

Read Each 5-Minute Overview in Titus

A CALL FOR AUTHENTIC BELIEFS AND LEADERSHIP (1:1–16)

Paul greets Titus as his true son in the faith and bestows upon Titus grace, mercy, and peace from Jesus. He quickly addresses the reason he left Titus in Crete. Paul reviews necessary qualifications for elders, including the ability to convict those who contradict the truth of the Gospel. Paul tells Titus why it is important to select qualified leaders, and he rebukes Jewish believers who, motivated by dishonest gain, are giving heed to Jewish fables and human traditions. Their minds and consciences are becoming defiled; they profess to know God, but their works don't line up with what they say they believe. ⏳ *TITUS 1:1–16*

A CALL FOR AUTHENTIC BEHAVIOR AND RELATIONSHIPS (2:1–3:15)

Paul provides guidelines for different groups within the church and some personal encouragement for Titus in the challenging position he holds. Titus is given instruction for what to teach each different generation within the congregation, as well as what to teach servants. There is one Gospel of grace for all people; it instructs to expect and prepare for the blessed hope of Christ. Paul concludes his letter to Titus with a call for believers to remember life before Christ and the miraculous, unexplainable salvation of God. ⏳ *TITUS 2:1–15; 3:1–15*

90 BC	80 BC	70 BC	60 BC	50 BC	40 BC	30 BC	20 BC	10 BC	0 BC

• 65 Buddhism rises in China • 44 Julius Caesar assassinated • 2 Magi visit

• 63 Pompey conquers Jerusalem • 37 Herod the Great (Israel)

• 102 Chinese ships reach India • 51 Cleopatra VII reigns in Egypt • 31 Augustus (Rome) • 4 Jesus' birth

Read Each 5-Minute Overview in Philemon

FORGIVENESS AND SECOND CHANCES (1–25)

A slave named Onesimus has run away from his master, Philemon, apparently after stealing from him. In God's providence, Onesimus meets Paul, who facilitates his conversion to Christianity and sends him back to Philemon with this letter. After sharing with Philemon how Paul prays for him and is thankful for him because of his love and faith toward Jesus and all the saints, Paul pleads for Philemon to forgive Onesimus. Paul is hopeful Philemon will welcome Onesimus back to him, and he promises to pay back anything that Onesimus has stolen. ⏳ *PHILEMON 1–25*

Slaves and masters: Did Paul endorse slavery?

Because Paul did not explicitly oppose slavery, some have argued that he actually endorsed it. Paul (who was often in jail himself) was more interested in spending his energy fighting for the Gospel's advancement rather than pushing social changes. Elsewhere Paul wrote, "Each person should remain in the situation they were in when God called them. Were you a slave when you were called? Don't let it trouble you—although if you can gain your freedom, do so" (1 Corinthians 7:20–21). To Paul, a person's status mattered less than their ability to make the most of whatever situation they were in. However, Paul also seemed to recognize that freedom was preferable to enslavement.

AD 10	AD 20	AD 30	AD 40	AD 50	AD 60	AD 70	AD 80	AD 90	AD 100
	✦ 8 Jesus visits temple	✦ 30 Jesus raised	✦ 45 James written		✦ 60 Eph–Col	✦ 68 Paul & Peter martyred		✦ 90 Revelation	
✦ 5 Birth of Paul (?)		✦ 32 Stephen martyred		✦ 55 1&2 Corinthians	✦ 64 Rome burns	✦ 70 Temple destroyed			
	✦ 14 Tiberius (Rome)		✦ 37 Paul converts	✦ 57 Romans		✦ 65 1 Peter & 1 Timothy		✦ 85 1–3 John written	

The Supremacy of Christ	Jesus Compared to Moses	Jesus Compared to the Priests of Israel
1:1–2:18	3:1–4:13	4:14–6:20

INTRODUCTION TO HEBREWS

Author: Unknown
Date Written: AD 65?

Although it is fundamentally a sermon, the book of Hebrews is actually a letter written to a specific group of people to address problems and concerns of that community. No one can say with certainty who wrote Hebrews or where the letter was written, but it appears clear Hebrews was written prior to the destruction of Jerusalem in AD 70. Some attribute it to Paul, yet in every other Pauline letter, the apostle opens by identifying himself. The language, style, and theological perspective are very different from Paul's. Perhaps the best insight comes from the early Christian theologian Origen. Concerning the author of Hebrews, he commented, "God alone knows."

The original recipients of this letter, as the title indicates, are Jewish Christians. They are being persecuted for their new faith. Although they start out standing firm, they begin to waver and are tempted to return to the comfort of their old, familiar ways. Some have apparently already left the Christian faith to return to Judaism, adding pressure to Jews still in the church.

The writer of Hebrews urges these Jewish Christians to press on and grow to maturity in Christ, basing his appeal on the superiority of Christ over the traditional Judaic system. The writer argues Jesus is better than angels, for even the angels worship Him. He is better than Moses, for Jesus created Moses. He is even better than the Aaronic priesthood, for Jesus' sacrifice is once for all time. And finally, Jesus mediates a better covenant, making Him better than the Mosaic Law. Thus, the word that sums up the theme of Hebrews is *better*. Jesus offers a

90 BC	80 BC	70 BC	60 BC	50 BC	40 BC	30 BC	20 BC	10 BC	0 BC

◆ 65 Buddhism rises in China   ◆ 44 Julius Caesar assassinated   ◆ 2 Magi visit

◆ 63 Pompey conquers Jerusalem   ◆ 37 Herod the Great (Israel)

◆ 102 Chinese ships reach India   ◆ 51 Cleopatra VII reigns in Egypt   ◆ 31 Augustus (Rome)   ◆ 4 Jesus' birth

Jesus Compared to Melchizedek	A More Meaningful Sacrifice and Salvation	Noteworthy Faith and God's Loving Discipline
7:1–8:13	9:1–10:39	11:1–13:25

better revelation, position, priesthood, covenant, sacrifice, and power. This theme is developed to prevent readers from giving up on the reality of Christ and returning to the shadow of the old Judaic system. To reject Jesus is not only foolish but also spiritually dangerous. Jesus is the only option that offers lasting salvation.

Hebrews presents a masterful explanation of the preeminence of Christ—His superiority over all things. It is not so much a contrast between the "old" ways of the ancient Israelites and the "new" ways of the emerging Christian era, but rather the similarity between Old Testament and New Testament believers: Both received the Gospel, were saved by grace through faith, and look forward to the promised rest of God.

The writer of Hebrews often uses the tabernacle as a metaphor. This re-creation sits in Timna Park, Israel.

The Supremacy of Christ	Jesus Compared to Moses	Jesus Compared to the Priests of Israel
1:1–2:18	3:1–4:13	4:14–6:20

Read Each 5-Minute Overview in Hebrews

THE SUPREMACY OF CHRIST (1:1–2:18)

A number of Jewish Christians are leaving the church and returning to the familiarity of their traditions. The author of Hebrews sends this letter to make clear exactly what they are abandoning. Jesus brings a revelation of God superior to even the prophets, and Jesus' claims about His divinity were confirmed with signs and wonders. The author gives a sevenfold description of the Son and culminates his argument of Jesus' superiority by comparing Him to angels. The writer also addresses Jesus' humanity as well as His role as high priest—an Old Testament shadow now a reality in Christ. ✗ HEBREWS 1:1–14; 2:1–18

JESUS COMPARED TO MOSES (3:1–4:13)

The Jews held Moses in such high regard because of his faithfulness to God and great accomplishments, but the author shows even Moses' deeds pale when contrasted with Jesus Christ. The writer reminds his readers of Israel's history in the wilderness and of the people's failure to enter God's rest

90 BC	80 BC	70 BC	60 BC	50 BC	40 BC	30 BC	20 BC	10 BC	0 BC

◆ 65 Buddhism rises in China ◆ 44 Julius Caesar assassinated ◆ 2 Magi visit

◆ 63 Pompey conquers Jerusalem ◆ 37 Herod the Great (Israel)

◆ 102 Chinese ships reach India ◆ 51 Cleopatra VII reigns in Egypt ◆ 31 Augustus (Rome) ◆ 4 Jesus' birth

Jesus Compared to Melchizedek	A More Meaningful Sacrifice and Salvation	Noteworthy Faith and God's Loving Discipline
7:1–8:13	9:1–10:39	11:1–13:25

because of their unbelief. Salvation has always been through grace, by faith; the author calls his readers to cease from trying to gain salvation through external works. ⌛ *HEBREWS 3:1–19; 4:1–13*

JESUS COMPARED TO THE PRIESTS OF ISRAEL
(4:14–6:20)

The author uses various temple analogies to show how Jesus correctly interprets what many generations of Jews had practiced. Jesus meets the biblical requirements for the high priest, but He is also their great high priest forever. Jesus even comes from the superior order of the priesthood: Melchizedek. Alluding to the temple veil, the author shows how Jesus provides access to God's presence; through Jesus, believers can approach God for mercy and grace any time they are in need. The writer warns against falling away. God's promises are reliable, and believers should have eternal hope in Christ. ⌛ *HEBREWS 4:14–16; 5:1–14; 6:1–20*

A priest of the ancient Samaritan community holds up the Torah.

Mysterious imagery: What should we make of the references to the tabernacle and priesthood in Hebrews?
The book of Hebrews showed its readers that it was better to serve God by putting faith in Jesus than by following Old Testament rituals. Jesus is better because He did what the Law could not do: save people and transform them. Jewish believers in Jesus, the original audience of the book of Hebrews, were tempted to return to temple worship and abandon Christ. Hebrews drew comparisons between the old and new covenants to show believers that Jesus had already fulfilled the Law. Therefore, if they returned to the Law while ignoring Jesus, they would lose everything.

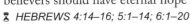

AD 10	AD 20	AD 30	AD 40	AD 50	AD 60	AD 70	AD 80	AD 90	AD 100

◆ 8 Jesus visits temple   ◆ 30 Jesus raised   ◆ 45 James written   ◆ 60 Eph–Col ◆ 68 Paul & Peter martyred   ◆ 90 Revelation

◆ 5 Birth of Paul (?)   ◆ 32 Stephen martyred   ◆ 55 1 & 2 Corinthians   ◆ 64 Rome burns   ◆ 70 Temple destroyed

◆ 14 Tiberius (Rome)   ◆ 37 Paul converts   ◆ 57 Romans   ◆ 65 1 Peter & 1 Timothy   ◆ 85 1–3 John written

The Supremacy of Christ	Jesus Compared to Moses	Jesus Compared to the Priests of Israel	Jesus Compared to Melchizedek	A More Meaningful Sacrifice and Salvation	Noteworthy Faith and God's Loving Discipline
1:1–2:18	3:1–4:13	4:14–6:20	7:1–8:13	9:1–10:39	11:1–13:25

JESUS COMPARED TO MELCHIZEDEK (7:1–8:13)

Jesus is superior to the Levitical priests because He provides salvation. The author emphasizes Melchizedek's appearance in scripture and how his ministry prefigures that of Jesus. The author compares and contrasts the role of Jesus as high priest with the Levitical priesthood, and he speaks of the need for a new priesthood. The Levitical priesthood never really made anything perfect, but this new priesthood offers everlasting salvation. ⏳ *HEBREWS 7:1–28; 8:1–13*

A MORE MEANINGFUL SACRIFICE AND SALVATION (9:1–10:39)

The law is described as a shadow; it can never permanently remove sin. Through the offering of Jesus' body, those who trust in Him are cleansed from sin forever and begin an inner transformation. The perfect heavenly sanctuary receives the perfect cleansing sacrifice. At His first coming, Jesus' sacrifice cleansed sin; when He returns, he will rescue His people. Using temple analogies again and imagery from the Day of Atonement, the writer speaks of hearts sprinkled and bodies washed; through Jesus, God's people can once again draw near to Him. The people of Israel are to remember past experiences to gain strength for the future. ⏳ *HEBREWS 9:6–28; 10:1–13, 19–22, 32*

NOTEWORTHY FAITH AND GOD'S LOVING DISCIPLINE (11:1–13:25)

The writer next provides many examples of faithful Old Testament saints who never received what they had been promised. He hopes to inspire the Jews who have put their faith in Jesus to imitate their ancestors. He provides practical insight for his listeners as they begin to return to the faith they are being lured away from. Using the example of Jesus, the writer exhorts these believers to press on and not become discouraged. He adds a severe warning for anyone who continues to resist God, and he gives reason for God's chastening. The writer concludes with a sermon on the necessity of persevering in faith. ⏳ *HEBREWS 11:1–31, 39–40; 12:1–3, 7–8; 13:20–21*

90 BC	80 BC	70 BC	60 BC	50 BC	40 BC	30 BC	20 BC	10 BC	0 BC

• 65 Buddhism rises in China • 44 Julius Caesar assassinated • 2 Magi visit

• 63 Pompey conquers Jerusalem • 37 Herod the Great (Israel)

• 102 Chinese ships reach India • 51 Cleopatra VII reigns in Egypt • 31 Augustus (Rome) • 4 Jesus' birth

INTRODUCTION TO JAMES

Author: James
Date Written: AD 45

This letter is replete with Old Testament teachings and allusions, but it is also clear James writes from a distinctly Christian perspective, as one who has spent time with Jesus. The audience is clearly experiencing persecution for their faith. James writes to them to encourage them in the face of trials and to help them know how to stand firm. The letter's tone is one of pastoral exhortation. James instructs his brothers and sisters in Christ with care and concern. Because of its teaching flavor, many scholars consider the book of James more of a written sermon than a letter.

James is the natural son of Joseph and Mary and the younger half brother of Jesus. Although James did not believe in Jesus during His early earthly ministry, after the resurrection James puts his faith in Christ and becomes the leader of the Jerusalem church from AD 44–62. He presides over the Jerusalem Council and is considered by Paul to be a pillar of the church, alongside Peter and John.

Martyrdom of St. James
by Albrecht Dürer (1471–1528)

AD 10	AD 20	AD 30	AD 40	AD 50	AD 60	AD 70	AD 80	AD 90	AD 100
◆ 8 Jesus visits temple		◆ 30 Jesus raised		◆ 45 James written		◆ 60 Eph–Col	◆ 68 Paul & Peter martyred		◆ 90 Revelation
◆ 5 Birth of Paul (?)			◆ 32 Stephen martyred	◆ 55 1 & 2 Corinthians	◆ 64 Rome burns		◆ 70 Temple destroyed		
	◆ 14 Tiberius (Rome)		◆ 37 Paul converts	◆ 57 Romans		◆ 65 1 Peter & 1 Timothy		◆ 85 1–3 John written	

Facing Trials and Living Out Faith	Love, Faith, and Action
1:1–27	2:1–26

Addressed to the twelve tribes scattered abroad, it is apparent James is written to Hebrew Christians outside Palestine; the whole epistle reflects Jewish thought and expressions. These Jewish believers are surrounded by problems that are testing their faith, and James is concerned with the impatience, bitterness, and disunity brewing among them. He writes this letter out of the overflow of this concern.

Repeating Jesus' own teaching but echoing instruction found in the Old Testament, James develops the theme of true faith in his letter. Faith without works cannot be called faith; without works, faith is dead and not really faith at all. Faith must be visible and produce fruit; it must inspire action. James gives his wise instruction in the distinctive rubber-meets-the-road way that only a firsthand witness can give. Faith is more than words, more than knowledge; genuine faith produces real changes in a person's conduct and character. James's overall concern is consistency in practicing faith through obedient acts that produce results.

James writes his letter during Paul's first missionary journey, when the church is still primarily Jewish, somewhere between AD 45 and the end of his life in AD 62. This letter is as relevant today as it was in the first century and is the most practical book in the New Testament. It addresses trials and temptations, response to the Word, preferential treatment because of social status, controlling the tongue, and the lure of worldliness.

Actions vs. faith: How do we reconcile the teachings of James and Paul?
Some readers have wondered if Paul and James contradicted each other. Paul wrote that people are justified by faith, while James noted the uselessness of faith without deeds. The answer to the apparent contradiction can be found in Galatians 5:6, which says, "For in Christ Jesus neither circumcision nor uncircumcision has any value. The only thing that counts is faith expressing itself through love." Paul did not want people to think salvation came through works of the Law. On the other hand, true faith is not just a mental acceptance of something. True faith produces active love. In other words, Paul and James taught the same thing. James offered practical examples of what love looks like. His message to the church? Loveless faith is absolutely useless. Faith must produce love for others or it is not saving faith.

90 BC	80 BC	70 BC	60 BC	50 BC	40 BC	30 BC	20 BC	10 BC	0 BC

◆ 65 Buddhism rises in China   ◆ 44 Julius Caesar assassinated   ◆ 2 Magi visit

◆ 63 Pompey conquers Jerusalem   ◆ 37 Herod the Great (Israel)

◆ 102 Chinese ships reach India   ◆ 51 Cleopatra VII reigns in Egypt   ◆ 31 Augustus (Rome)   ◆ 4 Jesus' birth

Wise Living	Wealth, Waiting, and Prayer
3:1–18	4:1–5:20

Read Each 5-Minute Overview in James

○ 1:1–27	Facing Trials and Living Out Faith	Page 249
○ 2:1–26	Love, Faith, and Action	Page 249
○ 3:1–18	Wise Living	Page 250
○ 4:1–5:20	Wealth, Waiting, and Prayer	Page 250

FACING TRIALS AND LIVING OUT FAITH (1:1–27)

Jewish and Gentile believers in the growing church are gaining their identity apart from Jews, but this new identity comes with persecution. James urges believers to persevere in trials and strengthen their faith. Trials produce patience that leads to maturity. James motivates his readers to endure temptation and describes the true source of temptation that leads to sin and spiritual death. He counsels readers to be swift to hear, slow to speak, and slow to become angry. James also expounds on a major theme of this epistle: being doers, not just hearers, of the Word. ⌛ *JAMES 1:1–27*

LOVE, FAITH, AND ACTION (2:1–26)

Some believers are displaying favoritism toward the rich in their assemblies while despising the poor. James provides several reasons why prejudice is unbecoming of those who believe in Jesus; favoritism is worthy of condemnation. James addresses the foolishness of professing faith unaccompanied by works. He uses several examples of Old Testament saints whose faith was accompanied by an outpouring of loving, good deeds. James declares three times that faith without works is dead. ⌛ *JAMES 2:1–26*

AD 10	AD 20	AD 30	AD 40	AD 50	AD 60	AD 70	AD 80	AD 90	AD 100
◆ 8 Jesus visits temple		◆ 30 Jesus raised		◆ 45 James written		◆ 60 Eph–Col ◆ 68 Paul & Peter martyred		◆ 90 Revelation	
◆ 5 Birth of Paul (?)			◆ 32 Stephen martyred		◆ 55 1 & 2 Corinthians	◆ 64 Rome burns		◆ 70 Temple destroyed	
	◆ 14 Tiberius (Rome)		◆ 37 Paul converts		◆ 57 Romans		◆ 65 1 Peter & 1 Timothy		◆ 85 1–3 John written

| MATT | MARK | LUKE | JOHN | ACTS | ROM | 1 COR | 2 COR | GAL | EPH | PHIL | COL | 1 THESS | 2 THESS |

Facing Trials and Living Out Faith	Love, Faith, and Action	Wise Living	Wealth, Waiting, and Prayer
1:1–27	2:1–26	3:1–18	4:1–5:20

NAVIGATING THE BIBLE

WISE LIVING (3:1–18)

James cautions his readers against becoming teachers; teachers will be strictly judged. James provides a series of illustrations demonstrating the power and danger of the tongue. He warns of the potential damage the tongue can bring. It can be as unmanageable as a raging fire and as harmful as poison. Wisdom and understanding are reflected in one's conduct and should be done in meekness. There are two kinds of wisdom: earthly "wisdom" that causes confusion and evil, and heavenly wisdom that produces the peaceable fruit of righteousness.
⧗ JAMES 3:1–18

WEALTH, WAITING, AND PRAYER (4:1–5:20)

James writes to believers who don't always get along. His words address the heart of the problem and probably the most basic human sin: pride. James challenges believers to submit to God wholeheartedly, draw near to Him humbly and with clean hands and purity of heart, and repent. He extends a warning to the wealthy who find their security in the here and now, and he encourages believers to endure in the present by focusing on Christ. Finally, James calls readers to trust God, confess sins to one another, and pray for healing for one another. Turning a sinner from error will save a soul from death; the sinner will be forgiven. ⧗ JAMES 4:1–17; 5:1–20

250

Striking a balance: How do faith and works relate to each other?
Faith and works are not competing truths that must be balanced; they are interconnected realities. True faith will connect us to the very nature of God. When we are connected to God, we will be connected to the love of God. This love takes over our hearts so that we engage this world with true works of love.

90 BC	80 BC	70 BC	60 BC	50 BC	40 BC	30 BC	20 BC	10 BC	0 BC

◆ 65 Buddhism rises in China   ◆ 44 Julius Caesar assassinated   ◆ 2 Magi visit

◆ 63 Pompey conquers Jerusalem   ◆ 37 Herod the Great (Israel)

◆ 102 Chinese ships reach India   ◆ 51 Cleopatra VII reigns in Egypt   ◆ 31 Augustus (Rome)   ◆ 4 Jesus' birth

God's Plan for Humanity	God's Plan for the Church	God's Call to the Submissive Life	Living Soberly
1:1–2:3	2:4–25	3:1–4:19	5:1–14

INTRODUCTION TO 1 & 2 PETER

Author: Peter
Date Written: AD 65–67

First Peter has been called the Job of the New Testament because of its themes of undeserved suffering and steadfast submission to the sovereignty of God. The letter was probably written shortly before or during the severe persecution instigated by the Roman emperor Nero. At this point in history, Christianity had not yet been officially banned, but hatred for Christ followers was quickly growing.

The proper response to Christian suffering is the focus of 1 Peter. Knowing their persecution would probably get worse before getting better, Peter gives Christians divine perspective so that they can endure persecution without their faith crumbling. Pointing to Jesus as the ultimate example of one who suffered, Peter tells them they should count it a privilege to share in His sufferings; their hardships are for their Christian testimony. Therefore they should rejoice in them and see them as a normal part of their service to God.

Peter also speaks of the Christians' position in Christ. Their hope is in the Lord's return, and their true destiny is eternal glory at the revelation of Jesus. Their character and conduct should reflect this knowledge. They should be above reproach, producing fruit rooted in submission. Godly submission should produce law-abiding citizens, obedient employees, submissive wives, and loving husbands.

The trials that Peter deals with in his first letter focus on conflict against the church coming from the outside in the form of persecution. Second Peter differs in that it deals with the conflict and the trials that arise within the church because

AD 10	AD 20	AD 30	AD 40	AD 50	AD 60	AD 70	AD 80	AD 90	AD 100

• 8 Jesus visits temple • 30 Jesus raised • 45 James written • 60 Eph–Col • 68 Paul & Peter martyred • 90 Revelation

• 5 Birth of Paul (?) • 32 Stephen martyred • 55 1 & 2 Corinthians • 64 Rome burns • 70 Temple destroyed

• 14 Tiberius (Rome) • 37 Paul converts • 57 Romans • 65 1 Peter & 1 Timothy • 85 1–3 John written

MATT MARK LUKE JOHN ACTS ROM 1 COR 2 COR GAL EPH PHIL COL 1 THESS 2 THESS

God's Plan for Humanity	God's Plan for the Church
1:1–2:3	2:4–25

NAVIGATING THE BIBLE

of false teaching. It concentrates on knowledge of the truth as the proper response to falsehood from within. Second Peter deals with problems that come when false teachers sneak into the Christian fold with the goal of turning people away from the message of Christ, enticing them with their own false message grounded in worldly wisdom and human achievement. Peter wants to give the standard of truth to the church so that once he and the rest of the apostles are gone, the church will be able to stand strong against heresy.

While 1 Peter encourages readers to hope in the Lord's return, 2 Peter urges believers to be confident in the certainty of the Lord's return in power and judgment. Both letters are written toward the end of Peter's life, most likely out of Rome, between AD 64 and 66.

252

Crucifixion of St. Peter *by Caravaggio*
(1571–1610)

Persecution: What kind of hardships did early Christians face?
The early church faced mounting persecution during its first few hundred years. For example, Acts 7:54–60 describes the death of Stephen, who was stoned by Jewish religious authorities. In Acts 12:1–2, we read of the killing of James. According to tradition, the apostle Peter was crucified upside down around AD 68. Jesus warned His followers that persecution was coming. He knew that some would hate His followers, just as they had hated Him. The early Christians faced isolation from their communities, beatings, imprisonment, and execution. Of the eleven remaining apostles, only one, John, is believed to have died from natural causes. The others were martyred by various means, including burning, beheading, the sword, and crucifixion.

90 BC	80 BC	70 BC	60 BC	50 BC	40 BC	30 BC	20 BC	10 BC	0 BC

♦ 65 Buddhism rises in China ♦ 44 Julius Caesar assassinated ♦ 2 Magi visit

♦ 63 Pompey conquers Jerusalem ♦ 37 Herod the Great (Israel)

♦ 102 Chinese ships reach India ♦ 51 Cleopatra VII reigns in Egypt ♦ 31 Augustus (Rome) ♦ 4 Jesus' birth

God's Call to the Submissive Life	Living Soberly
3:1–4:19	5:1–14

Read Each 5-Minute Overview in 1 Peter

GOD'S PLAN FOR HUMANITY (1:1–2:3)

Peter praises God for the believers' living hope, incorruptible inheritance, and glorious salvation to be revealed at the coming of Christ. Despite severe trials, the power of God through genuine faith is protecting them and filling them with joy. Salvation to come was foretold by the prophets, but it is preached through the Gospel by those inspired by the Holy Spirit. Peter calls believers to focus their minds and hope on the grace that will be given to them at the revelation of Jesus Christ. They should imitate their Father, who is holy, by conducting themselves appropriately and loving one another fervently. ⏳ *1 PETER 1:1–25; 2:1–3*

GOD'S PLAN FOR THE CHURCH (2:4–25)

Peter admonishes his readers to grow. Christians are being built up as a spiritual house of living stones, a holy priesthood. Jesus is the chief cornerstone, precious to those who believe but a stumbling stone for those who don't. Peter instructs believers to turn from fleshly lusts and make sure their conduct is honorable among the nations and glorifying to God. They should submit to governmental authorities. Christian slaves need to submit to their masters, even under harsh circumstances. Peter reveals such submission

AD 10	AD 20	AD 30	AD 40	AD 50	AD 60	AD 70	AD 80	AD 90	AD 100

◆ 8 Jesus visits temple ◆ 30 Jesus raised ◆ 45 James written ◆ 60 Eph–Col ◆ 68 Paul & Peter martyred ◆ 90 Revelation

◆ 5 Birth of Paul (?) ◆ 32 Stephen martyred ◆ 55 1&2 Corinthians ◆ 64 Rome burns ◆ 70 Temple destroyed

◆ 14 Tiberius (Rome) ◆ 37 Paul converts ◆ 57 Romans ◆ 65 1 Peter & 1 Timothy ◆ 85 1–3 John written

God's Plan for Humanity	God's Plan for the Church	God's Call to the Submissive Life	Living Soberly
1:1–2:3	2:4–25	3:1–4:19	5:1–14

is commendable before God and follows the example set by Jesus, whose own suffering delivered humankind from sin. ⏳ *1 PETER 2:4–25*

GOD'S CALL TO THE SUBMISSIVE LIFE (3:1–4:19)

Peter reminds his readers to be submissive. He counsels wives to submit to their husbands and adorn themselves with a meek and quiet spirit. A wife's chaste and respectful attitude may influence her unbelieving husband to respond to the Gospel. Husbands are instructed to honor their wives as the weaker vessels and as fellow heirs of the promise. Duties toward brothers in Christ are summarized: Believers should overflow with unity, compassion, love, kindness, and simple courtesy. Peter reminds his readers that God uses suffering to mold His children into the image of Christ. ⏳ *1 PETER 3:1–22; 4:1–19*

LIVING SOBERLY (5:1–14)

Finally, Peter commands elders to willingly and eagerly shepherd the flock of God among them as overseers and examples. Younger members are commanded to humbly submit to their elders and to one another. Peter encourages them to trust that God, who cares for them, will exalt them in due time. They are to remain sober and vigilant; Satan is just waiting to attack. Peter closes his letter by offering believers final instructions concerning living in this world. ⏳ *1 PETER 5:1–14*

254

90 BC	80 BC	70 BC	60 BC	50 BC	40 BC	30 BC	20 BC	10 BC	0 BC

◆ 65 Buddhism rises in China   ◆ 44 Julius Caesar assassinated   ◆ 2 Magi visit

◆ 63 Pompey conquers Jerusalem   ◆ 37 Herod the Great (Israel)

◆ 102 Chinese ships reach India   ◆ 51 Cleopatra VII reigns in Egypt   ◆ 31 Augustus (Rome)   ◆ 4 Jesus' birth

The True Knowledge of God Explained	The True Knowledge of God Attacked and Protected
1:1–21	2:1–3:18

Read Each 5-Minute Overview in 2 Peter

○ 1:1–21	The True Knowledge of God Explained	Page 255
○ 2:1–3:18	The True Knowledge of God Attacked and Protected	Page 255

THE TRUE KNOWLEDGE OF GOD EXPLAINED (1:1–21)

Peter's second epistle speaks of God's divine power as the source of all things that pertain to life and godliness. It includes precious promises for those who have escaped worldly lusts. Peter exhorts his readers to abound in grace, rendering them fruitful in the knowledge of Jesus Christ. He explains that in light of his impending death, he wants to motivate his readers to make sure they are mindful of these things after he is gone. He reminds them of his testimony concerning the power and coming of the Lord. Peter then bids them to give careful heed to the prophetic Word; it will serve as a light in a dark place until the day dawns and the morning star rises in their hearts. Peter exhorts them to pay attention to such things spoken of by the prophets and apostles, because they come from men who were moved by the Holy Spirit. ⏳ *2 PETER 1:1–21*

THE TRUE KNOWLEDGE OF GOD ATTACKED AND PROTECTED (2:1–3:18)

Peter warns of destructive false teachers, who will deny their Redeemer and secretly introduce heresy into the church. Many will follow them, and truth will be blasphemed; they will, however, bring destruction on themselves. Peter uses examples from antiquity of what happens to people who sin. God will reserve the wicked for the day of punishment but will also deliver the godly out of temptation. False teachers will denounce God's authority and will revel in pleasure as they move among Christians they seek to negatively influence. They are empty of true

AD 10	AD 20	AD 30	AD 40	AD 50	AD 60	AD 70	AD 80	AD 90	AD 100
✦ 8 Jesus visits temple		✦ 30 Jesus raised		✦ 45 James written		✦ 60 Eph–Col	✦ 68 Paul & Peter martyred		✦ 90 Revelation
✦ 5 Birth of Paul (?)			✦ 32 Stephen martyred		✦ 55 1 & 2 Corinthians	✦ 64 Rome burns		✦ 70 Temple destroyed	
	✦ 14 Tiberius (Rome)		✦ 37 Paul converts		✦ 57 Romans		✦ 65 1 Peter & 1 Timothy		✦ 85 1–3 John written

substance, like wells without water. Peter describes how false teachers deceive in both their methods and their promises. He again charges believers to listen to the words of the prophets and apostles, especially concerning Jesus' return. In the last days, these false teachers will mock and forget the Word of God, which speaks of judgment by fire. A delay in Jesus' return is not unplanned; rather, it is evidence of God's long-suffering. His return will be unexpected, and in the meantime, Christians are to focus on living holy and godly lives and look forward to the day when all of God's promises come to pass. Someday, righteousness will dwell in the new heaven and on the new earth. ⚱ *2 PETER 2:1–22; 3:1–18*

The Last Judgment. *Unknown artist (AD 1250). Image portrays Christ welcoming the saints to heaven while the lost are tormented in hell.*

90 BC	80 BC	70 BC	60 BC	50 BC	40 BC	30 BC	20 BC	10 BC	0 BC

✦ 65 Buddhism rises in China   ✦ 44 Julius Caesar assassinated   ✦ 2 Magi visit

✦ 63 Pompey conquers Jerusalem   ✦ 37 Herod the Great (Israel)

✦ 102 Chinese ships reach India   ✦ 51 Cleopatra VII reigns in Egypt ✦ 31 Augustus (Rome)   ✦ 4 Jesus' birth

God Is Life and Love	A Reliable Testimony	Understanding God's Love
1 John 1:1–3:24	1 John 4:1–5:21	2 John 1–3 John 14

INTRODUCTION TO 1, 2 & 3 JOHN

Author: John
Date Written: AD 85–90

It is well accepted that the apostle John wrote 1, 2, and 3 John, the same John who wrote the Fourth Gospel and Revelation. These three short but powerful letters reflect the apostle's heart for his fellow brothers and sisters in the faith.

Both 1 and 2 John are penned in response to false teachers. John's first letter is to a community of faith that knows him well. This particular Christian community has undergone a split, and a good portion of the group has withdrawn from fellowship over doctrinal issues. John writes to reassure those who did not break off, and he warns them to resist the proselytizing efforts of false teachers by bolstering their understanding of the truth. John assures believers that they do indeed possess eternal life. Prevalent themes include walking in light, confessing Jesus as Christ, and fellowship with God.

Second John is a personal letter, written to warn a sister congregation some distance away of missionary efforts of false teachers. In it, John offers specific instruction for how to deal with these traveling preachers and warns about the dangers of welcoming them when they do arrive. Second John is probably written around the same time as 1 John, around AD 90, while John is in Ephesus. Themes familiar to John's writing are threaded throughout the letter: how to know the truth, how to live a life of love within that truth, and how to identify false teaching regarding the Christian faith.

1 JOHN

257

AD 10	AD 20	AD 30	AD 40	AD 50	AD 60	AD 70	AD 80	AD 90	AD 100

- 8 Jesus visits temple
- 30 Jesus raised
- 45 James written
- 60 Eph–Col
- 68 Paul & Peter martyred
- 90 Revelation
- 5 Birth of Paul (?)
- 32 Stephen martyred
- 55 1&2 Corinthians
- 64 Rome burns
- 70 Temple destroyed
- 14 Tiberius (Rome)
- 37 Paul converts
- 57 Romans
- 65 1 Peter & 1 Timothy
- 85 1–3 John written

God Is Life and Love	A Reliable Testimony
1 John 1:1–3:24	1 John 4:1–5:21

John writes 3 John to encourage fellowship with Christian brothers and sisters. It is the shortest book of the New Testament and the only one of John's letters addressed to a named individual: Gaius. John writes this third letter to commend Gaius and another church leader, Demetrius. John also writes to send a warning about Diotrephes, who opposes John's leadership and is trying to diminish his authority. Third John highlights the theme of hospitality toward traveling teachers who are spreading the Gospel in the first century. It also speaks to pride and its effect on leadership within a community.

While 2 and 3 John do not bring doctrinal contributions to the Word of God that are not already found in 1 John, all three letters offer important insight into the life and struggles of the early apostolic church. As today, these churches are constantly threatened by eccentric doctrine and behavior.

The Bible records that the apostle John reclined near Jesus at the Last Supper. That seating reveals a close relationship between Jesus and John. This painting of the Last Supper was created by Juan de Juanes (ca. 1510–1579) in 1560.

90 BC	80 BC	70 BC	60 BC	50 BC	40 BC	30 BC	20 BC	10 BC	0 BC

◆ 65 Buddhism rises in China   ◆ 44 Julius Caesar assassinated   ◆ 2 Magi visit

◆ 63 Pompey conquers Jerusalem   ◆ 37 Herod the Great (Israel)

◆ 102 Chinese ships reach India   ◆ 51 Cleopatra VII reigns in Egypt   ◆ 31 Augustus (Rome)   ◆ 4 Jesus' birth

Understanding God's Love		
2 John 1–3 John 14		

Read Each 5-Minute Overview in John's Epistles

○ 1 John 1:1–3:24	God Is Life and Love	Page 259
○ 1 John 4:1–5:21	A Reliable Testimony	Page 259
○ 2 John 1– 3 John 14	Understanding God's Love	Page 260

GOD IS LIFE AND LOVE (1 JOHN 1:1–3:24)

John takes his readers to eternity past to meet the One who was from the beginning. He describes Jesus as eternally existent, physically present, and the Word of life, who is God yet distinct from the Father. John hopes to draw his readers into fellowship with God's people and God Himself. His focus shifts to a discussion on hindrances to fellowship with God. John exhorts his readers to abstain from sin, mature spiritually, guard themselves against sinful humanity united in rebellion against God, and recognize the greatness of God's love. True love for God and for one another brings assurance and confidence in Christ.
⌛ *1 JOHN 1:1–10; 2:9–17; 3:1–20*

A RELIABLE TESTIMONY (1 JOHN 4:1–5:21)

Jesus' followers must guard themselves against false prophets, according to John. True prophecy and true teaching will present a true Jesus. True fellowship with God leads to knowing and believing His love and grace. Jesus' love for humanity should motivate God's children to love Him in return. A person is born of God by believing Jesus is the Christ, the Messiah. Loving God and keeping His commandments demonstrates Christ's love to the body of believers. John acknowledges that Christians live in a dark world, but he proclaims the key to conquering the world is faith in Jesus' sacrificial death on the cross. This faith

AD 10	AD 20	AD 30	AD 40	AD 50	AD 60	AD 70	AD 80	AD 90	AD 100

♦ 8 Jesus visits temple   ♦ 30 Jesus raised   ♦ 45 James written   ♦ 60 Eph–Col   ♦ 68 Paul & Peter martyred   ♦ 90 Revelation

♦ 5 Birth of Paul (?)   ♦ 32 Stephen martyred   ♦ 55 1 & 2 Corinthians   ♦ 64 Rome burns   ♦ 70 Temple destroyed

♦ 14 Tiberius (Rome)   ♦ 37 Paul converts   ♦ 57 Romans   ♦ 65 1 Peter & 1 Timothy   ♦ 85 1–3 John written

God Is Life and Love	A Reliable Testimony	Understanding God's Love
1 John 1:1–3:24	1 John 4:1–5:21	2 John 1–3 John 14

is based on the most reliable testimony possible: the witness of God. ⏳ *1 JOHN 4:1–21; 5:1–21*

UNDERSTANDING GOD'S LOVE (2 JOHN 1–3 JOHN 14)

Most likely speaking to the churches in his region, John supports Jesus' commandment to "love one another." He cautions believers to watch for deceivers and antichrists who are abundant in the world and actively spread false teachings. Some teachers refuse to remain in Jesus' teaching and go beyond the truth of apostolic teaching. John makes it clear that these people are anti-Christ and do not know the Lord. He also reminds his readers of their responsibility as Christians to love other Christians. Above all things, John desires for them to walk in truth. Next, he criticizes a prideful false teacher who rejected one of his letters. John closes his third epistle with confident intentions of making a visit to discuss many more topics "face to face," rather than by pen. ⏳ *2 JOHN 1–13; 3 JOHN 1–14*

St. John the Evangelist on Patmos
by Hieronymus Bosch (ca. 1450–1516)

How is unbelief like spiritual blindness?
In the New Testament, blindness is frequently a spiritual condition associated with deliberate disbelief. Particularly applicable to verses 9–11 is John 12:39–40, where deliberate refusal to believe, in spite of the miracles Jesus had performed, led to an inability to believe. Just as those who refuse to come to the light are left in darkness, so those who refuse to love fellow members of the Christian community are said to be in darkness.

90 BC	80 BC	70 BC	60 BC	50 BC	40 BC	30 BC	20 BC	10 BC	0 BC

• 65 Buddhism rises in China   • 44 Julius Caesar assassinated   • 2 Magi visit

• 63 Pompey conquers Jerusalem   • 37 Herod the Great (Israel)

• 102 Chinese ships reach India   • 51 Cleopatra VII reigns in Egypt   • 31 Augustus (Rome)   • 4 Jesus' birth

The fate of Jesus' followers: What happened to John and the other disciples?

1. **James** was the second recorded martyr after Christ's death. His death is recounted in Acts 12:2, which reports that Herod Agrippa killed him with a sword. Date of martyrdom: AD 44–45.

2. **Peter** was crucified by Roman executioners because he would not deny his Master a second time. According to Eusebius, Peter thought himself unworthy to be crucified as his Master, so he asked to be crucified "head downward." Date of martyrdom: ca. AD 64.

3. **Andrew** was hanged from an olive tree at Patrae, a town in Achaia. Date of martyrdom: AD 70.

4. **Thomas** was impaled with pine spears, tormented with red-hot plates, and burned alive. Date of martyrdom: AD 70.

5. **Philip** evangelized in Phrygia, where a hostile audience had him tortured and crucified. Date of martyrdom: AD 54.

6. **Matthew** was beheaded at Nad-Davar in Ethiopia. Date of martyrdom: AD 60–70.

7. **Nathanael (Bartholomew)**, unwilling to recant of his proclamation of a risen Christ, was flayed and crucified. Date of martyrdom: AD 70.

8. **James the Lesser** was cast down from the top of the temple in Jerusalem and beaten to death with a fuller's club to the head. Date of martyrdom: AD 63.

9. **Simon the Zealot** was crucified by a governor in Syria. Date of martyrdom: AD 74.

10. **Judas Thaddaeus** was beaten to death with sticks. Date of martyrdom: AD 72.

11. **Matthias** replaced Judas Iscariot as the twelfth apostle of Christ (Acts 1:26). He was stoned to death while being crucified. Date of martyrdom: AD 70.

12. **John** is thought to have been exiled to the island of Patmos during the reign of Emperor Domitian. He was tortured but died of natural causes around AD 100.

2–3 JOHN

261

AD 10	AD 20	AD 30	AD 40	AD 50	AD 60	AD 70	AD 80	AD 90	AD 100

• 8 Jesus visits temple   • 30 Jesus raised   • 45 James written   • 60 Eph–Col   • 68 Paul & Peter martyred   • 90 Revelation

• 5 Birth of Paul (?)   • 32 Stephen martyred   • 55 1 & 2 Corinthians   • 64 Rome burns   • 70 Temple destroyed

• 14 Tiberius (Rome)   • 37 Paul converts   • 57 Romans   • 65 1 Peter & 1 Timothy   • 85 1–3 John written

INTRODUCTION TO JUDE

Author: Jude
Date Written: AD 65–70

The author of this letter is widely accepted to be Jude, the brother of James. Jude and James are most likely the same brothers listed in scripture as Jesus' half brothers. While these two brothers did not have faith in Jesus as Lord during Jesus' lifetime, they both became leaders in the first-century Christian church.

Jude does not point out any particular audience of readers, and there are no geographical hints; regardless, the author was probably targeting a specific region infiltrated with false teachers. This epistle is a passionate plea for readers to contend for what they believe. In light of a growing heresy that understood grace to be a license for immorality, Jude writes to this unidentified group of Christ followers to call them back to faith.

Many estimate Jude was written around AD 65. The content of Jude and 2 Peter is closely related, and this has prompted discussion about which letter came first; perhaps one provided reference for the other. While it had been Jude's intent to write to this particular group of believers on the topic of salvation, what prompts this letter is the news of false teaching.

Truth and discernment are two key themes of this book. Jude opens and closes his letter by addressing the believer's security in God's love, but the meat of the content pertains to false teachers in the church's midst and the need for believers to stand firm in the truth. Only believers who are spiritually strong can answer the call. Jude reminds these false teachers of how God has dealt with unbelieving Israel and wicked Sodom and Gomorrah in the past.

90 BC	80 BC	70 BC	60 BC	50 BC	40 BC	30 BC	20 BC	10 BC	0 BC

◆ 65 Buddhism rises in China ◆ 44 Julius Caesar assassinated ◆ 2 Magi visit

◆ 63 Pompey conquers Jerusalem ◆ 37 Herod the Great (Israel)

◆ 102 Chinese ships reach India ◆ 51 Cleopatra VII reigns in Egypt ◆ 31 Augustus (Rome) ◆ 4 Jesus' birth

Contend for the Faith and Finish Well

1–25

Jude references Old Testament characters a number of times in his short letter. He closes with one of the greatest doxologies in the Bible, emphasizing the power of Christ to keep those who trust in Him from being deceived by error.

The Destruction of Sodom and Gomorrah
by John Martin (1789–1854)

Predicting the future: What does Jude say about the end times?

The book of Jude warns that false teachers will come in the last days. These teachers will be known by several qualities:

- Mocking: These teachers are really con artists.
- Controlled by their own desires: False teachers will follow after their passions and lusts.
- Divisive: These individuals will establish themselves as spiritual elites who claim to have received special blessings and power from God.
- Worldly: They will follow their appetite for worldly lust without any self-control. They will have sensual minds.
- Devoid of the Spirit: These teachers will not have the most distinctive mark of a true believer—the Holy Spirit. These individuals will not possess the kind of power they claim to have.

Jude warns us that false teachers are coming. Christians would do well to remember this warning. We must not be ignorant of their tricks or be trapped by their deceptions. The best way to protect ourselves is to continue walking in the love of God.

AD 10	AD 20	AD 30	AD 40	AD 50	AD 60	AD 70	AD 80	AD 90	AD 100

- 8 Jesus visits temple
- 30 Jesus raised
- 45 James written
- 60 Eph–Col
- 68 Paul & Peter martyred
- 90 Revelation
- 5 Birth of Paul (?)
- 32 Stephen martyred
- 55 1 & 2 Corinthians
- 64 Rome burns
- 70 Temple destroyed
- 14 Tiberius (Rome)
- 37 Paul converts
- 57 Romans
- 65 1 Peter & 1 Timothy
- 85 1–3 John written

Contend for the Faith and Finish Well

1–25

Read the 5-Minute Overview in Jude

○ 1–25	Contend for the Faith and Finish Well	Page 264

CONTEND FOR THE FAITH AND FINISH WELL (1–25)

Heretical practices and doctrines are putting the Gospel of Jesus Christ in peril, prompting Jude to write this letter. Jude exhorts each believer to contend for the faith, as if trying to win a wrestling match. Men who deny the Lord Jesus Christ are secretly slipping in among the body of believers and are deceiving them with their teaching and lifestyles; these men need to be avoided. Jude reminds readers how God delivered Israel out of slavery in Egypt. At the threshold of the promised land, the people refused to trust God. As a result, almost the entire adult generation that left Egypt did not enter the land. However, Jude points out the ones who did: those who endured till the end. He exhorts his readers to do the same and finish the race well. Those who cause trouble will be judged, no matter how much they have been blessed in the past. Jude emphasizes the need for the community to be discerning and merciful toward false teachers. Finally,

Jude focuses on God's sustaining power. He closes with a doxology reminding believers of their eternal victory and triumph in God. ☒ *JUDE 1–25*

The Marriage of the Lamb by a Flemish artist (ca. AD 1400)

90 BC	80 BC	70 BC	60 BC	50 BC	40 BC	30 BC	20 BC	10 BC	0 BC

◆ 65 Buddhism rises in China ◆ 44 Julius Caesar assassinated ◆ 2 Magi visit

◆ 63 Pompey conquers Jerusalem ◆ 37 Herod the Great (Israel)

◆ 102 Chinese ships reach India ◆ 51 Cleopatra VII reigns in Egypt ◆ 31 Augustus (Rome) ◆ 4 Jesus' birth

Eternal Hope in Christ	The Heavenly Throne	The Day of the Lord	Two Witnesses, Satan, and the Antichrist	Final Justice	All Things Beautiful Again
1:1–3:22	4:1–6:17	7:1–10:11	11:1–13:18	14:1–19:21	20:1–22:21

INTRODUCTION TO REVELATION

Author: John
Date Written: AD 90

The word *revelation* means "unveiling" or "disclosure." This book uncovers how the person, righteousness, and judgment of Jesus will someday be unveiled in all the fullness, glory, and power of God. Some consider the book daunting and scary; its underlying theme, however, is filled with hope. As Genesis is the book of the beginnings, Revelation is the book of consummation. God's divine program of redemption will be brought to completion, and God's holy name will be vindicated before all creation.

As with most New Testament books, there has been discussion regarding the authorship of Revelation. There is no irrefutable evidence, however, to sway conservative scholars from accepting John as the author.

Many of the original apostles have been martyred for the faith, and John has been arrested and placed in exile on the island of Patmos. Persecution is rampant, and the immediate future for Christians looks dim. First-century believers need a boost of encouragement to stand firm in their trials; John writes this letter to affirm the kingdom of God will overcome the kingdoms of the world, and all who oppose God and oppress God's children will be brought to justice.

John's letter reveals significant aspects of the character and future work of Jesus Christ. The idea that God is outside of time and sovereign over human history emboldens these first-century Christians; they are encouraged in knowing that

AD 10	AD 20	AD 30	AD 40	AD 50	AD 60	AD 70	AD 80	AD 90	AD 100
✦ 8 Jesus visits temple		✦ 30 Jesus raised		✦ 45 James written		✦ 60 Eph–Col	✦ 68 Paul & Peter martyred	✦ 90 Revelation	
✦ 5 Birth of Paul (?)			✦ 32 Stephen martyred		✦ 55 1 &2 Corinthians	✦ 64 Rome burns	✦ 70 Temple destroyed		
	✦ 14 Tiberius (Rome)		✦ 37 Paul converts		✦ 57 Romans	✦ 65 1 Peter & 1 Timothy		✦ 85 1–3 John written	

Eternal Hope in Christ	The Heavenly Throne	The Day of the Lord
1:1–3:22	4:1–6:17	7:1–10:11

God is above the things driving them down. No matter how much it looks like evil is winning, that is not reality.

Revelation is especially clear in its presentation of the awesome resurrected Christ, who is given all authority to judge the earth. The book begins with a vision of His glory, wisdom, and power. Revelation portrays Jesus' authority over the entire church and shows how He is the Lamb who was slain and declared worthy to open the book of judgment. Jesus' righteousness will be poured out over the entire earth when He returns in power to judge His enemies and reign as Lord forever in the heavenly city—in the presence of all who know Him.

More relevant than ever before—especially in light of modern-day political, economic, military, technological, and communicative developments—Revelation offers a symbolic and rich vision of the end of the age. John concludes with an epilogue reassuring his readers of the good news that Jesus is coming quickly.

RECIPIENTS OF THE 7 LETTERS

PERGAMUM · THYATIRA · SARDIS · SMYRNA · PHILADELPHIA · EPHESUS · LAODICEA

Black Sea · ITALY · ASIA · GALATIA

90 BC	80 BC	70 BC	60 BC	50 BC	40 BC	30 BC	20 BC	10 BC	0 BC

◆ 65 Buddhism rises in China ◆ 44 Julius Caesar assassinated ◆ 2 Magi visit

◆ 63 Pompey conquers Jerusalem ◆ 37 Herod the Great (Israel)

◆ 102 Chinese ships reach India ◆ 51 Cleopatra VII reigns in Egypt ◆ 31 Augustus (Rome) ◆ 4 Jesus' birth

Two Witnesses, Satan, and the Antichrist	Final Justice	All Things Beautiful Again
11:1–13:18	14:1–19:21	20:1–22:21

Read Each 5-Minute Overview in Revelation

ETERNAL HOPE IN CHRIST (1:1–3:22)

John opens his revelation with the truth of God's power and eternal nature. God has a plan and He will be victorious in the end, no matter how much it looks like evil is winning. Seven churches in Asia Minor face different problems, and John relays a message from the Lord for each. Jesus presents Himself in a way that is relevant to each problem. The Lord will reward those who overcome these obstacles. ⏳ *REVELATION 1:4–20; 3:19–22*

THE HEAVENLY THRONE (4:1–6:17)

A voice like a trumpet tells John things concerning the future. John recounts a vision of God's heavenly throne, which is surrounded by a rainbow, reminding readers of God's commitment to His covenant promises. Impressive light and thunder are reminiscent of God's presence at Mount Sinai. All of heaven praises His power as the One who conquers and grants victory. John's visions transition from God the Creator to Jesus the Redeemer, Judge, and Savior of the world. The Lamb, which appears as though it had been slain, is given a scroll, indicating no person can understand scripture apart from Jesus Christ. The scroll is unrolled and its seals broken, marking the beginning of God's judgment upon the earth. ⏳ *REVELATION 4:1–8; 5:1–14; 6:1–17*

AD 10	AD 20	AD 30	AD 40	AD 50	AD 60	AD 70	AD 80	AD 90	AD 100
		◆ 8 Jesus visits temple	◆ 30 Jesus raised	◆ 45 James written	◆ 60 Eph–Col	◆ 68 Paul & Peter martyred	◆ 90 Revelation		

◆ 5 Birth of Paul (?)   ◆ 32 Stephen martyred   ◆ 55 1 & 2 Corinthians   ◆ 64 Rome burns   ◆ 70 Temple destroyed

◆ 14 Tiberius (Rome)   ◆ 37 Paul converts   ◆ 57 Romans   ◆ 65 1 Peter & 1 Timothy   ◆ 85 1–3 John written

Eternal Hope in Christ	The Heavenly Throne	The Day of the Lord
1:1–3:22	4:1–6:17	7:1–10:11

THE DAY OF THE LORD (7:1–10:11)

A pause between the sixth and seventh seal sets up events just prior to the wrath of God being poured out on the earth; the servants of the Lord are sealed. A great multitude worship God before the heavenly throne, recognizing Him alone as the source for salvation. Four trumpets bring terrible plagues on the earth and the heavens, revealing the severity of God's judgment. God will judge the leaders of the world system whose agenda is against Him. Three more trumpets sound, initiating more plagues. Yet humankind does not repent. John is called to prophesy to all nations, peoples, tongues, and kings. ⌛ *REVELATION 7:1–8; 8:1–12; 9:1–11, 20–21; 10:1–11*

TWO WITNESSES, SATAN, AND THE ANTICHRIST (11:1–13:18)

John is instructed to measure the temple of God and the altar. Two witnesses emerge giving testimony, and John continues to describe God's judgment on the earth. God now deals directly with Satan and those who have intentionally and directly supported Satan's efforts to oppose Jesus. Satan's final attempt in destroying the Messiah is through a false messiah, or the antichrist. ⌛ *REVELATION 11:1–14; 12:1–12; 13:5–18*

Apocalyptic mystery: How should we read the book of Revelation?
Three things can help us when we open the book of Revelation. First, the book helps Christians view history from God's point of view. God has revealed His message to us in Revelation so that every believer in every age can live for His glory, regardless of his or her circumstances.

Second, the author, John, wrote Revelation as a witness to what God revealed to him. The things Jesus showed John in Revelation will come true.

Finally, Revelation offers a blessing to those who read it. Those who value this letter and make it a priority to read it will find encouragement. The original recipients of Revelation were facing extreme persecution. They needed to be reminded that God is the sure winner in the cosmic battle. In the end, the kingdom of God will prevail, not the kingdom of this world.

90 BC	80 BC	70 BC	60 BC	50 BC	40 BC	30 BC	20 BC	10 BC	0 BC

◆ 65 Buddhism rises in China ◆ 44 Julius Caesar assassinated ◆ 2 Magi visit

◆ 63 Pompey conquers Jerusalem ◆ 37 Herod the Great (Israel)

◆ 102 Chinese ships reach India ◆ 51 Cleopatra VII reigns in Egypt ◆ 31 Augustus (Rome) ◆ 4 Jesus' birth

Two Witnesses, Satan, and the Antichrist	Final Justice	All Things Beautiful Again
11:1–13:18	14:1–19:21	20:1–22:21

Consequences of the Fall & The Hope of Heaven

Connection with God Severed
Genesis 3:22–24

Connection with God Restored
Isaiah 59:1–2

Relationships with Others Damaged
Genesis 3:7

Relationships with Others Repaired
Isaiah 2:4;
Isaiah 11:6

BROKEN **RESTORED**

A World Broken
Genesis 3:17–19

A World Restored
Revelation 21:4;
Isaiah 25:8

Revelation promises a new world in which God will restore our broken, sinful world.

AD 10	AD 20	AD 30	AD 40	AD 50	AD 60	AD 70	AD 80	AD 90	AD 100

◆ 8 Jesus visits temple ◆ 30 Jesus raised ◆ 45 James written ◆ 60 Eph–Col ◆ 68 Paul & Peter martyred ◆ 90 Revelation

◆ 5 Birth of Paul (?) ◆ 32 Stephen martyred ◆ 55 1 & 2 Corinthians ◆ 64 Rome burns ◆ 70 Temple destroyed

◆ 14 Tiberius (Rome) ◆ 37 Paul converts ◆ 57 Romans ◆ 65 1 Peter & 1 Timothy ◆ 85 1–3 John written

Eternal Hope in Christ	The Heavenly Throne	The Day of the Lord
1:1–3:22	4:1–6:17	7:1–10:11

NAVIGATING THE BIBLE

270

CAST OF CHARACTERS

Paul

Apostle of Christ. Paul was sent to become a Jewish rabbi at a young age. He grew to be a man of firm conviction and a fiery temperament. He hated Christians, but after a life-changing encounter with the living Christ, Paul began preaching the Gospel to both Jews and Gentiles.

Stephen

First Martyr. Stephen, full of the Holy Spirit, preached about the kingdom of God and performed miracles. However, many Jews did not like him, and they brought him to court to be tried. Stephen replied to their angry words using Old Testament scriptures, but they still stoned him to death.

90 BC	80 BC	70 BC	60 BC	50 BC	40 BC	30 BC	20 BC	10 BC	0 BC

◆ 65 Buddhism rises in China ◆ 44 Julius Caesar assassinated ◆ 2 Magi visit

◆ 63 Pompey conquers Jerusalem ◆ 37 Herod the Great (Israel)

◆ 102 Chinese ships reach India ◆ 51 Cleopatra VII reigns in Egypt ◆ 31 Augustus (Rome) ◆ 4 Jesus' birth

Two Witnesses, Satan, and the Antichrist	Final Justice	All Things Beautiful Again
11:1–13:18	14:1–19:21	20:1–22:21

IN ACTS–REVELATION

Timothy

Paul's Disciple. Timothy devoted himself to the Old Testament scriptures, aided by his devout mother, Eunice, and his grandmother, Lois. The apostle Paul chose young Timothy to accompany him on his journey. Timothy eventually went on to become the pastor of the church at Ephesus.

John

The Beloved Apostle. John left his profession as fisherman to become Jesus' disciple and beloved friend. He was with Jesus when Jairus's daughter was raised from the dead, at the transfiguration, and during Jesus' agony in Gethsemane. Jesus left His mother in John's care after His death and resurrection.

AD 10	AD 20	AD 30	AD 40	AD 50	AD 60	AD 70	AD 80	AD 90	AD 100

- ✦ 8 Jesus visits temple
- ✦ 30 Jesus raised
- ✦ 45 James written
- ✦ 60 Eph–Col
- ✦ 68 Paul & Peter martyred
- ✦ 90 Revelation
- ✦ 5 Birth of Paul (?)
- ✦ 32 Stephen martyred
- ✦ 55 1 & 2 Corinthians
- ✦ 64 Rome burns
- ✦ 70 Temple destroyed
- ✦ 14 Tiberius (Rome)
- ✦ 37 Paul converts
- ✦ 57 Romans
- ✦ 65 1 Peter & 1 Timothy
- ✦ 85 1–3 John written

Two Witnesses, Satan, and the Antichrist	Final Justice	All Things Beautiful Again
11:1–13:18	14:1–19:21	20:1–22:21

FINAL JUSTICE (14:1–19:21)

The beast's goal is to stop the Messiah, destroy the Jews, and persecute the church. Now God begins His final harvest. Seven angels pour out bowls of God's wrath. God is seen as the One with ultimate power and with the choice to decide when to display that power. Humankind is convinced it doesn't need God, seen through the image of the destruction of Babylon. The great marriage ceremony of the Lamb and the return of Jesus results in worship, victory, and the final destruction of the beast and his prophet ⌛ *REVELATION 14:14–20; 16:1–21; 17:1–6; 19:1–2, 6–16*

272

ALL THINGS BEAUTIFUL AGAIN (20:1–22:21)

Satan receives his judgment; victory is complete. John describes a new heaven, a new earth, and a new Jerusalem, spoken of by ancient prophets, established and ruled by God. There will be no more separation or evil between God and man. The new Jerusalem will be God's glorious dwelling place. John uses the most striking, beautiful image he can think of to describe Jesus' return: a bride coming down the aisle, ready to meet her husband. Jesus is coming soon! He will wipe away every tear and make all things new. ⌛ *REVELATION 20:1–15; 21:1–5; 22:1–21*

The Last Judgment *by Jan Van Eyck (1395–1441)*

90 BC	80 BC	70 BC	60 BC	50 BC	40 BC	30 BC	20 BC	10 BC	0 BC

◆ 65 Buddhism rises in China   ◆ 44 Julius Caesar assassinated   ◆ 2 Magi visit

◆ 63 Pompey conquers Jerusalem   ◆ 37 Herod the Great (Israel)

◆ 102 Chinese ships reach India   ◆ 51 Cleopatra VII reigns in Egypt   ◆ 31 Augustus (Rome)   ◆ 4 Jesus' birth

APPENDIX: THE BIG PICTURE

W hat would happen if you arranged the Bible books in chronological order? What big themes would you see in God's actions as history unfolds? The books of the Bible (and some big-picture lessons we can learn from them) can be organized into seven major time periods based on the specific historical eras in which they were written. Key stories are told in these books, and major life-transforming lessons can be learned from reading each section of scripture.

What Can We Learn about God and His Plan in the First Books of the Bible?
Books: Genesis and Job
Time period: Creation–1446 BC
Genesis contains events that occurred before 1500 BC. The story of Genesis begins with God's kingdom existing in perfect peace—everything relates to Him perfectly as He intended. However, humanity's sin severs this intimate relationship between God and His creation, resulting in a separation that seems beyond repair. God begins to make His name great. He initiates a plan of redemption and restoration through a promise, and He establishes a special people—Israel—as the object of His redeeming love. (Note: The events of Job may have taken place around the same time as the events of Genesis. In the book of Job, sickness, death, and pain show the effects of a broken world in dramatic fashion.)

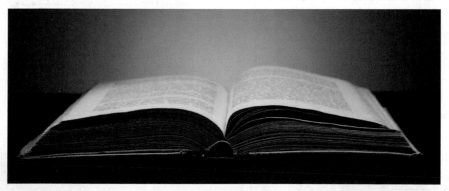

AD 10	AD 20	AD 30	AD 40	AD 50	AD 60	AD 70	AD 80	AD 90	AD 100

◆ 8 Jesus visits temple   ◆ 30 Jesus raised   ◆ 45 James written   ◆ 60 Eph–Col   ◆ 68 Paul & Peter martyred   ◆ 90 Revelation

◆ 5 Birth of Paul (?)   ◆ 32 Stephen martyred   ◆ 55 1 & 2 Corinthians   ◆ 64 Rome burns   ◆ 70 Temple destroyed

◆ 14 Tiberius (Rome)   ◆ 37 Paul converts   ◆ 57 Romans   ◆ 65 1 Peter & 1 Timothy   ◆ 85 1–3 John written

What Can We Learn about God and His Plan through the Books of the Law?
Books: Exodus, Leviticus, Numbers, and Deuteronomy
Time period: 1446–1406 BC

God reveals more of His plan of restoration through the books of Exodus, Leviticus, Numbers, and Deuteronomy. God is holy and righteous, and He expects His people to be set apart from the rest of the world. The nation of Israel, God's "treasured possession," is to look different, be a light to the surrounding nations, and cause the world to consider the God of Abraham, Isaac, and Jacob as the one true God. Israel is a nation set free from sin, paid for by a substitutionary blood sacrifice; this becomes the blueprint of how God will provide redemption for all nations.

What Can We Learn about God and His Plan through the Early Historical Books?
Books: Joshua, Judges, Ruth
Time period: 1406–1051 BC

Joshua, Judges, and Ruth envelop readers in a period of time in which the everyday characters learn to truly embrace God's promises. We see God's people cycle from trusting in God, to rebelling and turning from Him, and then falling to a place of exile and wandering. God's people experience the consequences of sin before repenting and returning to His presence and safety. During this period of time, God's people repeat this pattern again and again; but even so, God continued to show His commitment to preserve His creation—Jews and Gentiles alike—and restore His kingdom.

What Can We Learn about God and His Plan through the Rise and Fall of the Biblical Nation of Israel?
Books: 1 & 2 Samuel, 1 & 2 Kings, 1 & 2 Chronicles, Psalms, Proverbs, Ecclesiastes, Song of Songs, Isaiah, Jeremiah, and Lamentations
Time period: 1051–586 BC

God's story focuses on the promise of a King who will come and bring earthly peace. We learn God is more concerned with the state of His people's hearts than

the state of their earthly kingdoms. Through the prophetic writings, God establishes a pattern for what His rule will be in His new, restored kingdom.

What Can We Learn about God and His Plan through Israel's Exile and Restoration?
Books: Ezra, Nehemiah, Esther, Ezekiel, Daniel, Hosea, Joel, Amos, Obadiah, Jonah, Micah, Nahum, Habakkuk, Zephaniah, Haggai, Zechariah, and Malachi
Time period: 586–4 BC
God cannot let sin go unpunished; He disciplines His people when they choose to rebel against Him. God reveals how He allows the people of Israel to go into a period of exile and wandering as a means of discipline. However, He waits patiently for His people to return to Him and promises a fresh start. When they turn from their wicked, prideful ways, He graciously restores them to a place of dependence on Him alone.

What Can We Learn about God and His Plan through the Gospels?
Books: Matthew, Mark, Luke, and John
Time period: 4 BC–AD 30
God reveals one gospel of good news fulfilled in the person of Jesus Christ. Through Jesus' life, death, and resurrection, God offers a perfect solution for sin: Himself, through the final substitutionary blood sacrifice of His body. God's plan of redemption was always one single theme of restoration, centered on Jesus our Savior, the Creator of the universe and the one true God.

What Can We Learn about God and His Plan through the Church Age?
Books: Acts–Revelation
Time period: AD 30–90
God invites people from every tribe and tongue to be part of His church. At the end of time, God will restore the world to its perfect, sinless state. The books of Acts through Revelation speak of a time to come, when Jesus will return and set up His kingdom on earth. The restoration of His people will be complete, and all creation will be renewed.

INDEX TO PEOPLE
& PLACES